Colloquial
English

THE COLLOQUIAL SERIES
Series Adviser: Gary King

The following languages are available in the Colloquial series:

Afrikaans	French	Portuguese of Brazil
Albanian	German	Romanian
Amharic	Greek	Russian
Arabic (Levantine)	Gujarati	Scottish Gaelic
Arabic of Egypt	Hebrew	Serbian
Arabic of the Gulf and Saudi Arabia	Hindi	Slovak
Basque	Hungarian	Slovene
Breton	Icelandic	Somali
Bulgarian	Indonesian	Spanish
Cambodian	Irish (forthcoming)	Spanish of Latin America
Cantonese	Italian	Swahili
Catalan	Japanese	Swedish
Chinese	Korean	Tamil
Croatian	Latvian	Thai
Czech	Lithuanian	Turkish
Danish	Malay	Ukrainian
Dutch	Mongolian	Urdu
English	Norwegian	Vietnamese
Estonian	Panjabi	Welsh
Filipino	Persian	Yoruba (forthcoming)
Finnish	Polish	
	Portuguese	

COLLOQUIAL 2s series: *The Next Step in Language Learning*

Chinese	German (forthcoming)	Spanish
Dutch	Italian	Spanish of Latin America
French	Russian	

All these Colloquials are available in book & CD packs, or separately. You can order them through your bookseller or via our website www.routledge.com.

Colloquial
English

A Complete English Language Course

Gareth King

Routledge
Taylor & Francis Group
LONDON AND NEW YORK

First edition published 2005
by Routledge
2 Park Square, Milton Park, Abingdon, Oxon OX14 4RN

Simultaneously published in the USA and Canada
by Routledge
270 Madison Ave, New York NY 10016

Reprinted 2007

*Routledge is an imprint of the Taylor & Francis Group,
an informa business*

© 2005 Gareth King

Typeset in Times by
Florence Production Ltd, Stoodleigh, Devon

Printed and bound in Great Britain by
TJ International Ltd, Padstow, Cornwall

All rights reserved. No part of this book may be reprinted
or reproduced or utilised in any form or by any electronic,
mechanical, or other means, now known or hereafter invented,
including photocopying and recording, or in any information
storage or retrieval system, without permission in writing from
the publishers.

British Library Cataloguing in Publication Data
A catalogue record for this book is available from the
British Library

Library of Congress Cataloging in Publication Data
King, Gareth.
　Colloquial English: a complete English language course /
Gareth King.
　　p. cm.
　Includes index.
　　1. English language – Textbooks for foreign speakers.
2. English language – Spoken English – Problems,
exercises, etc.　I. Title.　II. Series.
PE1128.K43 2004
428.2′4 – dc22   2004010470

ISBN 978–0–415–29953–4 (pbk)
　　　978–0–415–29952–7 (CDs)
　　　978–0–415–45389–9 (pack)

LEEDS LIBRARIES AND INFORMATION SERVICES	
LD39020746	
HJ	16/05/2008
428.24	£20.28
S035179	

I dedicate this book
to the memory of my dear friend
Buzz Burrell 1956–2003
who loved the English language always

Contents

Acknowledgements	ix
Introduction	x
English spelling	xi
IPA symbols	xii
Grammatical terms used in this book	xiii

1	Pleased to meet you!	1
2	Where are you from?	20
3	Could you tell me where the bank is?	33
4	Have you got any bread?	47
5	What shall we do today?	64
6	Hello, could I speak to Vicki?	81
7	What date is it today?	98
8	Can I make an appointment?	117
9	I've lost my passport!	135
10	Which do you prefer?	155
11	I'll see you at half past five!	175
12	You can't be serious!	194

13	The people we met were fantastic!	209
14	What would you do?	226
15	I said you'd phone back later	241

Key to exercises	259
Reference grammar	276
Irregular verbs – alphabetical list	280
Irregular verbs by type	283
Grammar index	286

Acknowledgements

I thank Sophie Oliver and Suzanne Cousin at Routledge Language Reference Editorial for their unstinting support and encouragement throughout this project; the various reviewers of the original proposal for their positive response and helpful feedback; Linda Paulus, Production Editor, for her hard work and accuracy; the *Guardian* and *Daily Mirror* newspapers for permission to use material; my friends and colleagues in the bunker for populating a significant proportion of the book; my fellow CaRPistas in cix:carp for real and useful pedantry of a consistently high order; and of course Adam, Liam and Jonquil for being the best family in the world.

Introduction

Although this book is a member of the Colloquial series, and conforms broadly with the format and approach of other titles in the series, *Colloquial English* necessarily departs in some respects from its fellows.

For a start, it is written *in* the target language, and an assumption of prior knowledge of the language must therefore be made. Nonetheless, I have tried to keep explanations simple and succinct, allowing the context of the dialogues and exercises to show the user how the language works.

Presentation of vocabulary is another problematic issue in a book aimed at users from diverse linguistic backgrounds. There can be no two-way glossary at the back of *Colloquial English*, and instead I must depend on the student's having access to a good learner's dictionary of English – fortunately there are a number of comprehensive and reliable works readily available on the TEFL market, and at a reasonable price.

I have made sparing use of the IPA phonetic alphabet (and in a broad rather than narrow transcription) where I have thought the disparity between the spelling of common words and their pronunciation warranted it; and I have listed the IPA symbols and combinations of symbols at the front of the book for reference. Naturally the accompanying CDs/tapes will also be of benefit in this regard, and I strongly recommend their use in conjunction with the course.

This book does not shy away from grammar, and a glance at the index will show how central a component of the course it is. In explaining the grammar in the body of the book, while aiming to keep technical language to a minimum, I have not held back from using grammatical terminology where I think this helps make the system and mechanisms of the language clearer for the learner.

English spelling

You will see that sometimes phonetic symbols have been used to help you with pronunciation in this book. This is because English spelling (like French and Danish, and unlike German and Russian) is a historic rather than a phonetic system, which means that it does not always correspond very well to pronunciation – the words have changed in sound while the old spelling has stayed the same. This is a difficulty for people learning English, but it is something that must be accepted from the start – you will have to learn pronunciations as well as spellings. But the *important* thing to remember is that English spelling *does* have a system – it isn't completely illogical. It's just that the system is sometimes a bit more complicated than you might expect, and there are a lot of apparent exceptions to rules.

For example, we use a 'silent e' as a regular component of the system: a silent **e** *after* a single consonant changes the sound of the vowel *before* the consonant: **pan** /pæn/ but **pane** /pɛin/; **hop** /hɔp/ but **hope** /hǝup/. And sometimes we spell the same sound in different ways – look at the different possible spellings there are for /ɑi/: **my night time**; and for /ǝu/: **hole throw boat only soul**. Or (to take an extreme example) look at the different pronunciations of the combination **-ough**: **through** /θruː/ **though** /ðǝu/ **bough** /bɑu/ **bought** /bɔːt/ **cough** /kɔf/ **enough** /ɪˈnʌf/. But don't worry – millions of people learn English all over the world, and they all manage pretty well with the spelling, because the more contact you have with the language, the easier it is. If you approach this aspect of English with a positive frame of mind, you'll be surprised how quickly you get used to it!

IPA symbols 🎧

Vowels

/ə/	butter, sofa
/æ/	cat, hand
/ɑː/	father, farm
/ɛ/	get, send
/ɪ/	sit, win
/i/	happy
/iː/	feel, machine
/ɔ/	long, top
/ɔː/	fall, thought
/ʊ/	full, book
/uː/	do, cool
/ʌ/	cup, some
/ɜː/	bird, hurt

Diphthongs

/ɛi/	say, eight
/ɑi/	my, night
/ɔi/	boy
/əʊ/	boat, home
/ɑu/	now, found
/ɪə/	hear, here
/ɛə/	hair, where
/ʊə/	sure

/ˈ/ (precedes stressed syllable)

Consonants

/b/	book, able
/k/	come, look
/tʃ/	children, which
/d/	red, down
/f/	fall, if
/g/	go, leg
/dʒ/	Gerry, Jenny
/h/	have, hand
/l/	look, milk
/m/	man, come
/n/	now, run
/ŋ/	bring, running
/p/	paper, cup
/kw/	quite, quick
/r/	red, arrive
/ʳ/	car, four[†]
/s/	send, miss
/ʃ/	should, wish
/t/	it, time
/θ/	think, three
/ð/	the, with
/v/	very, give
/w/	want, when
/j/	yes, you
/z/	prize, rose
/ʒ/	measure

[†] silent before consonant and at end of sentence

Grammatical terms used in this book

action verb – a verb that describes a dynamic action or event: *run, read, throw, phone.*
active – a sentence structure where the doer of the action is the subject: *the dog bit the postman.*
adjective – a word that describes a noun: *red, heavy, electronic, difficult.*
adverb – a word that describes how, where or when an action or event takes place: *quickly, here, tomorrow.*
auxiliary – a special verb that is used with another (main) verb: *I was going, he didn't come*; compare **modal auxiliary**.
base-form – the normal dictionary form of the verb, without any endings: *come, go, study, drive, stop.*
C1 – a type of conditional tense: *if he arrives late.*
C2 – a type of conditional tense: *if he arrived late.*
clause – a part of a sentence that includes a verb.
comparative – the form of the adjective that shows a higher degree: *cheaper, bigger, more expensive.*
conditional – a tense of the verb that indicates hypothetical situations: *I'd read a book.* There are two main conditional tenses in English: C1 and C2.
consonant – in writing, the following letters: **b c d f g h j k l m n p q r s t v w x y z**; compare **vowel**. But consonant **sounds** can sometimes be written as vowels: *university.*
definite article – the word *the*.
degree words – words that describe the degree of an adjective: *very small, quite expensive, awfully clever.*
direct object – the person or thing that receives the action of the verb: *we saw the concert.*
direct speech – the actual words someone said, put in the sentence as a quote: *She said: He isn't coming*; compare **reported speech**.

ed-form – the regular past tense form of the verb: *smiled, stopped, studied, asked*.

empty it – in some sentence structures, an *it* that doesn't refer to anything specific, but is required for grammatical reasons: *it's raining, it's nice to see you*.

full form – *see* **short form**.

future – a tense of the verb – there are three main ways of doing the future in English: *I will write, I'm writing, I'm going to write*.

genitive – a form of the noun denoting possession or relationship: *John's book, the middle of the road*.

indefinite article – the word *a/an*.

indirect object – the person or thing that receives the direct object of the verb: *we gave the girl* (INDIRECT OBJECT) *a book* (DIRECT OBJECT).

indirect speech – another term for **reported speech**.

ing-form – the form of the verb ending in **-ing**: *coming, going, studying, driving, stopping*; used in the continuous tenses, and in other ways.

irregular verb – a verb that doesn't form its past simple tense by adding *-ed*: *flew (fly), came (come), went (go), made (make)*.

modal auxiliary – special auxiliary verbs that have their own meanings, but are used with other verbs: *he can speak English, you shouldn't go*.

negative – the form of the verb that tells you that something doesn't, didn't or won't happen.

noun – a word that names a thing, person, place or idea: *cat, James, London, honesty*.

object – the thing or person that *receives* the action in a sentence: *Liz fed the cats*; compare **subject**.

passive – a sentence structure where the receiver of the action is the subject: *the postman was bitten by the dog*; compare **active**.

past continuous – a tense of the verb that indicates ongoing action in the past: *I was reading*.

past participle – the form of the verb used with *have* to form the present perfect tense: *I've arrived, she's gone*.

past perfect – a tense of the verb one stage back in the past from the present perfect: *I had broken my leg*.

past simple – a tense of the verb that indicates completed action in the past: *I stopped*.

phrasal verb – a combination of verb + adverb which has a special meaning: *blow up, turn off, take off*.

possessive adjective – words that tell you who something belongs to: *my*, *your*, *his*.

preposition – a word that shows the relationship between nouns, or nouns and pronouns: *at*, *by*, *for*, *to*, *with*.

present continuous – a tense of the verb that indicates ongoing action at the time of speaking, or future intention: *I'm reading*.

present perfect – a tense of the verb indicating an action or event that has happened very recently: *I've broken my leg*.

present simple – a tense of the verb that indicates habitual action in the present, or state: *I read every day*.

pronoun – a word which stands in place of a noun: *I*, *me*, *you*, *he*, *him*, *she*, *her*, *we*, *us*, *they*, *them*.

regular verb – a verb that forms its past simple tense by adding *-ed*.

relative clause – a clause that adds information about the main clause in a complex sentence: *The man we saw yesterday is here again today*.

reported speech – someone's actual words incorporated into a sentence: *She said he wasn't coming*; compare **direct speech**.

s-form – the BASE-FORM of the verb with **-s** or **-es** added: *comes*, *goes*, *studies*, *drives*, *stops*.

short form – colloquial shortened forms of verbs, such as *I'm* for *I am*, and *wasn't* for *was not*; *I am* and *was not* are **full forms**.

statement – the positive form of the verb, stating that something does, did or will happen.

state verb – a verb that describes a continuing physical or mental state, or an unchanging situation: *know*, *belong*, *mean*, *contain*; compare **action verb**.

strong form – some common words have two pronunciations: a full pronunciation used only when emphasising the word (STRONG FORM), and a weak pronunciation used in all other circumstances; *see* Language point 13.

subject – the doer of the action in a sentence: *the postman delivered the letter*; compare **object**.

superlative – the form of the adjective that shows the highest degree: *the cheapest*, *the biggest*, *the most expensive*.

to-form – the BASE-FORM of the verb with *to* added to the front: *to come*, *to go*, *to study*, *to drive*, *to stop*. Sometimes called the to-INFINITIVE.

verb – a word that describes an action or event.

vowel – in writing, the following letters: **a e i o u**.

weak form – the normal pronunciation of a word that also has a full pronunciation for emphasis; *see* **strong form** and Language point 13.

wh-word – any of these question words: *who?, what?, where?, why?, when?, which?, whose?, how?*.

1 Pleased to meet you!

In this unit you will learn how to:

- greet people
- say goodbye to people
- introduce yourself to someone
- introduce someone to someone else
- identify people

Dialogue 1

VICKI: Hello, I'm Vicki.
HELEN: Hello, Vicki. My name's Helen.
VICKI: Pleased to meet you.
HELEN: And you.

Dialogue 2

STUART: I'm Stuart.
JENNY: Hello Stuart. I'm Jenny.
STUART: Nice to meet you.
JENNY: And you.

Dialogue 3

Paul introduces himself to Mo.

PAUL: Hello – you're Mo, aren't you?
MO: Yes, I am. And what's *your* name?
PAUL: I'm Paul – pleased to meet you.
MO: Pleased to meet you too.

Language point 1 – short forms

Introducing yourself and finding out people's names always involves the verb **be**. For example, if Jenny wants to tell someone her name, she can just say **I'm Jenny**, or she can say **My name's Jenny**. To find out someone else's name, she says **What's your name?** All these phrases contain special SHORT FORMS of the verb **be**. Let's have a look at how they work.

In colloquial English – when we are speaking in informal situations – we use special SHORT FORMS for some verbs. So, in Dialogue 1, Vicki says:

I'm Vicki

- **I'm** is the short form for the FULL FORM **I am**.

And in Dialogue 3, Paul says:

you're Mo

- **you're** is the short form for the full form **you are**.

With verbs that have short forms (not only **be** but also **have**, **do** and some others that we will meet later) we do not normally use the full form in speaking except when we want to put special emphasis on the verb. (But we *have* to use the full form in TAG RESPONSES – see next Language point.)

So, for the present tense of **be** we have short forms for all persons:

Full form		*Short form*	
I am	/aɪ æm/	I'm	/aɪm/
you are	/juː ɑːʳ/	you're	/jɔːʳ/
he is	/hiː ɪz/	he's	/hiːz/
she is	/ʃiː ɪz/	she's	/ʃiːz/
it is	/ɪt ɪz/	it's	/ɪts/
we are	/wiː ɑːʳ/	we're	/wɪəʳ/
they are	/ðeɪ ɑːʳ/	they're	/ðeəʳ/

Pay attention to the pronunciation of these short forms in British English, and notice that all the full forms have two syllables, while the short forms all have one.

Be careful with the he/she short form **'s** – you *can't* use it after a name ending in **-s**, **-ch**, **-sh**, **-x** or **-z**. So we say:

Fred's here   **Fiona's here**   **Terry's here**

Brian's here   **John's here**

but

James is here   **Rich is here**   **Trish is here**

Max is here   **Baz is here**

not

~~**James's here**~~   ~~**Rich's here**~~   ~~**Trish's here**~~

~~**Max's here**~~   ~~**Baz's here**~~

We will see some more short forms in the next unit. It is important to know how to use them as they form a common and typical feature of colloquial English everywhere.

Exercise 1

Turn the full forms into short forms in these sentences. Be careful – one of them *can't* be changed to a short form! The first one has been done for you.

1 Brian is in work today.   **Brian's in work today.**
2 Hello, I am Fred.
3 Sue is over there.

4   Terry is by the door.   *Terry is by ~~Terry's~~* .
5   They are in the kitchen.   *They're* .
6   Chris is next door.   *Chris is* .
7   We are in town tomorrow.   *We've* .
8   Stuart is at his desk.   *Stuart's* .
9   My brother is on holiday at the moment.   *My brother's / brothers*
10 This CD is broken.   *This CD's* .

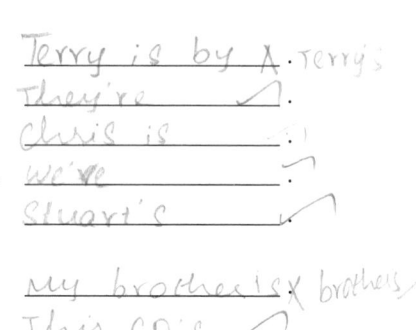

Language point 2 – question tags and tag responses

In Dialogue 3, Paul says: **You're Mo, aren't you?**, and Mo answers: **Yes, I am**. In English, when we want to check that something we have said is true, we can add a QUESTION TAG after a STATEMENT which invites the other speaker to confirm what has been said. There are many different types of tag, so for now we will just look at one.

Paul makes a statement:

You're Mo

but he wants to make sure this is true, so he adds:

aren't you?

so that Mo can tell him that he's right:

Yes, I am

Here are some more examples of TAGGED STATEMENTS:

You're a nurse, aren't you?
You're James, aren't you?
You're a computer technician, aren't you?
You're from Germany, aren't you?

Mo responds to the tag using the FULL FORM of the verb **be**: **Yes, I am**; we *don't* use the short form in tag responses, so it is wrong to say '~~Yes, I'm~~'. We will look at question tags in more detail in Unit 2.

Exercise 2

Add the correct question tags to these sentences – the first one has been done for you.

1. You're a teacher, **aren't you**?
2. Simon's a footballer, _____ ? *isn't he?*
3. Suzie's a nurse, _____ ? *isn't she?*
4. Pete and Dave are lawyers, _____ ? *aren't they?*
5. Ela's from Poland, _____ ? *isn't she?*
6. This food's delicious, _____ ? *isn't it?*
7. We're a bit late, _____ ? *aren't we?*
8. It's cold this morning, _____ ? *isn't it?*
9. You're from Finland, _____ ? *aren't you?*
10. Ilse's from Austria, _____ ? *isn't she?*

Dialogue 4

Rosemary wants to introduce Justine and Tim to Stuart, who doesn't know them.

ROSEMARY: Stuart, this is Justine.
STUART: Hello, Justine.
JUSTINE: Pleased to meet you, Stuart.
ROSEMARY: And this is Tim.
TIM: Hello, Stuart.

Dialogue 5

Justine introduces Vicki to Chris.

JUSTINE: Vicki – do you know Chris?
VICKI: I don't think so.
JUSTINE: Chris, this is Vicki.
CHRIS: Hello Vicki.
VICKI: Hello Chris. Pleased to meet you.

Language point 3 – introducing people

You can find out if someone knows someone else, or introduce two people who don't know each other, by asking one of them **Do you know...?** followed by the name of the other person.

Vicki answers with **I don't think so**, not because she isn't sure but because this is a more indirect way of saying **No** – it would sound rather short just to say 'No'. Let's look at another example of two people being introduced to each other:

Dialogue 6 🎧

Stuart is seeing if he can remember the names of everyone in the room.

STUART: Now then, are you Helen?
HELEN: Yes, I am.
STUART: And is that Su by the door?
HELEN: Yes, it is.

Stuart turns to another person.

STUART: And are you Jenny?
JENNY: Yes, I am!

Stuart points to someone else.

STUART: And is she Ann?
JENNY: Yes she is! Well done!

Dialogue 7 🎧

Su is talking to Shamira in the office.

SU: Is the coffee ready?
SHAMIRA: Yes, it is.
SU: Good. Where's the sugar?
SHAMIRA: It's over there on the table.

Su looks for the sugar.

SU: Are you sure, Shamira?

Shamira looks as well.

SHAMIRA: Oh no – here it is, on Tim's desk.
SU: Is Tim off today?
SHAMIRA: Yes, he is. He's ill.
SU: Poor Tim. Coffee for two, then?

Language point 4 – questions with the verb 'be'

We turn statements using the verb **be** into questions by simply changing the order of the pronoun (**I, you, he, she, it,** etc.) and verb in the full form. So:

Statement (full form)	Question
I am	am I?
you are	are you?
he is	is he?
she is	is she?
Kevin is	is Kevin?
we are	are we?
they are	are they?
Ann and Jenny are	are Ann and Jenny?

Notice that there is no short form for questions: for example, instead of **he is** we usually say **he's**, but we cannot say '~~'s he?~~' instead of **is he?**

(Most verbs in English *don't* form questions in this way, as we will see in later units – but this is always the way to make questions with **be**.)

Exercise 3

Turn these statements into questions – remember to use *full* forms! The first one has been done for you.

1 I'm late. **Am I late?**
2 Dave's off work today.
3 It's cold outside.
4 We're in the right place.
5 Everyone's ready.
6 You're tired.
7 They're in the garden.
8 Morgan and Eddie are here.
9 Oliver's outside.
10 Jenny's inside.

Dialogue 8

Brian is having trouble with names and faces.

BRIAN: Is that Gerry over there?
STUART: Yes, it is.
BRIAN: And who's that with him?
STUART: That's Ben.
BRIAN: And where's Sandra?
STUART: She's over there, by the window.
BRIAN: Oh yes – and who's that with her?
STUART: That's Dave.

Dialogue 9

Ben has a list of names of people in the office, but he doesn't know who's who! He asks Justine to help, and she points them out as he reads out the names.

BEN: Right. Where's Helen?
JUSTINE: That's her, by the door.
BEN: And Stuart?
JUSTINE: That's him, at the computer.
BEN: And what about Gerry and Adrian?
JUSTINE: That's them, by the coffee-machine.
BEN: And finally what about Justine?
JUSTINE: That's me, silly!

Language point 5 – personal pronouns

When we looked at the verb **be** earlier in this unit we saw the PERSONAL PRONOUNS that are used with verbs in English. Here they are again:

   I you he she we they

These are mostly used before verbs. Notice that in English we have different pronouns in the singular for males and females, but we do not make a distinction in the plural: **they** is used for all third person subjects, whether male or female. And notice that **you** is both singular and plural, and both informal and formal – we *don't* have a special form for addressing strangers; **you** is correct in all circumstances.

All the personal pronouns except **you** have two forms: the SUBJECT FORM and the OBJECT FORM:

SUBJECT FORM	**I**	**you**	**he**	**she**	**we**	**they**
OBJECT FORM	**me**	**you**	**him**	**her**	**us**	**them**

We use the object form of a personal pronouns when it is the OBJECT of the sentence (see Grammatical terms) – we will look at this in a later unit – but we also use object forms in identification sentences, for example after **That's ...** , as in Dialogue 9, where Justine is pointing people out:

That's him	*not*	'That's he'
That's her	*not*	'That's she'
That's them	*not*	'That's they'
That's me	*not*	'That's I'

It is *wrong* to use the subject forms in this kind of sentence.

Exercise 4

Fill in the pronoun. The first one has been done for you.

1 Where's Terry?   That's **him**!
2 Where's Janet?   That's ___!
3 Where's George?   That's ___!

4 Where are Paul and Gerry? That's ___!
5 Where's Su?   That's ___!
6 Where are Ann and Tim?   That's ___!

Idiom – what about . . . ?

In Dialogue 9, Ben asks Justine **Where's Helen?**. Then he wants to ask the same about other people – he says **What about Gerry and Adrian?** and **What about Justine?**. We use **What about . . . ?** to indicate that we're asking the same question as before.

Here's another example: Gerry wants to find out what kind of ice cream Adrian likes. This is how the conversation goes:

GERRY: Just answer yes or no, OK Adrian?
ADRIAN: OK.
GERRY: Do you like vanilla ice cream?
ADRIAN: Yes.
GERRY: What about strawberry?
ADRIAN: Yes.
GERRY: What about chocolate?
ADRIAN: Yes.
GERRY: What about lemon?
ADRIAN: No.
GERRY: And what about raspberry?
ADRIAN: Yes.
GERRY: Thanks for your help.
ADRIAN: Don't mention it.

Dialogue 10

Shamira introduces herself to someone who has just started work in the same office as her.

SHAMIRA: Excuse me, I don't know your name.
KATH: It's Kath – hello!
SHAMIRA: Hello, Kath – my name's Shamira. Pleased to meet you.
KATH: And you.

SHAMIRA:	Do you know the people in our office?
KATH:	I know their faces, but I don't know all their names.
SHAMIRA:	Maybe I can help you out there?
KATH:	Yes. That person by the photocopier – what's her name?
SHAMIRA:	That's Helen. And the man sitting with her . . .
KATH:	I know his name – that's Adrian, isn't it?
SHAMIRA:	Yes – he's our boss.

Language point 6 – possessive adjectives

Between them, Shamira and Kath cleverly manage to use all the POSSESSIVE ADJECTIVES that correspond to the PERSONAL PRONOUNS we've already met:

Personal pronouns		Possessive adjective
Subject	Object	
I	me	my
you	you	your
he	him	his
she	her	her
we	us	our
they	them	their

Exercise 5

Fill in the blanks from the words in the box – some are personal pronouns and some are possessive adjectives.

1 Excuse ___, I don't know ___ name.
2 Do ___ know that man over there? What's ___ name?
3 ___ recognise those people, but I don't know ___ names.
4 Do ___ know Helen? That's ___ by the window.
5 Hello, ___ name's John – pleased to meet ___.
6 ___ don't know James – can you introduce ___ ?

your	his	their	us
her	me	we	my
you	you	you	I

Dialogue 11

Stuart and Rosemary are at a party. Stuart doesn't know anyone, so Rosemary is pointing out who's who.

STUART: Who's that over there, then?
ROSEMARY: That's Dave.
STUART: And the two people with him?
ROSEMARY: Those are friends of his – but I don't know their names. And then ... you see that woman by the window?
STUART: With the funny hat?
ROSEMARY: Yes ... that's Miranda – her husband works with Steve in the garage down the road.
STUART: And which one is Steve?
ROSEMARY: Steve's not here – he's off on a course[1] somewhere. But there's his brother, Mike. He's in computers.
STUART: Really? Like me!
ROSEMARY: Let's go and introduce ourselves, shall we?
STUART: Good idea.

1 **off on a course** = 'away from home doing a training programme'

Language point 7 – pointing people out

When we are indicating or pointing a person out, we use **that** rather than the pronouns **he** or **she**. So when Stuart indicates Dave to Rosemary for the first time, he doesn't say **Who's he?** – he says **Who's that?** And Rosemary replies with **That's Dave**. This is the normal way of pointing a person out in English, and it isn't rude or impolite. It *is* okay to use **he** or **she**, but it's more natural and much more common to use **that**. In the same way, we say **What's that?** when we point to a thing, but in this case we *never* say 'What's it?'.

However, when we point out more than one person, we *do* use the pronoun **they** or **those people**; but the answer can still be **that**:

Who are they over there?	– That's Mick and Sandra.
	not 'Those are Mick and Sandra.'
Who are those people in the corner?	– That's the Smiths.
	or – Those are the Smiths.

Who are they in the other room? — That's the Chinese students.
or — Those are the Chinese students.
Who are they at the bar? — That's the rugby club.
not 'Those are the rugby club.'

Notice that you have to be careful with the answers – you can use **Those are** with plurals, but *not* with single individuals, for example **Mick and Sandra** (even though together they are plural), nor with singular NOUNS denoting groups, for example **the rugby club** (even though it contains many individuals).

Language point 8 – 'Let's . . .'

When Rosemary says **Let's go . . ., shall we?**, she's making a suggestion to Stuart. This is a very common way of doing this in English – you start with **Let's** and then add the verb in its BASE-FORM (the dictionary form with nothing added):

Let's go for a walk
Let's phone James
Let's order a pizza
Let's have a barbecue

Then Rosemary adds the tag **. . ., shall we?** at the end to make the suggestion more open, inviting Stuart to agree or disagree with it. In this case, Stuart agrees by saying **Good idea** – he could also have said any of these other phrases:

OK (, then)
All right (, then)
Fine
Fine by me
Why not?

Idioms

The adverb **off** has a number of idiomatic meanings in colloquial English. In Dialogue 7, Su asks **Is Tim off today?**, and in Dialogue 11, Rosemary says that Steve is **off on a course** – in this kind of-phrase, **off** means **away**, and it can be used when someone *is* away or when they are *going* away. For example, we can say:

I'm off to London tomorrow = 'I'm going to London tomorrow'
I'm off in London tomorrow = 'I will be in London tomorrow'
Jenny's off in the morning = 'Jenny is going away/leaving in the morning'

Sometimes the same phrase can mean two different things: **Jenny's off today** can mean either that Jenny is leaving to go somewhere today, or that she is away from work.

Rosemary tells Stuart that Mike's **in computers** – this is an informal way of saying what kind of work he does; it means that his work is something to do with computers, but that Rosemary doesn't know exactly what his job is. Compare these two statements:

Mike's in computers
Mike's a software designer

The first description is vague or unspecific, while the second description is precise.

Here are some more examples of general descriptions of someone's job:

Harry's in publishing
Fiona's in fashion
Kath's in education
Paul's in politics
Vicki's in banking
James is in advertising

Finally, notice the difference between **in** and **into** in this type of sentence:

Mike's in computers = Mike's job involves computers
Mike's into computers = Mike's interested in computers

Stuart says **Really?** in response to a statement by Rosemary – this is not a true question (he's not *asking* Rosemary if what she's said is true), but is simply a way of expressing interest in a fact not previously known. Look at some more examples:

I'm going to sail to New Zealand in my yacht	– Really?
Norman's bought another horse	– Really?
Chocolate is an aphrodysiac	– Really?
More than a billion people speak Chinese	– Really?

Stuart adds **Like me!** to say that what Rosemary has just told him is true of Stuart as well. He could also have said **Me too!**, **Same here!** or **So am I!** Here are some more examples:

Posh and Becks are English	– Like me!
Terry's a long-distance lorry driver	– Me too!
My brother's an accountant	– Same here!
Gerry's going to Spain this summer	– So am I!

The first three responses can be used in all situations; but be careful with **So am I!** – it can only be used in answer to a statement using the verb **be** (on its own or in conjunction with another verb, as in the last example above).

Dialogue 12

Now Ann introduces Marian to Rosemary.

ANN: Rosemary, this is Marian – she's from Brighton.
ROSEMARY: Hello, Marian – what do you do for a job?
MARIAN: I'm a teacher.
ROSEMARY: So am I! Where do you teach?
MARIAN: In the college here. What about you?
ROSEMARY: I teach in a primary school.

Language point 9 – 'a'/'an' and 'the'

In Dialogue 9, Rosemary says **I teach in a primary school** – she uses the INDEFINITE ARTICLE with the noun because it is the first time it has appeared in the conversation. This is why we use the indefinite article when we say what someone's job is:

I'm a doctor	Suzi's a teacher
James is an airline pilot	she's a nurse
he's a footballer	Paul's a university lecturer

Jeremy's a poet
Jane's an orthodontist
Fiona's an archaeologist
Harold's an estate agent
Mike's a surgeon

The indefinite article has two forms: **a** and **an** – you can tell which one to use by the *sound* of the word that follows:

- if the following word begins with a CONSONANT sound, we use **a**
- if the following word begins with a VOWEL sound, we use **an**

Remember that it is the *sound* that is important, not the spelling. In the list above you can see that Paul is **a university lecturer** – the word **university** begins with a vowel in writing, but the first sound of the word is /j/, which is a consonant sound, so **a** is correct here.

Pronunciation

Many very commonly used words in English have both STRONG and WEAK pronunciations. In normal speech we use the weak pronunciation of these words, unless we want to emphasise them for some reason.

The weak pronunciations of the indefinite article are /ə/ and /ən/ – make sure you use these when you are speaking! We will meet a lot more weak pronunciations in Unit 2 (Language point 13).

Exercise 6

Look at these people's jobs – complete these sentences using **a** or **an**.

1 John's _a_ doctor.
2 Fiona's _a_ nurse.
3 My sister's _a_ university student.
4 My father's _a_ pilot.
5 Dave's _an_ architect.
6 Simon's _a_ writer.
7 Suzie's _an_ optician.
8 My father's _an_ airline pilot.
9 Kath's _a_ psychologist.
10 Roger's _an_ assistant librarian.

Exercise 7

Listen to the audio of people telling you their names and their jobs, then fill in the information.

1 Pete   is a   **lawyer**
2 Gerry   is an   architect
3 James   is a   Doctor
4 Helen   is a   teacher
5 Susan   is a   scientist
6 Nigel   is a   taxi driver
7 Brian   is an   actor
8 Allison   is a   farmer
9 Henry   is a   policeman
10 Lisa   is a   journalist

We use the DEFINITE ARTICLE **the** when talking about something that has already been mentioned, or that we know about anyway:

James is taking a taxi to the airport
Tom works in an office in the city

We already know about the airport, and about the city, but not about the taxi or the office – these are 'new information'.

old information – 'the'
new information – 'a'/'an'

We also use **a/an** to talk about *one thing out of many*, and **the** to talk about a *unique thing*:

The sun is a star
(There is only *one* sun, but there are *many* stars)

This is a large room, but that is the largest room in the hotel
(There are many large rooms in the hotel, but only *one* of them can be the largest)

> ⚠️ **Be careful!** The definite article **the** is used with *both* singular *and* plural nouns, but the indefinite article is *only* used with singular nouns.

17

Pronunciation

The is pronounced /ðə/ before CONSONANT sounds, but /ðɪ/ before VOWEL sounds:

the nurse	/ðə nɜːs/
the architect	/ðɪ ˈɑːkɪtɛkt/
the university	/ðə juːnɪˈvɜːsɪti/
the hour	/ðɪ ˈauwə/

Exercise 8

Complete these sentences using **a/an** or **the**. Don't worry if you don't completely understand the sentences – concentrate on the types of nouns.

1. Please could you tell me where ___ bank is?
2. We're going to ___ cinema after lunch.
3. ___ streets in ___ town centre are flooded.
4. We're staying in ___ large room on ___ fifth floor.
5. You need ___ telescope to see ___ Moon in detail.
6. Would you like ___ cup of tea?
7. What's ___ weather like today?
8. Have you got ___ ten-pound note I could borrow?
9. Paris is ___ capital of France.
10. ___ Russian Federation is ___ very large country.

Dialogue 13

Vicki's leaving early, but she doesn't forget to say goodbye to Helen, Jenny, Stuart and Rosemary.

VICKI: I'm off now – bye, everybody!
HELEN: Bye, Vicki!
JENNY: Bye, Vicki – see you tomorrow!
STUART: See you, Vicki!
ROSEMARY: Bye, Vicki!

Language point 10 – saying goodbye

You may have noticed that *none* of the speakers in Dialogue 13 actually said **Goodbye** – in colloquial English this phrase is usually shortened to **Bye**. It is always okay to use this when you are leaving someone and want to say goodbye.

We can also use the phrase **Bye bye**, particularly when talking to little children.

Another very common phrase is **See you!** – you can say just this, or, if you know when you'll see the person again, you can add a time phrase like **tomorrow**, **on Friday** or **next week**. In normal speech **See you** is usually pronounced /ˈsiːjə/ – make sure you use this pronunciation when you're speaking. If you don't know when you'll next see the person, you can also say **See you round** or **See you around** – nobody in Dialogue 13 says this, because they all expect to see Vicki tomorrow.

2 Where are you from?

In this unit you will learn how to:
- use the negative
- find out information about people
- talk about things that happen regularly or all the time
- use question words
- say that something belongs to someone

Dialogue 1

Gerry is talking to the wrong person.

GERRY:	Hello, Ian.
ADRIAN:	I'm not Ian, I'm Adrian.
GERRY:	Oh! ... Sorry!

Gerry looks round the room.

	... who's Ian, then?
ADRIAN:	That's Ian, over there.
GERRY:	Thanks!

Dialogue 2

Gerry goes to talk to the man Adrian has pointed out.

GERRY:	Hello – you're Ian, aren't you?
IAN:	Yes, I am. Isn't your name Steve?
GERRY:	No, no – I'm Gerry.

IAN: Oh, you're Gerry, are you?
GERRY: Yes, I am. I work with Steve.
IAN: Do you? Where's Steve, then?
GERRY: I don't know.

Language point 11 – negative short forms

In Unit 1 we saw how the verb **be** has special SHORT FORMS in the present tense when making statements. Another important set of short forms with the verb **be** involves the NEGATIVE word **not**:

Full form	Short form
I am not	**I'm not**
you are not	**you're not** *or* **you aren't**
he is not	**he's not** *or* **he isn't**
she is not	**she's not** *or* **she isn't**
it is not	**it's not** *or* **it isn't**
we are not	**we're not** *or* **we aren't**
they are not	**they're not** *or* **they aren't**

As you can see, when we add **not** to the present tense of **be**, we have a choice of how to do it – we're allowed *one* SHORT FORM, and we can:

either   keep the short form of the verb and simply add **not**:
            he's + **not** = **he's not**

or   use the full form of the verb and add **not**:
            he is + **not** = **he isn't**

Both these ways are correct, and there is normally no difference in meaning or use. But there is no choice with **I am not** – the only short form possible here is **I'm not** and it is wrong to say '~~I amn't~~'.
Another short form you need to know is **don't** (**do** + **not**) – we'll see why later in this unit.
Notice that the short form **n't** is written with the verb as *one word*:

         we aren't
not   '~~we are n't~~'

Exercise 1

Turn the statements into negatives, using both SHORT forms we have learnt. Be careful – in one of them you can *only* use *one*. The first sentence is done for you.

1. Pete's in the office today.   **Pete isn't in the office today.**
   Pete's not in the office today.

2. We're ready to go.

3. I'm at home tomorrow.

4. They're in the kitchen.

5. You're very late.

6. Suzie's back at work.

7. It's very cold today.

8. She's in the garden.

Dialogue 3

Jo wants to introduce Mark to Di.

Jo: Mark – this is Di, a friend of mine from work.
MARK: Pleased to meet you, Di.
DI: Hello, Mark. How do you know Jo?
MARK: We go to the same fitness club ... don't we, Jo?
Jo: That's right.

Dialogue 4

Andy is asking Bob about his daily routine.

ANDY: When do you usually get up, Bob?[1]
BOB: I get up at seven during the week, but I don't get up so early at the weekend.
ANDY: So ... when do you leave for work?
BOB: I leave the house at about eight.

ANDY:		And how do you get to work?
BOB:		I walk to work, because I live close to my office.
ANDY:		And when do you get back?
BOB:		About six.
ANDY:		What do you do in the evenings?
BOB:		Sometimes I go and work out[2] in the gym. Or I watch TV. Or I go and see friends.

1 **get up** = 'rise', 'get out of bed in the morning'
2 **work out** = 'do exercises'

Language point 12 – present simple

There are two present tenses in English: the PRESENT SIMPLE and the PRESENT CONTINUOUS. Mark uses the PRESENT SIMPLE when he says **We go to the same fitness club**, because he is talking about an action that happens regularly.

The present simple is easy to form in English: with **I**, **you**, **we** and **they** we use the BASE-FORM of the verb (the form of the verb without any endings, as listed in the dictionary); and with **he**, **she**, **it** and nouns (names of people and things) we add **-s** or **-es**. We only add **-es** if the verb ends in a vowel (e.g. **go**) or in **-ch**, **-s**, **-sh**, **-x** or **-z**; otherwise we use **-s**. Here are some examples of the present simple:

	live	work	run	go	finish
	I live	**I work**	**I run**	**I go**	**I finish**
but	**he lives**	**he works**	**he runs**	**he goes**	**he finishes**

The verb **have** has an irregular s-form **has** /hæz/.

Pronunciation

The **-s** ending is pronounced /s/ after VOICELESS sounds (**works** – /wɜːks/), but /z/ after VOICED sounds (**lives** /lɪvz/, **runs** /rʌnz/); the **-es** ending is pronounced /ɪz/ after a CONSONANT: **finishes** /ˈfɪnɪʃɪz/, but /z/ after a VOWEL: **goes** /ɡəʊz/. The s-forms of two verbs, **does** and **says**, have irregular pronunciations: /dʌz/ and /sɛz/.

We form questions in the present simple by using the AUXILIARY verb **do**, which is also used for the TAGS:

Do you **live** in Heathfield?
(TAG RESPONSE: 'Yes, I do'/'No, I don't')

Does James **work** in an office?
(TAG RESPONSE: 'Yes, he does'/'No, he doesn't')

And we also use **do** when we start a sentence with a question word such as **how ...?**:

How **do** you **know** Jo?
How **does** Charlie **go** to work?

The negative of the present simple uses **don't/doesn't** /'dəʊnt/ /'dʌznt/:

I **don't speak** Italian.
My sister **doesn't speak** Italian either.

> ⚠ **Be careful!** The present simple is *not* used to describe actions that are taking place now. We will see how to do this in the next unit.

Exercise 2

Look at the answers and complete the questions. The first one is done for you.

1 Where **does Fred work**?   (Fred)
                                        He works in a shop.
2 _Do you drink tea_?   (drink tea)
                                        No, I don't.
3 _Does this bus go_?   (that bus/station)
                                        Yes, it goes to the station.
4 _Does she speak Spanish_?   (Spanish)
                                        No, she only speaks French.
5 _Do Pete & Sally speak Italian_?   (Pete and Sally/Italian)
                                        No, they speak Esperanto.
6 Where _do you teach_?
                                        I teach in a school.

7 Where _does this bus go_? (this bus)
It goes to the town centre.
8 _Does Su live nearby_? (Su/nearby)
Yes, she lives next door.
9 When _do Mick and Sandra leave_? (Mick and Sandra)
They leave at nine o'clock.
10 When _does the post arrive_? (the post)
It arrives early in the morning.

Exercise 3

Here are some things Stephen and his friends do and don't do. Complete the sentences using the information from the box.

	does [+]	*doesn't do* [–]
Stephen	speak Russian	play the piano
James	drink coffee	speak Russian
Oliver	wear glasses	drink coffee
Jenny	play the piano	wear glasses

1 [+] Stephen **speaks Russian**
2 [–] Oliver _____
3 [–] James   _____
4 [+] Jenny   _____
5 [–] Stephen _____
6 [–] Jenny   _____
7 [+] James   _____
8 [+] Oliver _____

Dialogue 5

Chris and Julie are looking through Chris's family photos.

JULIE: That's your brother Dave, isn't it?
CHRIS: Yes, it is.
JULIE: And who's that with him?
CHRIS: That's his wife. She's called Debbie, and she's from Australia.
JULIE: Do they live here?
CHRIS: No, they live in Australia – in Sydney. He's a lorry driver, and she's a nurse.
JULIE: Do they both work in Sydney?
CHRIS: No – Debbie works in one of the hospitals, but Dave drives all over the country.
JULIE: Have they got any children?
CHRIS: Two boys.
[*Julie turns the page*] Here they are – Simon and James.
JULIE: How handsome they are!
CHRIS: Thank you!

Language point 13 – weak forms

A number of very common short words in English have two pronunciations: a FULL PRONUNCIATION when they are given special emphasis, and a more common WEAK PRONUNCIATION otherwise. Here are some that we have had already – if you have the cassettes/CDs, listen again to the Dialogues we have had so far and see if you can hear the weak pronunciations.

	Full	*Weak*
the	/ðiː/	/ðɪ/, /ðə/
to	/tuː/	/tə/
at	/æt/	/ət/
for	/fɔːʳ/	/fə/
and	/ænd/	/ən(d)/
do	/duː/	/də/
or	/ɔːʳ/	/ə/
of	/ɔv/	/əv/
your	/jɔːʳ/	/jəʳ/
him	/hɪm/	/ɪm/
her	/hɛːʳ/	/əʳ/
from	/frɔm/	/frəm/

Dialogue 6

Two people meet one morning in a crowded café in London.

ANDY: Do you mind if I sit here?
BETH: Not at all.
ANDY: It's busy in here, isn't it?
BETH: It's always like this in the mornings.
ANDY: Do you live round here?
BETH: No – I live a few miles away. But I work just round the corner. What about you?
ANDY: I'm visiting friends for the day.
BETH: Where do you come from, then?
ANDY: From Bristol. But I live in Cambridge now, because that's where I work.
BETH: So what do you do?
ANDY: I'm a doctor. What about you?
BETH: I work for a publisher's.

Language point 14 – forms of the verb

There are *five* main forms of the verb in English – let's look at them quickly, using an ordinary REGULAR VERB, **talk**:

BASE-FORM	**talk** –	this is the simplest form of the verb, with no endings added
S-FORM	**talks**	
ING-FORM	**talking**	
ED-FORM	**talked**	
TO-FORM	**to talk** –	this is the same as the base-form, but with **to** in front

However, a lot of common verbs in English are IRREGULAR in the ED-FORM (for example, **speak** changes to **spoke**, *not* 'speaked'), and there are spelling rules as well (for example, **stop**, but **stopping** *not* 'stoping').

We will deal with all these things as the course goes on – all you have to do for now is remember the names of the forms and what they look like with a regular verb.

In this unit we have seen the base-form and the S-FORM. We saw that the s-form is used in the PRESENT SIMPLE in the third person singular, but that otherwise the present simple is the same as the base-form; and we saw Andy in Dialogue 6 use the base-form after **Do you mind if I . . . ?**

In the next unit we will look at the ING-FORM.

Dialogue 7

Jane brings the coffees over – but she can't remember who ordered what.

JANE:	Here we are, then. Now . . . whose is the latte?
FRED:	That's mine.
JANE:	And the cappuccino is yours, Su, isn't it?
SU:	No, that's mine there – the mocha.
JANE:	Right. And mine is the Americano, so the espresso is yours, Rod.
ROD:	That's right. Now . . . where's the sugar?

Language point 15 – wh-questions

When we ask for information, there is a set of special words that can be used to start the question:

where?	/weə^r/	
what?	/wɔt/	
when?	/wɛn/	
why?	/waɪ/	
who?	/huː/	
whose?	/huːz/	(this word means 'belonging to who?')
which?	/wɪtʃ/	(this word is used to *identify* things)

Because they all begin with **wh-**, the questions they ask are called wh-questions. There is also a question word that doesn't begin with **wh-**, which is **how?**, but we include it in the WH-WORDS anyway.

We've already met **what?** and **who?** in Unit 1 when we were talking about finding out people's names:

What's your name?
Who's that over there?

Here are some more examples with the verb **be**:

What's the time?
Why is James late?
Where are my gloves?
Whose car is that over there?
Which is mine?

If we use the present simple after these words, we need **do/does**, because this is how we form questions with the present simple.

Where <u>do you</u> live?	– I live in Heathfield
What <u>do you</u> think?	– I think it's a great idea!
How <u>does this</u> work?	– It works on batteries
Which <u>do you</u> prefer?	– I prefer this one

Exercise 4

Complete these sentences with the correct wh-word.

1. Wh___ knows the answer?
2. Wh___ does this word mean?
3. Wh___ shall I put these bags?
4. Wh___ does the next train leave?
5. Wh___ is he looking at me like that?
6. Wh___ dress do you like?
7. Wh___ do they live now?
8. Wh___ book is this?
9. Wh___ do you think of that idea?
10. Wh___ is that man's name?

Exercise 5

Match the meanings of these wh-words with the words in the box.

1. **What?** is used to identify **a thing**
2. **Who?** is used to identify _____
3. **Where?** is used to identify _____
4. **When?** is used to identify _____
5. **Why?** is used to identify _____
6. **Whose?** is used to identify _____
7. **Which?** is used to identify _____
8. **How?** is used to identify _____

a place	an owner	a time	a person
a choice	a thing	a reason	a way/method

Language point 16 – mine and yours

In Dialogue 7, Fred says **That's mine**, meaning **That's my latte**. Look at these two sentences:

This is my coffee
This coffee is mine   *not*   'This coffee is my'

And these two:

Is this your coffee?
Is this coffee yours?   *not*   '~~Is this coffee your?~~'

my and **your** are POSSESSIVE ADJECTIVES (Unit 1) and are used *before the noun*; but **mine** and **yours** are POSSESSIVE PRONOUNS and stand alone. Here are the others:

Adjective	*Pronoun*
her	**hers**
his	**his** (no difference)
our	**ours**
their	**theirs**

Other possessives have the same form whether they are adjectives or pronouns:

This is Anna's coffee
This coffee is Anna's

We will meet the possessive **'s** in the next unit (Language point 19).

> ⚠ **Be careful!** Although **my**, **your,** etc. are adjectives, they *can't* be used with **a**, **some**, **this**, **that**, **these**, or **those** – instead we have to use **of** + PRONOUN after the noun. So, in Dialogue 3, Jo calls Di **a friend of mine**, *not* '~~a my friend~~'.

Here are some more examples:

this house		**this house of yours**
	not	'~~this your house~~'
	not	'~~your this house~~'
some friends		**some friends of ours**
	not	'~~some our friends~~'
	not	'~~our some friends~~'
those children		**those children of hers**
	not	'~~those her children~~'
	not	'~~her those children~~'

Exercise 6

Correct the following sentences. Be careful! One of them doesn't need correcting.

1. I'm pleased with my present, but are you pleased with yours?
2. Where do you want to go – my place or your?
3. Is this book his or her?
4. This drink is your and that one's my.
5. I've forgotten mine mobile phone.
6. His workbook is not as neat as my.

Exercise 7

Look at the possessive adjectives and nouns and rewrite them as a phrase. The first one has been done for you.

1	this + your good news	**this good news of yours**
2	that + his kind mother	_____
3	some + our close friends	_____
4	a + my great idea	_____
5	those + her friends	_____
6	this + their stupid idea	_____

Exercise 8

Listen to the audio of this group of friends deciding what to order at the café, then fill in the details of the orders next to the names.

	Drink	Food
Henry	_____	_____
Dave	_____	_____
Su	_____	_____
Kath	_____	_____

3 Could you tell me where the bank is?

In this unit you will learn how to:

- ask and say where things are
- ask the way to places in town
- talk about things that are happening now
- give and understand instructions
- tell people not to do something

Dialogue 1

Jac stops a passer-by to ask the way.

JAC: Excuse me, could you tell me where the bank is?
PASSER-BY: The bank? It's just over there, next to the supermarket.
JAC: Ah yes – thanks very much.

Dialogue 2

Meanwhile, Nina can't find the tourist information office.

NINA: Excuse me – could you tell me how to get to the tourist information office?
PASSER-BY: Hang on[1] ... let's see now. Right, go back to the post office and turn right. And then go along the road till you get to a big supermarket. The tourist information office is opposite.
NINA: And what's the supermarket called?

PASSER-BY:	MegaSave, I think. Shall I write it down for you?
NINA:	No, I think I've got it. Thanks a lot.
PASSER-BY:	Bye!

1 **Hang on** = 'Wait a moment'

Language point 17 – commands

The BASE-FORM of the verb can be used on its own to tell someone to do something:

Open the door
Close the window
Lock the door

But in colloquial English this way of giving commands is rather short and can sound rude.

If we want to give someone *directions* or *instructions*, however, it *is* okay to use the base-form:

Turn left at the traffic lights
Go straight ahead
Plug the computer in and switch on

It doesn't matter whether you are talking to one person or more than one – the base-form stays the same.

> ⚠ **Be careful!** Normally, except with close friends, or when telling someone to do something nice, we *don't* use the base-form when we want someone to do something, as it sounds very short and a bit rude. See Language point 18 on how to do this.

If we want to tell someone *not* to do something, we can always use **Don't** + base-form:

Don't wait for me
Don't pay the bill
Don't worry

Exercise 1

Say where you think you would find the following orders. Write the correct letters in the blanks.

1	library	_j_	a	Don't annoy the teacher!
2	park	___	b	Don't smoke near the patients!
3	bar	___	c	Don't forget to turn off your mobile!
4	restaurant	___	d	Don't forget your passport!
5	hospital	___	e	Don't forget the present!
6	classroom	___	f	Don't drink too much!
7	airport	___	g	Don't complain about the food!
8	swimming pool	___	h	Don't pick the flowers!
9	cinema	___	i	Don't dive!
10	birthday party	___	j	~~Don't make too much noise!~~

Language point 18 – asking people to do things

Instead of giving commands (Language point 17), we usually *ask* people to do things for us. To do this, we put an AUXILIARY before the base-form: **Could you ...?** Or **Would you ...?**, and at the end of the sentence we can add **please**:

Could you open the window (please)?
Would you close the door (please)?

Or we can use the auxiliary as a TAG, and start with the base-form:

Open the door, could you?
Close the door, would you?

Don't forget the auxiliary tag here – otherwise it will sound rude.

Exercise 2

Correct these instructions and requests. Be careful! One of them *doesn't* need correcting.

1 Slip not on the ice! _____
2 Wait please here a minute. _____

3   Be not rude to customers!
4   Do this work now, please.
5   Don't please throw litter.
6   Open the door, you could?
7   You could close the door, please?
8   Do wait not for me.

Dialogue 3

Terry is looking for the bus station.

TERRY: Excuse me, am I going the right way for the bus station?
PASSER-BY: Let's see now ... yes – keep going down here till you reach the traffic lights, then turn right and you'll see the bus station at the end of the road.
TERRY: Thanks a lot.
PASSER-BY: Quite all right.

Idiom

We use the phrase **Let's see now** to signal to the person we're talking to that we need a moment to think.

Language point 19 – genitive

In Dialogue 3 the passer-by says:

the end of the road *not* 'the road's end'

But we say

John's book *not* 'the book of John'

So we have two GENITIVE constructions in English:

POSSESSIVE: **John's book**   (X's Y)
OF-PHRASE: **the end of the road**   (the Y of X)

How do we decide which to use?

We prefer the possessive (X's Y):

> when X is a *person*: **Laura's exam results**
> when Y *belongs* to X: **Gerry's hand**, **Fred's car**

but otherwise we generally prefer **of** (the Y of X)

> **the door of the school**
> **the middle of the night**
> **the end of the war**

Exercise 3

Decide which of the two options is correct for each phrase.

1 John's book   ~~The book of John~~
2 The road's end   The end of the road
3 My sister's clothes   The clothes of my sister
4 The house's top   The top of the house
5 The week's end   The end of the week
6 Alice's new car   The new car of Alice
7 The pool's bottom   The bottom of the pool
8 The night's middle   The middle of the night
9 My brother's house   The house of my brother
10 Our cat's ears   The ears of our cat

Dialogue 4

Sasha is lost – she's looking for the art gallery. In the end, a passer-by notices her.

PASSER-BY: You look lost – can I help?
SASHA: Oh thank you – yes, I *am* a bit lost, I'm afraid. I'm trying to find the art gallery.
PASSER-BY: That's miles away! No wonder you look lost! Get the 22 bus from the corner here, and get off at Southwold Terrace. Then turn left into York Avenue, and carry on until you get to the gallery.
SASHA: Could you write it down for me? I'm bound to get lost again otherwise.

Passer-by:	Certainly . . . [*writes it down for Sasha*] . . . there you are.
Sasha:	Thank you for your help.
Passer-by:	Not at all. Enjoy the art gallery!
Sasha:	I will. Bye!
Passer-by:	Bye!

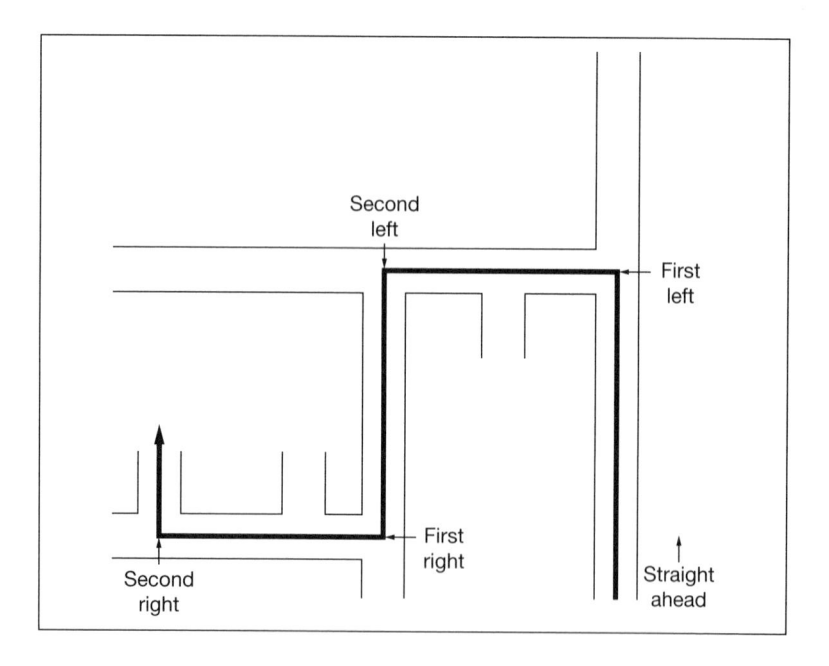

Idioms

– **no wonder** means 'I'm not surprised that . . .'

– **I'm bound to . . .** means 'I'm certain to . . .' *or* 'It's certain that I'll . . .'

– We use **There you are** when we *give* someone something, or when we *finish doing* something for them.

– **otherwise** means 'if not':

Hurry up, otherwise we'll miss the bus.
= 'Hurry up – <u>if</u> we <u>don't</u> hurry up, we'll miss the bus.'

Language point 20 – phrasal verbs

A PHRASAL VERB is a VERB + ADVERB which together have a special meaning. For example, **carry on** in Dialogue 4 means **continue** – it has nothing to do with **carry**.

Phrasal verbs are very important in colloquial English – they are often used instead of more formal 'standard' words. Here are some more examples:

find out	=	'discover'
turn up	=	'arrive'
let down	=	'disappoint'
fall out	=	'argue'
break down	=	'stop working' (machine)

It's usually the very common verbs in English that form phrasal verbs – verbs such as:

come	go	put	set	take
turn	give	let	find	make

and the ADVERBS that go with them to make phrasal verbs are usually adverbs of *place* or *motion*:

about	away	in	over
across	back	off	through
along	by	on	under
around	down	out	up

Remember: the important thing about phrasal verbs is that they often (though not always) have a meaning that is *different* from the separate meanings of the verb and adverb. For example, **turn up** means **arrive** – it has nothing to do with **turning**, or with motion **up** – we simply have to learn that **turn up** is a *single idea* that means **arrive**.

Another characteristic of phrasal verbs is that many of them have *more than one meaning*. For example, **set off** can mean 'start (a journey)', but it also means 'activate' – you can tell which meaning is intended by considering the rest of the sentence:

We set off at nine o'clock (start journey)
The burglar set off the alarm (activate)

You can buy special dictionaries of phrasal verbs in English, with examples of all their different meanings. You have to be careful where you put pronoun objects (**me**, **him**, **her**, etc. – see Language point 5) with phrasal verbs. In Dialogue 2 the passer-by uses the phrasal verb **write down**, and says

> **Shall I write it down for you**
> *not* 'Shall I write down it for you'

She puts the object **it** *before* the adverb part of the phrasal verb, not after. We'll look at this aspect of phrasal verbs in more detail in Unit 7.

You will meet phrasal verbs in most of the units that follow, and you will find a short section at the end of the unit explaining their meanings.

Dialogue 5

This time it's Helen looking for the tourist information office – it's a popular place!

HELEN:	Excuse me – I'm looking for the tourist information office. Could you tell me how to get there?
PASSER-BY:	Yes – go down this road and take the first right, then the second left and you'll see the information office on the corner.
HELEN:	So: down here, first right, second left and it's on the corner.
PASSER-BY:	That's right!
HELEN:	Thanks for your help.
PASSER-BY:	Bye.

Language point 21 – -ing and the present continuous

In Dialogue 5 Helen says **I'm looking for the tourist information office** – she uses the PRESENT CONTINUOUS rather that the present simple, because she's describing an action *happening now*. Compare these:

PRESENT SIMPLE	**Steve drinks coffee**	(every day)
PRESENT CONTINUOUS	**Steve's drinking coffee**	(at the moment)

We form the present continuous by adding the verb **be** to the ING-FORM of the main verb:

I'm drinking tea   **you're drinking coffee**
he's drinking milk   **she's drinking orange juice**
we're drinking hot chocolate   **they're drinking water**

The ing-form never changes, but the AUXILIARY **be** does. (Go back and revise this if you need to – Language points 1, 4 and 11.)

We form questions and negatives like this:

(+) **He's drinking milk**
(?) **Is he drinking milk?**
(−) **He isn't drinking milk**   *or*   **He's not drinking milk**

We form the ing-form of the verb simply by adding **ing** to the base-form:

drink   drinking
eat   eating
talk   talking

But there are some changes sometimes:

Spelling rules

A base-form ending in a silent **e** *drops* this before adding **ing**:

come   coming   *not* 'comeing'
release releasing   *not* 'releaseing'

One-syllable base-forms ending in a single vowel + single **b p m n r t** *double* this letter before adding **ing**:

stop   stopping   *not* 'stoping'
run   running   *not* 'runing'
slam   slamming   *not* 'slaming'
hit   hitting   *not* 'hiting'
rob   robbing   *not* 'robing'

Exercise 4

Write the ing-form of the following verbs.

1 remove _____
2 write _____
3 read _____
4 hurry _____
5 fit _____
6 open _____
7 fly _____
8 chase _____
9 pay _____
10 ask _____

Exercise 5

Write the following sentences in the correct present tense.

1 I (eat/'m eating) lunch now.
2 Dave (reads/'s reading) a book every week.
3 These plants (grow/are growing) better outside.
4 This bus always (goes/is going) to the airport.
5 Terry (reads/'s reading) the paper – don't disturb him.
6 My granny was born in Russia – she (speaks/'s speaking) Russian.

Exercise 6

Change these present continuous sentences into questions.

1 She's going to the library. **Is she going to the library?**
2 They're waiting for us. _____?
3 Dave's studying Law. _____?
4 The children are having breakfast. _____?
5 Jack and Jill are washing the car. _____?
6 The weather's improving. _____?
7 This music is disturbing them. _____?
8 I'm driving too fast. _____?

Exercise 7

Change these sentences as indicated.

1	These flowers smell very nice	[–]	**These flowers don't smell very nice**
2	I understand you	[–]	
3	She's asking a question	[?]	
4	These shoes belong to Suzie	[?]	
5	You understand me	[?]	
6	Am I reading the paper?	[–]	
7	Is Gerry reading the paper?	[+]	
8	We aren't listening	[+]	

Language point 22 – get

In Dialogue 5, Helen says **Could you tell me how to ge̲t there?** – she means **arrive** or **reach**. And in Dialogue 2 Nina says **I've go̲t it** – she means that she has understood.

The passer-by in Dialogue 4 tells Sasha to **get the 22 bus from the corner here** – she means **take** – and Sasha says she doesn't want **to ge̲t lost again** – she means **become** lost.

Get is a verb with many different meanings in colloquial English – have a look in a dictionary and see how many are listed. Here are just a few of the more common ones:

receive	arrive
understand	take
become	fetch

Using **get** instead of these (sometimes more formal) verbs is a typical feature of colloquial English.

In this unit we also see **get** as a PHRASAL VERB – here are some very useful ones which you should learn:

get on	James is getting on the bus	(enter vehicle)
get off	Let's get off at the next stop	(leave vehicle)
get up	I get up at seven o'clock every morning	(rise)

get in	**Get in the car, boys!**	(enter vehicle)
get out	**Let's get out of here**	(leave; go away)
get away	**The thieves tried to get away**	(escape)

Life and living – a trip down the high street

If you're too **shy** to ask the way, or if you're simply not **pushed for time**, you can get to know where everything is in town by having a look round and keeping your eyes open. Let's take a short walk down a **typical** high street, shall we? I'll **lead the way** and we'll see if we can **spot** any useful or interesting places.

Over here on the left, on our side of the street, is the **supermarket**, and **right next to** it there's the **post office** – every town has one of these somewhere, and you can **tell** it by its red **sign**. Over there on the other side of the street you can see some smaller shops: there's a **newsagent's** on the **corner**, and a **couple of** cafés – we might go in one of those later for a cup of tea ... what do you think? **Further** down on the right is the bus station, and just behind that you can probably **just see** the **sports and leisure centre**, which is open to everyone; you can often find **private** sports and health clubs in towns as well – they're smaller and you have to pay to be a **member**.

Now – can you see that big old building **coming up** on the left, opposite the bus station? That's the public **library**. Actually, that **reminds** me – I've got to take some books back there today or tomorrow, otherwise I'll get a **fine**. Anyway, just **a bit** further on, there are two banks, one on **either side** of the street, and then you can see some **traffic lights**. Then there are some more small shops just past the lights, including a **butcher's** and a **greengrocer's**, and some Indian and Chinese **restaurants**. Then if we stop here outside the **pub** and look straight ahead, that building in the distance is the **railway station** – it's about a ten-minute walk from the town centre.

There we are – a typical British high street. So now let's go back the way we came – I think I **could do with** that cup of tea now.

Glossary

shy – afraid to talk to people
pushed for time – with not much time; so 'I'm not pushed for time' means 'I've got plenty of time' or 'I needn't worry about time'
typical – usual, normal
lead the way – go first
spot – notice
over here – here near us
supermarket – large shop that sells all kinds of food
right next to – immediately next to, next door to
post office – public building where you can send letters and parcels
tell – recognise
sign – name board outside a shop
newsagent's – shop that sells newspapers
corner – point where two roads join
couple of – two

further – more far
just see – see with difficulty, see if you try hard
sports and leisure centre – public building where you can do sports and fitness exercises
private – not open to the public
member – someone who belongs to a club or organisation
coming up – approaching
library – public building which lends books
reminds me – makes me remember
fine – a penalty, money you have to pay as punishment for something
a bit – a little
either side – both sides
traffic lights – red, yellow and green lights to control the traffic
butcher's – shop that sells meat
greengrocer's – shop that sells vegetables
restaurants – places where you can sit down and eat a meal
pub – place where you can sit and drink alcoholic drinks and eat food
railway station – place where trains stop
could do with – need

4 Have you got any bread?

> **In this unit you will learn how to:**
> - use countable and uncountable nouns
> - ask for and buy things in shops
> - ask the price of something
> - use numbers
> - use British money
> - say that you want or don't want something

Dialogue 1

Helen is buying a few things in the corner shop.

HELEN:	Hello. Have you got any bread left?
ASSISTANT:	Yes – we've got white and brown, sliced and unsliced.
HELEN:	Give me a brown sliced loaf, please. Oh, and a box of matches, and a bottle of milk.
ASSISTANT:	Anything else?
HELEN:	Let's see ... some apples and some cat food.
ASSISTANT:	How many apples would you like?
HELEN:	Half a dozen.
ASSISTANT:	And how much cat food?
HELEN:	Two tins[1] will do, I think. How much does that come to?
ASSISTANT:	£5.86, please.
HELEN:	[*gives the assistant the money*] Thanks a lot.

ASSISTANT: Thank you. Bye.
HELEN: Bye.

1 **tin** – a sealed metal container for food. The food in the tin can be either uncountable (cat food, ham, rice pudding) or countable (carrots, potatoes), but the tin itself is always countable! Another word for **tin** is **can**, which is used in the UK particularly for drinks. For an explanation of uncountable and countable nouns, see Language point 23 below.

Idioms

- **will do** means 'will be enough'
- **come to** means 'add up to'; **how much does it come to?** means 'what is the total that I have to pay?'

Language point 23 – counting and quantity

There are two types of noun in English:

- nouns such as **cup, egg, garden, book, mouse** which are COUNTABLE (C)
- nouns such as **water, milk, butter, food** which are UNCOUNTABLE (UC)

They are used in different ways.

Countable nouns

- can have PLURALS: **cups, eggs, gardens, books, mice**
- are used in the singular with **a/an**: **a cup, an egg, a garden**
- can be used with numbers: **three mice, seven books**
- are used with **many**: **how many cups?, too many books**

Uncountable nouns

- usually *can't* have plurals: 'waters', 'milks', 'butters', 'foods'
- usually *can't* be used with **a/an**: 'a water', 'a milk', 'a food'
- are used with **much**: **how much water?, too much food**
- usually *can't* be used with numbers: 'three foods', 'seven waters'

Both uncountable and countable nouns:

- can be used with **the**: **the garden, the gardens, the milk**

Both uncountable and PLURAL countable nouns:

- can be used with **some, any** and **a lot of**:

    Have you got any bread?
    Have you got any eggs?
    Give me some apples and some cat food
    There are a lot of children here
    There's a lot of snow outside

- can be used with QUANTITY WORDS:

    a box of matches
    a pint of milk

> ⚠ **Be careful!** In colloquial English we *don't* use **much** and **many** on their own, except in NEGATIVE sentences – instead we say **a lot of**:
>
> **There's a lot of food on the table**
> *not* 'There's much food on the table'
>
> **There are a lot of people in the meeting**
> *not* 'There are many people in the meeting'
>
> But
>
> **There isn't much food on the table**
> **There aren't many people in the meeting**
>
> And we *do* say **how much, too much, how many, too many**, etc.

Notice in Dialogue 1 that Helen says:

   Have you got any bread left?
not 'Have you got bread left?'

We generally put **some** (statements) and **any** (questions and negatives) before plural nouns and uncountable nouns.

More examples:

> **I need some eggs**
> **I need some milk**
> **Has Sandra got any children?**
> **Has Sandra got any food in the house?**
> **We don't want any biscuits**
> **We don't want any cake**

Exercise 1

Candace has made shopping list. Look at the items on it and write whether they are countable nouns (C) or uncountable nouns (UC).

1. eggs   ____
2. milk   ____
3. apples   ____
4. newspaper   ____
5. butter   ____
6. carrots   ____
7. washing-up liquid ____
8. twelve bars of chocolate ____
9. cheese   ____
10. biscuits   ____
11. rice   ____
12. bottles of water ____
13. a chicken   ____
14. an English book ____
15. toothpaste   ____
16. light bulbs   ____
17. toothbrush   ____
18. playing cards ____
19. tin of rice pudding ____
20. box of soap powder ____

Exercise 2

Bert's also made a shopping list. Complete it by adding either **a/an** or **some** before each item.

1. ____ soap
2. ____ teabags
3. ____ loaf of bread

11. ____ eggs
12. ____ newspaper
13. ____ melon

4	____ rice		14	____ orange juice
5	____ bag of carrots		15	____ extra bottle of milk
6	____ butter		16	____ pencil
7	____ toothbrush		17	____ pizzas
8	____ box of matches		18	____ yoghurts
9	____ kilogram of ice cream		19	____ sour cream
10	____ coffee		20	____ bottle of wine

Dialogue 2

Back at home, Simon asks Helen how the shopping went.

SIMON:	Did you get any milk?
HELEN:	Yes, I got a pint.
SIMON:	And did they have any bread left?
HELEN:	Yes, they did. I got us a brown loaf.
SIMON:	And what else did you get?
HELEN:	I got some apples and two tins of cat food.
SIMON:	Good – we were right out of cat food.
HELEN:	And I got some matches.
SIMON:	Right – would you like a cup of tea?
HELEN:	[*suddenly remembers*] Oh hell! I didn't get any teabags! And we're out of them, aren't we?
SIMON:	Afraid so. I'll get some later.
HELEN:	OK.

Idioms

- **we're right out of** (**cat food**) means 'We haven't got <u>any</u> cat food left', 'the cat food has all gone'; and so **we're out of them** means 'we haven't gone any more of them left'.

- **left** means 'remaining':

    How many have you got left?
    There are three biscuits left
    There's nobody left in the building

- we use **oh hell!** when we are cross or angry about something that has happened – it's *not* rude, so you can use it when you like, but maybe avoid using it in formal or sensitive situations.

    Oh hell, I've locked myself out!
    Oh hell, we've missed the bus!
    Oh hell, we're out of milk!

- **afraid so**, or **I'm afraid so**, means 'Unfortunately you're right' or 'Unfortunately what you say is correct'.

Language point 24 – 'did' auxiliary

We have already seen **do** as an AUXILIARY in the present simple (Language point 12):

	<u>Do</u> you speak Italian?	(present simple question)
	I <u>don't</u> speak Italian	(present simple negative)
but	**I speak Italian**	*not* '<s>I do speak Italian</s>'

If we change **do** (present) to **did** (past) and use it with the BASE-FORM in the same way, we can talk about the past:

<u>Did</u> you get any milk?	(past simple question)
I <u>didn't</u> get any teabags	(past simple negative)

But in ordinary statements (in just the same way as the present simple) we *don't* use the **do** auxiliary – so in Dialogue 2 Helen says:

I got a pint	*not*	'<s>I did get a pint</s>'

– she uses the past simple **got**. We will see how to do past simple statements in Unit 9 – for now remember the difference between the **do** and **did** auxiliaries.

Exercise 3

Complete the sentences using either **do** or **did**.

1. ____ you see Gerry yesterday?
2. ____ you speak English?
3. ____ you know where the bank is?
4. ____ you get enough wine for the party?
5. ____ you go to work by bus usually?
6. ____ you go to work by bus today?
7. ____ you watch the film on TV last night?
8. ____ you know what the capital of Switzerland is?

Exercise 4

Fill in the blanks from the box – you can use each word only once.

1. **Do** your parents live nearby?
2. ____ Fiona speak French?
3. Su and Shamira ____ like the cold weather.
4. I ____ buy enough food for the party, I'm afraid.
5. We ____ usually buy a Sunday paper.
6. ____ Justine tell you about the party?
7. James ____ like hot food.
8. ____ they want to come to the party with us?

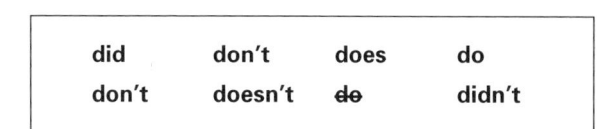

did	don't	does	do
don't	doesn't	~~do~~	didn't

Dialogue 3

Jenny's in the pub with her friends. She's ordering drinks at the bar.

JENNY: Two lemonades, please.
ASSISTANT: Would you like ice with those?
JENNY: Yes please. And a pint of lager ...

ASSISTANT: We haven't got any lager today.
JENNY: Oh. What kind of beer *have* you got, then?
ASSISTANT: We haven't got any.
JENNY: No beer? OK, I'll have a glass of wine.
ASSISTANT: Red or white?
JENNY: Red, please.
ASSISTANT: We haven't got any more red, unfortunately.
JENNY: Oh for goodness sake! – *white*, then!
ASSISTANT: We haven't got any white either.
JENNY: Just give me three bags of crisps, then.
ASSISTANT: Sold out.
JENNY: No beer, no wine, no crisps, What kind of pub is this?
ASSISTANT: A bad one.

Idiom

- When something is **sold out** it means the shop has sold it all and there's none left:

    We've sold out of oranges
    = 'We've sold all our oranges (so you can't buy any here)'

- We say **for goodness sake** when we are irritated or cross about something, or we are losing our patience with the situation. It's *not* rude when said to people that you are on informal or friendly terms with.

    Oh hurry up, for goodness sake!
    Oh for goodness sake, stop complaining!

Language point 25 – 'have'

We saw **got** in Language point 24 – but **got** is also used with **have** to show *possession* in colloquial English. In Dialogue 3 the barman says:

We haven't got any lager

Look at some more examples:

> **I've got five pounds**
> **Terry hasn't got any money at all**
> **Susan's got a Ferrari**
> **Have you got a ten-pound note?**

Notice that **got** doesn't change, but that **have** changes to **has** for the third person singular, and that we use SHORT FORMS of **have** in statements, and LONG FORMS + **n't** in the negative:

I've		**I haven't**	
you've		**you haven't**	
he's	got	**he hasn't**	got
she's		**she hasn't**	
we've		**we haven't**	
they've		**they haven't**	

This meaning of **got** is different from the one Helen uses in Dialogue 2, when she says **I got some apples**. Compare these two sentences:

I got some apples = 'I bought some apples' (action of getting)
I've got some apples = 'I have some apples' (possession)

We've already seen that **get/got** has a number of different meanings – and this is true of **have** as well. Jenny says:

> **I'll have a glass of wine**

Here she *isn't* talking about possession, she's using **I'll have** to order a drink or say what she wants. Similarly, if someone wants to buy someone else a drink, they often say:

> **What'll you have?**

Because this *isn't* possession, we *don't* use **have got**, so we *can't* say:

> ~~'I'll have got a glass of wine.'~~
> ~~'What'll you have got?'~~

We'll see other uses of **have** in later units.

Exercise 5

These sentences all use **have got** to talk about possession – change them as indicated. The first two are done for you.

1 Dave's got a new car.   [?] **Has Dave got a new car?**
2 You haven't got a phone.   [?] **Have you got a phone?**
3 Has he got time?   [+] _____
4 I haven't got enough time.   [+] _____
5 Have they got enough money?   [–] _____
6 Su's got a car.   [–] _____
7 We haven't got the tickets.   [?] _____
8 Has Fiona got them?   [+] _____

Exercise 6

Put a tick against the *possession* sentences, and a cross against the others.

1 I have eggs for breakfast every morning. __
2 Jenny's got a big paper bag. __
3 Have you got any money on you? __
4 I'll have a cup of coffee, please. __
5 My brother hasn't got a jacuzzi. __
6 Jenny got a big paper bag. __
7 The children are having fun. __
8 What'll you have? __
9 Henry got a letter this morning. __
10 Has your house got central heating? __

Dialogue 4

Dave isn't happy with the bill.

DAVE: Could you check this bill for me – I don't think it's right.
WAITER: Certainly. First, did you have two coffees?
DAVE: Yes. Then I had a Danish pastry and my friend here had a roll and butter.
WAITER: [*ticking them off on the bill*]
          OK. Then you had two mineral waters.
DAVE: No. I didn't have a mineral water. My friend had one, but I had another coffee.
WAITER: Ah ... sorry about that. You were right, and I was wrong.

> **Idiom**
>
> - We use **sorry**, of course, to apologise to someone. If we want to refer back to the situation or incident we're apologising for, we say **sorry about that**.

Language point 26 – 'two coffees'

We saw in Language point 23 that words such as **coffee** are UNCOUNTABLE (UC), and that this means that they:

- can't have plurals
- can't be used with numbers

But in Dialogue 4 the waiter says:

Did you have <u>two coffees</u>?

We also saw that UC nouns can't be used with **a/an**, but Dave says:

I didn't have <u>a</u> mineral water

These examples seem to break the rules, but they don't. Some uncountable nouns can *also* be countable (C) in special cases:

- **coffee** (UC) = the drink itself
- **coffee** (C) = 'a *cup* of coffee' – **cup** is a COUNTABLE noun, so **coffee** is countable when it means this, and it behaves like any other countable noun:

    a coffee
    two coffees

Another example of a UC/C noun is **paper**: it means the material itself when it's UC, but it means **newspaper** when it's C:

I'm going to buy <u>some</u> paper	(UC)	(to write on)
I'm going to buy <u>a</u> paper	(C)	(to read)

Most dictionaries for learners of English will tell you when a noun can be both UC and C. Some books and dictionaries call UC nouns MASS NOUNS.

Language point 27 – 'don't think'

In Dialogue 4, Dave is unhappy with the bill. He thinks to himself:

The bill <u>isn't</u> right

but then he says to the waiter:

I don't think <u>it's</u> right
not   '<s>I think it isn't right</s>'

In colloquial English we don't usually say **I think** when what follows is NEGATIVE – instead we change it round and say **I don't think** + POSITIVE. Here are some more examples:

I don't think Sarah's coming   (Sarah isn't coming)
I don't think you're right   (you aren't right)
I don't think we've got time   (we haven't got time)

Exercise 7

Change the following into 'I don't think . . .' sentences. The first one is done for you.

1 Kath isn't here.   **I don't think Kath's here**
2 My watch isn't working properly. _____
3 The children aren't hungry.   _____
4 That's not important.   _____
5 The coffee isn't very nice.   _____
6 We aren't on the right bus.   _____
7 This bus doesn't go to the airport. _____
8 You don't understand.   _____
9 Henry doesn't read books.   _____
10 The students aren't listening.   _____

Dialogue 5

Su is at the supermarket checkout, where the checkout assistant asks her if she has a card.

C/ASSISTANT:	Have you got a MegaSave card?
SU:	No. How do I get one?
C/ASSISTANT:	Just fill in this form – it's quite simple.
SU:	[*begins to fill it in*] What about my postcode – I can't remember what it is.
C/ASSISTANT:	Leave it out for now – we can fill that in for you later.
SU:	Oh look! Now I've made mistake with my phone number. Shall I tear it all up and start again?
C/ASSISTANT:	No, no! Just cross it out and write it in again over the top. [*Su fills in the form*]
SU:	What do I do with it now?
C/ASSISTANT:	Give it back to me. Your card will arrive in the post in a day or two.
SU:	Thanks.

Language point 28 – 'one', 'another' and 'other'

When a countable noun has already been mentioned, we can use one to refer to it again:

> Fred had <u>a coffee</u>, and I had <u>one</u> too
> I need <u>a pencil</u> – have you got <u>one</u>?
> I'll have a beer – what about you?   – I'll have <u>one</u> as well

Another /ə'nʌðəʳ/ is an ADJECTIVE used with SINGULAR C nouns – it is made up of **an** + **other**, but it is written as one word. It has two different meanings:

> I'll have another coffee, please   (= one more)
> Give me another cup, please   (= a different one)

When we use **another** without the noun, we often add **one**:

> This cup is dirty – can I have another?
> *or* This cup is dirty – can I have another one?

But other adjectives *can't* stand on their own in English – if the noun is not stated, then **one** must take its place:

(I prefer the red hat)   **I prefer the red <u>one</u>**
                    not   'I prefer the red'
(I need a blue shirt)   **I need a blue one**
                    not   'I need a blue'

Other is different from **another**:

- it can be used with both SINGULAR *and* PLURAL nouns:
  the other man, other men, the other men
- when it's used with **the**, we write it as two words, not one:
  another, but **the other** *not* 'theother'
- we *can't* use it to mean 'one more' –
  Can I have another biscuit?   (one more)
  Can I have the other biscuit?   (a different one)

There is a PLURAL PRONOUN **the others**:

Where are the others?   =   'Where are the other ones?'

but we *don't* normally use the singular:

Where is the other one?   *not*   'Where is the other?'

Exercise 8

Correct the following sentences. Be careful – two of them *don't* need correcting.

1. This fork is dirty – can I have other one?
2. I don't like these shoes – can I try the other?
3. Would you like other cup of tea?
4. Could you get me another one glass of milk?
5. This one's OK but I prefer other one.
6. Another tea and two coffees, please.
7. James is here but where are the others?
8. I don't like these – let me try another ones.
9. Another CD is better than this one.
10. Other one car is more expensive than this one.

Phrasal verbs

cross out – 'delete'; 'draw a line through'.
fill in – 'complete (a form)'.
give back (something) – 'return (something)'.
leave out – 'omit'; 'not include'.
tear up – 'destroy by tearing'.
sell out (of something) – 'sell all of something'.
tick off – 'make a mark with a pen or pencil against an item on a list'.
write (something) in – 'add something in writing'.

Life and living – numbers and money

Numbers

Just as in most places in the world today, you won't get far in the UK without *money*, especially when it's time to do the shopping. But before that, you need the numbers!

1 one	6 six	11 eleven	16 sixteen
2 two	7 seven	12 twelve	17 seventeen
3 three	8 eight	13 thirteen	18 eighteen
4 four	9 nine	14 fourteen	19 nineteen
5 five	10 ten	15 fifteen	20 twenty

Notice their pronunciation:

/wʌn/   /sɪks/   /ɪˈlɛvn/   /sɪksˈtiːn/
/tuː/   /ˈsɛvn/   /twɛlv/   /sɛvnˈtiːn/
/θriː/   /ɛit/   /θɜːˈtiːn/   /ɛiˈtiːn/
/fɔːʳ/   /nain/   /fɔːˈtiːn/   /nainˈtiːn/
/faiv/   /tɛn/   /fɪfˈtiːn/   /ˈtwɛnti/

21 – **twenty-one**, etc.

Now look at the *tens*:

30 **thirty** /ˈθɜːti/   70 **seventy** /ˈsɛvnti/
40 **forty** /ˈfɔːti/   80 **eighty** /ˈɛiti/
50 **fifty** /ˈfɪfti/   90 **ninety** /ˈnainti/
60 **sixty** /ˈsɪksti/   100 **a hundred** /ə ˈhʌndrəd/

200 – **two hundred**, etc.

We use **and** /n/ after **hundred**, but *not* after the tens:

501	**five hundred and one**	/faivhʌndrədn'wʌn/
346	**three hundred and forty-six**	/θri:hʌndrədnfɔ:ti'sɪks/

Although Britain is a **member** of the EU (European Union), it is not part of the European **single currency** (though it may join **eventually**), and so does *not* use the **euro** /'jʊərʌʊ/ , although some shops do accept them, especially in large cities.

The unit of currency in Britain is the pound (£) /paʊnd/ , which is divided into 100 pence /pɛns/ . Prices are said as follows:

£2.49	**two pounds forty-nine**
	/tu:paʊndzfɔ:ti'naɪn/ *or* /tu:fɔ:ti'naɪn/
53p	**fifty-three pence**
	/fɪftiθri:'pi:/ *or* /fɪftiθri:'pɛns/

British money comes in paper notes (£5, £10, £20 and £50) and metal **coins** (1p, 2p, 5p, 10p, 20p, 50p, £1 and £2).

In colloquial English a £10 note is called a tenner, and this is also used for a price of exactly £10:

How much do you want for this?   **– A tenner.**

Similarly, a £5 note is called a fiver. But you *can't* use these words in prices generally:

    £10.58   **ten fifty-eight**

As well as **cash**, you can pay for things with cheques or credit cards or debit cards. Credit cards are a way of borrowing money from the credit card company; debit cards are **issued** by your bank and simply allow you to use money from your **account** without having to write a cheque – the **transaction** goes through electronically. The commonest type of debit card is a Switch card – for example, you would say to the shop assistant, 'Can I pay by Switch?' or 'Can I use Switch for this?'

Glossary

member – someone or something that belongs to an organisation
single currency – the monetary system of the European Union
eventually – in the end; some time in the future
euro – the EU unit of currency
cash – banknotes and coins, *not* cheques
issued – given to you by an organisation
account – where you keep your money at the bank
transaction – the act of buying something and paying for it

5 What shall we do today?

In this unit you will learn how to:
- make suggestions to do things
- accept and decline suggestions
- discuss plans
- ask about and talk about likes and dislikes
- offer people things
- choose between things

Dialogue 1

Andrew and Kim are wondering what to do.

ANDREW: What shall we do this evening?
KIM: How about going out?
ANDREW: Good idea. Where shall we go?
KIM: We could go down the pub and have a drink, or we could go to the cinema.
ANDREW: Which would you prefer?
KIM: I don't mind really.
ANDREW: Well, let's go to the pub, then, shall we?
KIM: OK!

Dialogue 2

Meanwhile, Sarah and John are having a similar discussion, but they're hungry!

SARAH: Shall we eat in or go out for a meal?
JOHN: I don't know – I can't decide.

SARAH:	Why don't we go to the *Trattoria* – the food's nice there.
JOHN:	No, I don't really feel like Italian food tonight.
SARAH:	How about trying the new Chinese restaurant in the High Street, then?
JOHN:	OK, I'll get my shoes on.
SARAH:	And you'd better get your wallet as well – you're paying!

Dialogue 3

Mike and Sandra have got some friends from Belgium, Koen and Kim, staying with them.

MIKE:	What shall we do with Koen and Kim this evening?
SANDRA:	How about eating out?
MIKE:	Yes. Or we could eat in, and then take them out for a drink.
SANDRA:	I don't feel up to cooking tonight. Why don't we go around some of the pubs in town, then we can end up at the Indian for a late dinner?
MIKE:	Great idea. They can try out Indian food, and we can get a taxi back home.
SANDRA:	I'll go and ask them what they think.

Dialogue 4

Andy phones Bob, whose wife Nina is Danish, with a suggestion.

ANDY:	Are you free tonight, Bob?
BOB:	Why – what did you have in mind?
ANDY:	There's a Danish film on at the Arts Cinema.
BOB:	Really?
ANDY:	Yes – I thought Nina might like to come along.
BOB:	Sounds like a great idea, but I'll check with her first. Hang on a moment ... [*Bob goes off for a minute, then comes back*] Hello, Andy?
ANDY:	Yes.
BOB:	That's fine. When does the film start?
ANDY:	Eight. Shall we meet up at 7.30 in the cinema café?
BOB:	Perfect. See you later.
ANDY:	Bye.

> **Idiom**
>
> - **Hang on a moment** means 'Wait a moment'

Dialogue 5

Later, Andy, Bob and Nina arrive at the cinema. There's a huge queue!

BOB: Look! The place is going to be packed out!
ANDY: What shall we do? Wait and see if we get in, or give up and come another day?
BOB: [*looks at his watch*] Oh, I can't be bothered waiting. Let's go to the pub.
ANDY: Fine. I wouldn't mind having a drink – I'm quite thirsty, actually. What do you think, Nina?
NINA: OK by me. We can discuss Danish cinema over some beers, can't we?

> **Idioms**
>
> - **packed out** means 'completely full of people'
> - **I can't be bothered (doing)** means 'I'm not really interested in (doing)' or 'I don't want to make the effort to (do)'

Language point 29 – making suggestions to do things

There are a number of ways of making a suggestion to someone to do something. Three of the most common are:

    Shall we ...?　　(followed by the BASE-FORM of the verb)
    Why don't we ...?　(followed by the BASE-FORM of the verb)

and

    How about ...?　　(followed by the ING-FORM of the verb)

So:

  Shall we go out tonight?
or **Why don't we go out tonight?**
or **How about going out tonight?**

You can *agree* to someone else's suggestion by using any of these expressions:

 OK (, then)   **Why not?**
 Good idea   **All right (, then)**

If you *don't* want to do what the other person suggests, you can say one of the following:

       ... I don't want to
       ... I don't really feel like (doing) that
 No (thanks), **... I'd rather do something else**
       ... let's think of something else
       ... let's do something else

You can make a more definite suggestion by using **Let's ...** (with BASE-FORM of the verb). Here are some examples:

 Let's stay in tonight
 Let's go and see if Jeremy's in
 Let's phone for a pizza

When you make a suggestion using **Let's ...**, you can always check if it's okay with the person you're speaking to by adding the tag **..., shall we?**

 Let's stay in tonight, shall we?
 Let's go and see if Jeremy's in, shall we?
 Let's phone for a pizza, shall we?

Exercise 1

Complete the suggestions, using the right form of the verb. The first one has been done for you.

 1 How about (~~drive~~/driving) to the seaside?
 2 Why don't we (watch/watching) a film on DVD?

3 Shall we (buy/buying) an ice cream?
4 How about (take/taking) a walk in the park?
5 Shall we (catch/catching) a bus into town?
6 How about (meet/meeting) James and Terry for a drink?
7 How about (play/playing) a game of snooker?
8 Why don't we (phone/phoning) Jane to see if she's free?
9 Shall we (stay/staying) in tonight?
10 How about (go/going) for a swim?

Exercise 2

Fill in the blanks with the right words in these suggestions and responses. The first one has been done for you.

1 Shall **we** get a takeaway?   **No, I don't feel _like_ that today.**
2 How ___ going shopping?   ___ idea!
3 ___ ___ having a walk into town?   ___, ___ do something else.
4 ___ don't ___ go fishing?   ___!
5 Shall ___ order some food?   All right ___ .
6 ___ we organise a party?   Why ___ ?
7 ___ ___ hiring some bikes?   No, I'd ___ do something else.
8 Why ___ ___ call on Jerry?   Good ___!
9 ___ about listening to some music?   No, I don't ___ to.
10 ___ ___ go to the pub?   ___ then, let's do that.

Exercise 3

Make the following suggestions to someone using the words given. The first one has been done for you.

1 go to the cinema (how)   **How about going to the cinema?**
2 go swimming (shall)   _____ ?
3 organise a party (let's)   _____ ?
4 practise our English (why)   _____ ?
5 wash the car (shall)   _____ ?

6 call in on Sam and Fred _____ ?
   (why)
7 write some postcards home _____ ?
   (how)
8 cook an Indian meal _____ ?
   (shall)
9 invite James and Fiona to tea _____ ?
   (let's)
10 help with the washing-up _____ ?
   (why)

Dialogue 6

Dave and Neil are discussing what type of food they like.

DAVE: Do you like Indian food?
NEIL: Yes, I do! It's my favourite.
DAVE: Why don't we go out for a curry, then?
NEIL: No – we can't do that tonight.
DAVE: Why not?
NEIL: Paul's coming out with us tonight, and he doesn't like curry.
DAVE: Doesn't he? What kind of food does he like, then?
NEIL: I think he likes Chinese food. Shall we go to the *Peking*?

DAVE: No, I'd rather not – I don't like Chinese food very much.
NEIL: All right, then – let's all stay in and phone for a pizza, shall we?
DAVE: Does Paul like pizza?
NEIL: It's his favourite food!
DAVE: OK, that's what we'll do!

Language point 30 – liking things, and offering things

Look at these two questions and answers:

Do you like coffee? – **Yes, I do!**
Would you like some coffee? – **Yes, I would!**

The verb **like** is in both, but with different meanings. **Do you like ...?** asks someone if they *like* something, but **Would you like ...?** asks someone if they *want* something.

If you want to *offer* something to someone, you use:

Would you like ...?

If you just want to know if someone likes something, you use:

Do you like ...?

Exercise 4

How would you say these things to someone? The first one is done for you.

1 Offer someone a cup of tea: **Would you like a cup of tea?**
2 Ask if someone likes Indian food: _____?
3 Ask if someone likes apples: _____?
4 Offer someone a cheese sandwich: _____?
5 Offer someone some soup: _____?
6 Ask someone if they like milk in their coffee: _____?

7 Offer someone another
  cup of tea: _____ ?
8 Offer someone some more
  soup: _____ ?
9 Ask if someone likes tea: _____ ?
10 Offer Dave some pizza: _____ ?

Language point 31 – offering to let someone do something, or suggesting it

As well as offering *something* to somebody, we can offer to let somebody *do* something. Look at these two sentences:

Would you like a sandwich?
Would you like to go to the pub this evening?

When we offer to let someone do something, **Would you like** is followed by the TO-FORM of the verb. So we say:

Would you like   + NOUN
Would you like + to   + VERB

Here are some more examples:

(sit here)	**Would you like to sit here?**
(play a game of chess)	**Would you like to play a game of chess?**
(order the food)	**Would you like to order the food?**
(practise your English)	**Would you like to practise your English?**
(do some aerobics)	**Would you like to do some aerobics?**
(have lunch with us)	**Would you like to have lunch with us?**

Exercise 5

Unscramble each sentence to make a question. The first one is done for you.

1 come like would round you to tonight ?
  Would you like to come round tonight?

2   coffee more like you some would ?
    _____

3   like museum visit would to you the today ?
    _____

4   afternoon this swimming go to like you would ?
    _____

5   another would like cake you ?
    _____

6   the like you menu to would see ?
    _____

Language point 32 – asking if someone likes something, and saying you don't

In Dialogue 6, Dave says:

Do you like …?

and when he's talking about Paul he says:

… does he like?

like is a word describing a *mental state*, so we make present tense questions using **Do …?** and **Does …?**:

Do you like tomatoes?
not 'Are you liking tomatoes?'

Does Sally like black coffee?
not 'Is Sally liking black coffee?'

Do they like Indian food?
not 'Are they liking Indian food?'

Do your friends like fish and chips?
not 'Are your friends liking …?'

In Dialogue 6, Neil says:

… he doesn't like curry

and Dave says:

I don't like Chinese food

We make **like** negative by using **don't** and **doesn't**:

        I don't like salad
not   'I'm not liking salad'

        Geoff doesn't like Italian food
not   'Geoff isn't liking Italian food'

        she doesn't like hamburgers
not   'she isn't liking hamburgers'

        we don't like coffee
not   'we aren't liking coffee'

        they don't like cornflakes
not   'they aren't liking cornflakes'

Exercise 6

Change the sentences as indicated: (+) statement, (?) question, (−) negative. The first one has been done for you.

1. They like Indian food   (?)   **Do they like Indian food?**
2. James likes ice cream.   (?)   _____
3. My parents like fish   (−)   _____
4. Does Sarah like apples?   (+)   _____
5. Fiona doesn't like vegetables   (?)   _____
6. They don't like fish and chips   (+)   _____
7. Do Fred and Kim like sport?   (−)   _____
8. Pete doesn't like carrots   (?)   _____

Exercise 7

Some of these sentences have mistakes in them – can you see which ones? And can you correct them?

1. Does Susan like coffee?   _____
2. Would you liking some more coffee?   _____
3. I don't like fish and chips.   _____
4. Are you like English food?   _____
5. James isn't liking hot weather.   _____
6. Does you like ice cream?   _____
7. Would you like some ice cream?   _____
8. Do your sister like oranges?   _____
9. Would you liking an orange?   _____
10. Is Jerry liking milk with his tea?   _____

Language point 33 – liking doing things

As well as talking about liking things, you can also talk about liking *doing* things. Look at these two sentences:

Sue likes <u>ice cream</u> on a hot day
Sue likes <u>sitting under the trees</u> on a hot day

When we talk about liking *doing* things, **like** is followed by the ing-form of the verb. Here are some more examples:

(swim)	The children like <u>swimming</u> in the pool
(read)	Does your sister like <u>reading</u> magazines?
(play)	Terry likes <u>playing</u> tennis on his days off
(watch)	I don't like <u>watching</u> football on TV
(sit)	I like <u>sitting</u> in the garden
(work)	Do you like <u>working</u> for the company?

And when someone asks you if you like something, there are many answers you can give. Let's look as some of the possibilities, starting with positive answers and going through to negative answers:

<u>**Do you like fast food?**</u>	Yes, I love it!
	Yes, I quite like it
	It's OK, I suppose
	I'm not bothered
	Not really
	No, I don't like it at all
	I can't stand it!
	No, I hate it!

Exercise 8

Fill in the blanks with the verbs in the box – use the different forms of the verbs to help you decide which ones belong where. The first one is done for you.

1. Would you like to **help** me with the washing-up?
2. Do you like ____ football?
3. ____ Jerry like ____ on the beach?
4. ____ you like to ____ in this evening?
5. I like ____ my exercises in the morning.

6 Fiona ____ ____ with the washing-up.
7 Would you ____ to ____ cricket with us today?
8 I ____ like ____ in the evening.
9 Would you like to ____ some aerobics at the health club this evening?
10 ____ you like ____ to the radio?

helping	sunbathing	doing	play
~~help~~	playing	listening	do
don't	does	would	do
likes	like	working	stay

Exercise 9

Look at the answers to the question 'Do you like fast food?' at the end of Language point 33 – can you draw two lines to divide the answers into positive, neutral and negative?

Language point 34 – choosing between two things, and pointing them out

You can use the verb **prefer** to say which of two things or actions you think is better:

> **Which would you prefer – tea or coffee?**
> **I'd prefer coffee, thank you.**

We use **prefer** when we think something is better than something else:

> **I prefer coffee** = 'I think coffee is better'
> **I prefer coffee to tea** = 'I think coffee is better than tea'

We use **(woul)d prefer** when we want something more than something else:

> **I'd prefer coffee** = 'It would be better if you gave me coffee.'
> **Would you prefer tea?** = 'Would it be better if I gave you tea?'

Now look at these examples:

Do you like this hat or that one?
I like them both, but I prefer that one.

Notice that we put **this** in front of a noun when we want to talk about something that is near to the speaker, and that for something **that** is further away. So, if Anne is holding a red hat and Susan is holding a blue hat, Anne says **this hat** for the red one and **that hat** for the blue one. For Susan it's the other way round!

> ⚠️ **Be careful!** When the noun is *plural*, **this** changes to **these** and **that** changes to **those**:
>
> | Singular | Plural |
> |---|---|
> | **this hat** | **these hats** |
> | **that hat** | **those hats** |

Now look at these examples:

Which tie do you prefer?	– I like <u>this one</u>
Which trousers do you prefer?	– I like <u>these</u>
Which hat do you prefer?	– I like <u>that one</u>
Which shoes do you prefer?	– I like <u>those</u>

If the noun has already been mentioned, you don't need to repeat it – you can use **this/that** and **these/those** without the noun, *but* you have to put **one** after **this** and **that**.

Exercise 10

Can you match each sentence on the left to one on the right that means the same thing? The first one has been done for you.

1	**I prefer coffee**	a	Please give me some coffee
2	I wouldn't like coffee	b	I think coffee is nice
3	I'd like coffee	c	Please give me some coffee instead
4	I don't like coffee	d	**I think coffee is better**
5	I'd prefer coffee	e	Don't give me any coffee
6	I like coffee	f	I don't think coffee is nice

Exercise 11

Choose the right word in brackets to complete each sentence. The first one has been done for you.

1 How much are (that/those) apples?
2 Do you like (these/this) watch?
3 (Those/That) people are from Bangladesh.
4 I think (this/these) are too expensive.
5 Would you like some more of (this/these) cake?
6 I like (this/these) jumper, but I prefer (that/those) one.
7 Shall we sit at (this/those) table?
8 (This/those) children are very noisy, aren't they?
9 How much are (this/these)?
10 Would you prefer (this/those) restaurant or (those/that) one?

Dialogue 7

It's a lovely day, and Brian and Susan are wondering where to go for lunch. Pay attention to the tags in this conversation.

SUSAN: You like seafood, don't you?
BRIAN: Yes, I love it!
SUSAN: Well, why don't we go down to the beach and have lunch there?
BRIAN: OK, let's do that. Shall we ask Fiona if she'd like to come too?
SUSAN: No – Fiona doesn't like the beach, does she?
BRIAN: Ah – no, you're right. She doesn't. Perhaps James would like to come with us?
SUSAN: Maybe. How about phoning him to ask?
BRIAN: Wait a minute. Let's decide which restaurant to go to first, shall we?
SUSAN: I like the Jolly Roger – the food's excellent.
BRIAN: Hmm, yes ... but I don't like their prices! How about trying that new restaurant, further up the road.
SUSAN: You mean the Ocean View? They specialise in shell-fish, don't they?
BRIAN: Yes. I'd really like to give it a try, wouldn't you?
SUSAN: OK, let's go there. Shall we phone first to book a table?

BRIAN: That would be a good idea, wouldn't it? It's very popular at lunchtimes.
SUSAN: Right – why don't you phone James, and then I'll phone the Ocean View.

> **Idiom**
>
> - **give it a try** means 'try it out' or 'see what it's like'

Exercise 12

Read Dialogue 4 again, and then decide whether the following statements are True (T) or False (F).

1	Fiona wouldn't like to come to the beach	T / F
2	The Ocean View doesn't do shellfish	T / F
3	Brian doesn't like seafood very much	T / F
4	Brian doesn't like the food at the Jolly Roger	T / F
5	Susan is going to phone James	T / F
6	Lots of people have lunch at the Ocean View	T / F

Phrasal verbs

come along – 'accompany'; 'come with (other people)'. **Do you want to come along?** means 'We're going somewhere – do you want to come with us?'.

eat in – 'have food at home'.

eat out – 'have food in a restaurant, or anywhere away from home'.

end up – when we end up at a place, it means that we have visited several places, and this is the last one. **We ended up in the curry house** could mean, for example, that we went to the cinema, then to the pub, and *finally* to the curry house.

meet up – 'meet by arrangement'. **We met Keith, Greg and Carl** usually means that we met them *by chance* – we *weren't* expecting to see them; **We met up with Keith, Greg and Carl** means that we had *arranged* or *agreed* to meet them.

try out – when we try something out, we test it to see if it's okay, or if we like it.

Life and living

Once you've decided on what to eat, you'll have to decide where! If you don't feel like cooking, this will mean either **eating out** (which we'll talk about in the next unit) or a **takeaway** – and in Britain there are usually plenty of choices either way.

The cheaper **option** is a takeaway – going to a shop or restaurant and bringing the food back home to eat. In the big cities there are almost endless possibilities, but even in small towns you probably find examples of these:

a fish-and-chip shop
an Indian restaurant
a Chinese restaurant
a pizza house
a kebab house

If you want something typically British, why not go for **fish and chips**? You don't need to **order ahead** – simply go to the shop, ask for what you want and they'll cook it for you **there and then**. There are usually various kinds of **fried** fish available – cod is very popular, and so is plaice. Fish-and-chip shops usually sell other types of food as well: pies, sausages – in fact, anything that goes well with chips!

Indian food – curry – is now the most popular food in the UK, and you'll find Indian restaurants everywhere. You can order ahead by phone and then collect it, but if you are new to Indian **cuisine** it's probably better, and more fun, to decide on what to have once you have arrived at the restaurant. This way, you can ask the **restaurant staff** about different **dishes** as you look at the menu – it might be rather confusing as there are always a lot of different dishes available, and they all have **exotic** names! Also, some Indian dishes are very hot (spicy), so be sure to ask about this as well! You'll have to wait a while for the food, but this is all part of the **experience**.

Chinese takeaways are usually very quickly prepared – there is no real need to **order in advance**, as the food takes only a minute or two to arrive. Pizzas and kebabs take a little longer – order by phone about fifteen minutes ahead if you don't want to wait at the shop.

Glossary

eating out – going to a restaurant and eating there
takeaway – a meal bought at a restaurant and taken home to eat; also means the shop
option – choice
chips – potatoes cut up and cooked in oil
order ahead – use the phone to tell the restaurant your order before you go and collect it
there and then – at once; immediately
fried – cooked in oil
cuisine – style of cooking
restaurant staff – the people who work in the restaurant
dishes – items on a menu
exotic – unusual and from far away
experience – how it feels to do something
order in advance – order before you get to the restaurant

6 Hello, could I speak to Vicki?

In this unit you will learn how to:
- talk on the phone
- ask for permission to do things
- use pronoun indirect objects
- make gentle suggestions
- use time expressions

Dialogue 1

Dave phones Vicki's number to see if Nigel's there.

DAVE: Hello, could I speak to Vicki?
VICKI: Speaking.
DAVE: Oh, hello Vicki – I didn't recognise your voice. It's Dave.
VICKI: Hi, Dave. How's things?
DAVE: Not bad, thanks. Listen, I don't suppose Nigel's there, is he?
VICKI: No – but I'm expecting him round later on.
DAVE: OK – could you get him to ring me back?
VICKI: Of course. Can you give me your number?
DAVE: I think he's got it, but let me give you it now just in case.
VICKI: Hang on – let me get a pen ... OK.
DAVE: Six-seven-nine-oh-four-oh-four. Got that?
VICKI: Got it!

Idioms

- **I don't suppose** is used with a TAG to make a question sound less direct, especially questions where you expect the answer to be 'no':

    I don't suppose you've got any money, have you?
    = 'Have you got any money?'

    I don't suppose Brian can drive a lorry, can he?
    = 'Can Brian drive a lorry?'

    I don't suppose anyone here speaks Turkish, do they?
    = 'Does anyone here speak Turkish?'

- **Got that?** means 'Did you hear that OK?'

Dialogue 2

Julie's phone rings, and she answers.

JULIE: 247649.
TERRY: Ah, hello. Could I speak to Jim, please?
JULIE: Jim?
TERRY: Yes, Jim Fife. Is he there?
JULIE: I'm afraid there isn't anyone here by that name. Who am I speaking to?
TERRY: This is Terry Smith. Isn't that Marilyn's house?
JULIE: No – you've got the wrong number.
TERRY: Ah – I'm sorry.
JULIE: Quite all right.

> **Idiom**
>
> - **by that name** means 'with that name'

Language point 35 – phone language

Speaking on the phone in English is easy once you have learnt a few important phrases:

- Use **hello** /həˈlaʊ/ to greet the other person – this is okay on the phone even in more formal situations.
- Use **Is that . . . ?** to make sure you're talking to the right person. You can use a name or a job title:

    Is that John Smith?   **– Yes, it is.**
    Is that the manager?   **– No, it isn't . . . it's the caretaker.**

> ⚠️ **Be careful!** We *don't* use **Are you . . . ?** to find out who is on the other end of the phone:
>
>   **Is that Dave Rogers?**   **Yes, it is.**
> *not*   'Are you Dave Rogers?'   'Yes, I am.'
>
>   **Is that James?**   **No, it isn't . . . it's Gerry**
> *not*   'Are you James?'   'No, I'm not . . . I'm Gerry.'
>
> If you don't recognise the voice, either say
>
>   **Who is that?**
> *or*   **Who am I speaking to?**

Remember that in British English on the phone 'that' refers to the person on the other end of the phone, and **this** refers to yourself. So, for example, if Sue phones Maria, she will say:

This is Sue . . . is that Maria?

or if she doesn't recognise the voice at all:

This is Sue . . . who is that?

(In American English people use **this** for both people, and say **Who is this?**)

If the phone is answered by someone *other* than the person you want to speak to, say:

      Could I speak to ...?
or **Is ... there, please?**

To tell the other person who *you* are, say:

      It's ...
or **It's ... speaking**

If the person you want to speak to isn't there, you can say either:

      OK, I'll phone again later
or **Could you get him/her to phone me back?**

You can use **ring** instead of **phone** in these two sentences as well.

If someone phones you and asks to talk to someone else, they might say:

      Is ... there?
or **Could I speak to ...?**

and *you* can say:

      Can I ask who's calling?

They will say:

      Yes, it's ...

Exercise 1

Match the halves of the sentences to make phrases for phone conversations.

1	Who am I	a	ask who's calling?
2	Who is	b	there?
3	Can I	c	speaking to?
4	Is Miranda	d	her to phone back?

5	It's Adrian	e	John Smith?
6	Could you get	f	that?
7	Is that	g	back later.
8	I'll ring	h	speaking.

Language point 36 – direct and indirect objects

In Dialogue 1 Vicki says to Dave:

Can you give me his number?

We have already seen (Unit 1) that the personal pronouns have SUBJECT forms (**I**, **he**, **she**, etc.) and OBJECT forms (**me**, **him**, **her**, etc.). In English the object pronouns can also include the meaning **to**:

me	=	'to me'
you	=	'to you'
her	=	'to her'
him	=	'to him'

In this meaning we call them INDIRECT OBJECT pronouns. You will see them with verbs such as **give** – here are some examples:

Give me the tickets, please
Can you give her the books?

In the first example, **the tickets** is the DIRECT OBJECT (the things being given), and **me** is the INDIRECT object (the person the tickets are given to).

Notice that we place the indirect object pronouns *before* the direct object, *not* after:

    Give me the tickets, please
not 'Give the tickets me, please'

And we can put nouns and names in this special position:

Give Dave the tickets   (= to Dave)
Give the ticket collector the tickets (= to the ticket collector)

But in all these cases, if we use the word **to** we have to *change the word order*. There are two basic patterns:

| verb | + | indirect object | + | direct object |
| *or* verb | + | direct object | + | **to** | + | indirect object |

Let's summarise the possibilities:

Give me the tickets   *not*   'Give the tickets me'
Give the tickets to me   *not*   'Give to me the tickets'
Give Dave the tickets   *not*   'Give the tickets Dave'
Give the tickets to Dave   *not*   'Give to Dave the tickets'

Exercise 2

Complete the answers to the questions, using pronouns. The first is done for you.

1   What is Suzie showing Fiona?
    She's showing her her new watch.
2   What is James going to give Su?
    _____ a birthday present.
3   Where is Dave buying the food?
    _____ in the local shop.
4   When do your parents use the car?
    _____ every day.
5   Where does Alan keep his books?
    _____ on the shelf.
6   When is your brother buying his new jeans?
    _____ today.
7   When is Jenny picking up the kids?
    _____ this afternoon.
8   What is Jenny giving James?
    _____ a cup of tea.

Dialogue 3

Cynthia phones to speak to Bob at work. But she gets through to his secretary.

CYNTHIA: Hello, it's Cynthia Palmer here. Can I speak to Bob Watford please?

SECRETARY: Hold on, I'll see if he's available ...
... Hello? I'm afraid Mr Watford's in a meeting at the moment. Would you like to leave a message?
CYNTHIA: Yes – could you ask him to get back to me as soon as possible?
SECRETARY: Yes – has he got your number?
CYNTHIA: Yes, he has.
SECRETARY: Fine – I'll make sure he calls you as soon as he gets out of the meeting.
CYNTHIA: Thanks.

Idioms

- **at the moment** means 'now'
- **get back to me** means 'phone me back'

Language point 37 – 'as soon as'

In Dialogue 3 the secretary says she'll make sure Bob Watford calls:

as soon as he <u>gets</u> out of the meeting

In English we use the PRESENT SIMPLE to mean the FUTURE after:

when
before
as soon as
until/till

Here are some more examples:

Present   *Future*
Don't forget to lock the door <u>when you leave</u>
Let's do the washing-up <u>before Dave comes back</u>
Phone us <u>as soon as you hear</u> any news
Let's stay here <u>until the rains stops</u>

Remember to use the present simple, *not* the present continuous, with this type of word:

> **... until the rain stops**
> *not* 'until the rain is stopping'
> **... when you leave**
> *not* 'when you're leaving'

Learn the phrase **as soon as possible**. You will often hear people use the abbreviation as well:

a.s.a.p. (*or* **asap**) /eɪ es eɪ ˈpiː/

both in writing and when speaking:

Can you get back to me a.s.a.p.?

Exercise 3

Unscramble the sentences.

1. stops wait the let's until rain
2. soon as us get phone as you back
3. us to arrive when forget you don't ring
4. them see children the before presents the hide let's
5. you you could leave the shut when door ?
6. souvenirs before some home let's go buy we

Exercise 4

Make the correct choice from the expressions in brackets to complete the sentences. The first one is done for you.

1. Let's wait (till/as soon as) the weather gets better.
2. Let's go in the garden (before/when) the weather gets better.
3. Could you shut the door (until/when) you leave?
4. Phone us (as soon as/until) you arrive.
5. Give me back the book (before/when) you finish it.
6. Let's wait here (till/before) Suzie arrives.
7. Pay me back the money (until/when) you can.
8. I can't use the computer (until/when) the power comes back on.

Dialogue 4

Pete's in a crisis, and he needs Sally's help.

PETE:	Sally!
SALLY:	Yes, what is it?
PETE:	I can't find my mobile.
SALLY:	Honestly, can't you take better care of your things?
PETE:	Don't go on at me – can you help me look for it?
SALLY:	[*sighs*] All right. Where did you have it last?
PETE:	I had it in my pocket last night, but I *think* it was on the kitchen table this morning. But it's not there now.
SALLY:	[*thinks for a moment*] Is it switched on?
PETE:	I think so.
SALLY:	Well, why don't you use *my* mobile to phone *yours*? Then we can listen for the ring.
PETE:	Brilliant! Give us[1] your mobile, then. [*Sally feels in her pocket, then looks around*]
SALLY:	Er ... Pete.
PETE:	What?
SALLY:	I can't find *my* mobile either.

1 **us** is sometimes used in colloquial English to mean **me**

Idiom

- **What is it?** means 'What's the problem?' or 'What do you want to talk to me about?'
- **Don't go on at me** means 'Stop criticising me', 'Stop being annoyed with me' or 'Stop telling me what to do'

Language point 38 – 'Why don't you . . . ?'

In Dialogue 4 Sally makes a suggestion to Pete:

<u>Why don't you</u> use my mobile phone?

We can use **Why don't you** + BASE-FORM as a gentle or polite way of suggesting to someone that they do something. Here are some more examples:

Why don't you wait here for them?
Why don't you ask the receptionist?
Why don't you buy your wife a present?

You can also use **Why don't ...** with **we** and **I** in a similar way:

<u>Why don't we</u> go out tonight? = 'Let's go out tonight'
<u>Why don't I</u> order us a pizza? = 'Shall I order us a pizza?'

Although they look like questions and have a question mark (**?**) at the end, these phrases don't need a specific answer – if you want to agree to the suggestion, you can just say:

OK
Fine
All right, then
Good idea

or even:

Brilliant

(like Pete in the Dialogue) if you think it's a *really* good idea.

If you *don't* agree with the suggestion, just say:

No, let's not
No, I don't think so

Exercise 5

Use **Why don't ...?** with the correct pronoun **you**, **we** or **I** to write out what James says to Fiona in the following situations. The first one is done for you.

1   James offers to pay the bill.
    Why don't I pay the bill?
2   James suggests that Fiona
    should pay the bill.   _____ ?
3   James suggests that he and
    Fiona go to the cinema.   _____ ?
4   James offers to help Fiona
    with the cooking.   _____ ?

5   James suggests that he and
    Fiona watch TV.   _____ ?
6   James offers to do the
    washing-up.   _____ ?
7   James suggests that Fiona
    should switch channels.   _____ ?
8   James suggests that he and
    Fiona ask some friends
    round for coffee.   _____ ?

Language point 39 – time expressions

We use **this**, **last** and **next** with nouns of time to talk about when things happen:

last week	**last month**	**last year**
this week	**this month**	**this year**
next week	**next month**	**next year**

These phrases *don't* have **the** (so not '~~the last week~~'), and they *don't* use a preposition (**on**, **in**, etc.) so we say:

I'm going away next week
not '~~I'm going away on next week~~'
not '~~I'm going away in next week~~'

Here are the days of the week:

Monday	/ˈmʌndɪ/
Tuesday	/ˈtjuːzdɪ/
Wednesday	/ˈwɛnzdɪ/
Thursday	/ˈθɜːzdɪ/
Friday	/ˈfraɪdɪ/
Saturday	/ˈsætədɪ/
Sunday	/ˈsʌndɪ/

Notice that we have special pronunciations of these words in colloquial English.

- We always write them with a capital letter (*not* '~~friday~~').

> ⚠ **Be careful!** With **day** and **night**, and with **morning**, **afternoon** and **evening**, we have special words and phrases that must be learnt:
>
> | | *Day* | | *Night* |
> |---|---|---|---|
> | (last) | **yesterday** /ˈjɛstədɛi/ | | **last night** |
> | (this) | **today** /təˈdɛi/ | | **tonight** /təˈnait/ |
> | (next) | **tomorrow** /təˈmɔrəʊ/ | | **tomorrow night** |
> | | | | |
> | (last) | **yesterday morning** | **yesterday afternoon** | **yesterday evening** |
> | (this) | **this morning** | **this afternoon** | **this evening** |
> | (next) | **tomorrow morning** | **tomorrow afternoon** | **tomorrow evening** |
>
> It is *wrong* to say, for example, '~~this night~~', '~~last afternoon~~', '~~next night~~'.

- We can use them with other words:

    on Tuesday
    last Tuesday
    this Tuesday
    next Tuesday
    every Tuesday

- And remember that we *don't* use **on** when there is another word before the day:

        on Thursday
    but **last Thursday**
    not '~~on last Thursday~~'

- Notice the difference between **on Friday** (single point in time) and **on Fridays** (= every Friday, regularly). In Dialogue 5 you will see that the newsagent asks Damian **Are you prepared to work on Sundays?** – meaning 'every Sunday'. If he had said **Are you prepared to work on Sunday?** this would have meant only the following Sunday.

- Finally, notice the difference between:

        every week = each week, week after week
    and **all week** = from the start of the week to the end

- This usage is found with **day**, **night**, **month** and **year** as well. Here are some examples:

    I'm working in the garden <u>all day</u> today
    (Tuesday 0830–1800)

    I'm working in the garden <u>every day</u> this week
    (Monday to Sunday)

    James is in London all week
    (he went last Sunday, and he staying there till next Sunday)

    James goes to London every week
    (he makes a trip there and back at least once a week)

Exercise 6

Choose the correct word from the brackets to complete the sentences. The first one has been done for you.

1 Shamira's working in Brighton (~~all~~/every) day this week.
2 Kath's going to London (last/next) week.
3 We haven't got any bread till (this/next) week, I'm afraid.
4 Fiona's in Miami (last/this) week.
5 Candace is working at the office (all/every) day today.
6 Is Jenny coming in by car (yesterday/today)?
7 Stuart needs a lift to the office (yesterday/tomorrow) morning.
8 Ann's working in Eastbourne (on/last) Thursday.

Dialogue 5

Damian's short of money – he needs a job that'll fit in with school. He calls at the newsagent's, where they're advertising for someone to deliver papers in the mornings.

DAMIAN: I'm interested in the delivery job.
NEWSAGENT: OK. May I[1] ask you a few questions to see if you're suitable for the job?
DAMIAN: Of course – fire away!
NEWSAGENT: Right – first and foremost: are you good at getting up early?
DAMIAN: Oh yes.
NEWSAGENT: Good. And are you afraid of the dark?
DAMIAN: Not at all.
NEWSAGENT: Excellent. Are you used to riding a bike?
DAMIAN: I ride my bike all the time.
NEWSAGENT: Good. And are you prepared to work on Sundays as well?[2]
DAMIAN: Of course. I need the money.
NEWSAGENT: Fine. And one final question: are you good with animals?
DAMIAN: Good with animals? Why are you worried about that?
NEWSAGENT: Because some of our customers have vicious dogs.
DAMIAN: Look, I'm going to think it over for a bit. Can I get back to you later?
NEWSAGENT: OK. Don't put it off too long, though, or someone will get in before you.

1 **May I ...?** (+ BASE-FORM) is a more formal way of asking permission to do something.
2 **as well** = 'also'

Idioms

- **Fire away!** means 'Go ahead and ask the questions'
- **First and foremost** means 'first of all'

Language point 40 – adjectives with prepositions

Some adjectives are used with PREPOSITIONS – you have to learn these uses individually. For example, in Dialogue 5 we see:

      interested <u>in</u> the job
and **suitable <u>for</u> the job**

Sometimes the same adjective is used with different prepositions depending on what type of word follows:

good <u>with</u> animals	(noun)
good <u>at</u> getting up early	(ING-FORM of the verb)
ready <u>for</u> dinner	(noun)
ready <u>to</u> go out	(BASE-FORM of the verb)

Sometimes two adjectives use the same preposition, but different forms of the verb:

prepared <u>to work</u>
used <u>to working</u>

Good learners' dictionaries will always tell you this information for any adjective. Try making separate lists of your own to help you learn them. For example, you could make your own list of adjectives that are followed by **to**, and add to it as you come across new examples. Grammar books of English also often provide lists of adjectives in this way.

A lot of adjectives describing *personal feelings* are used with prepositions, such as **afraid <u>of</u> the dark** in the Dialogue. Here are some others:

surprised <u>at</u>	proud <u>of</u>
keen <u>on</u>	bored <u>with</u>
scared <u>of</u>	disappointed <u>with/about</u>
ashamed <u>of</u>	worried <u>about</u>

Usually these adjectives + prepositions are followed by a NOUN:

I'm disappointed about <u>the result</u>
Gerry's proud of <u>his work</u>
My sister is worried about <u>money</u>

but they can often also be followed by the ING-FORM of the verb:

I'm disappointed about <u>coming last</u>
Gerry's proud of <u>learning Spanish</u>
My sister's worried about <u>missing the plane</u>

Exercise 7

Complete these sentences using **in**, **about**, **with**, **to**, **for**, **on**, **of** or **at**. Use a dictionary if you need to.

1 Are you ready ___ another question?
2 You look bored ___ all that paperwork.
3 Are you interested ___ coming along with us?
4 This bag is full ___ doughnuts.
5 I'm angry ___ Stuart – he's throwing chocolates at me.
6 Is Satoko good ___ speaking English?
7 Are the children ready ___ leave yet?
8 You have to be good ___ animals to work in a zoo.
9 We're rather worried ___ Henry.
10 Gerry's very keen ___ biscuits, isn't he?

Exercise 8

Match the first half of the sentences on the left with the second halves on the right. The first one has been done for you.

1	**The team was amazed**	a	with people
2	Rosemary is terribly scared	b	for the main course yet
3	I'm so fed up	c	with the exam result
4	We were shocked	d	**by the score last week**
5	The room was crowded	e	with this job
6	We're not ready	f	at the terrible news
7	I'm disappointed	g	in applying for that job
8	I hear Nigel's interested	h	of big spiders

Phrasal verbs

fit in (with) – **Does this fit in with you?** means 'Does this coincide with what you've already arranged?'.
get back (to) – **I'll get back to you** means 'I'll contact you again soon'.

get through (to) – 'succeed in contacting'; **I got through to him in the end** means that I finally managed to speak to him on the phone.

go on (at) – when someone goes on at you, it means that they keep complaining to you or telling you something until you agree. **Stop going on at me!** means something like 'Stop talking – I don't want to listen!'.

put off – 'postpone'; 'change an arrangement 'so that it happens later. **Don't put it off** means 'Do it now – don't delay.'

ring back – 'return a phone call'.

switch off is what we do to lights and machines when we want them to *stop* working – we use the **off** **switch**. (We also say **turn off** to mean the same thing).

switch on is what we do to lights and machines when we want them to *start* working – we use the **on** **switch**. (We also say **turn on** to mean the same thing).

think over – when we think something over (*not* 'think over something'), we spend some time thinking carefully about it. If you make a suggestion to someone, and they say to you **I'll think it over**, it means that you will have to wait and come back to them later for an answer.

7 What date is it today?

In this unit you will learn how to:

- talk about the future
- tell someone what you plan or intend to do
- talk about necessity and having to do things
- use state verbs

Dialogue 1

James and Henry are talking about the Bank Holiday – James hasn't thought everything through.

JAMES:	What are you doing over the Bank Holiday,[1] Henry?
HENRY:	I'm going to do up the house – we're selling it next year. What about you and Fiona?
JAMES:	We're going to hire a car and go down to Cornwall.
HENRY:	That'll be fun. What are you going to do there?
JAMES:	I'm going to try and do some surfing – if the weather's OK. And Fiona's going to visit her sister.
HENRY:	Will you be back by Tuesday?
JAMES:	Fiona will, but I'm taking an extra day off work, so I'm not driving back till Tuesday.
HENRY:	How's Fiona getting home, then?
JAMES:	Good question – I'll ask her.

1 **Bank Holiday** – a public holiday in the UK when banks, schools and public offices are closed. See **Life and living – holidays** at the end of Unit 11 for more information about this and other holidays.

Language point 41 – present for future

James asks Henry:

What <u>are you doing</u> over the Bank Holiday?

He uses the PRESENT CONTINUOUS (Language point 21) to talk about something that will happen *in the future*. In the same way, Henry says about the house:

<u>We're selling</u> it next year

and later in the Dialogue, James says:

<u>I'm not driving</u> back till Tuesday

In Unit 3 we saw that the present continuous is used for actions and events *happening now*:

I'm reading a book
Jane's sitting in the garden
The children are playing football

but the same tense is used in colloquial English to talk about *future plans and arrangements*:

I'm going to Spain (on Friday)
Jane's selling her car (next week)
The children are going to the cinema (this afternoon)

So – PRESENT *form* but FUTURE *meaning*!

Then Henry uses *another* type of future when he says:

I'm going to do up the house

He uses **be going to** + BASE-FORM to talk about *intention* (what he has *decided* to do). Here are some more examples:

Abigail's going to learn Ancient Greek
We're going to meet Dave and Jane in the pub later
Are you going to help me?

Pronunciation

going to is often pronounced /ˈgənə/ in normal colloquial speech: **I'm going to learn Greek** /aim ˈgənə lɜːn griːk/. And sometimes you even see **going to** spelt **gonna**.

We'll meet another future in Language point 43. For now, remember:

- future plans or arrangements – PRESENT CONTINUOUS
- future intention – **be going to** + BASE-FORM

Exercise 1

Complete these sentences using **going to** – the first one has been done for you.

1 Terry's playing football today, and **he's going to play** football again tomorrow.
2 It's raining today, and _____ again tomorrow.
3 I'm doing the shopping this week, and _____ again next week.

4 My sister's eating a biscuit, and _____ another biscuit in a minute.
5 Diane's going to the opera this month, and _____ to the opera again next month.
6 Miranda's riding her horse today, and _____ her horse again tomorrow.
7 Otto's phoning Austria this evening, and _____ again tomorrow evening.
8 Terry and June are washing the car today, and _____ it again on Sunday.
9 I'm planting potatoes today, and _____ carrots tomorrow.
10 Andy's swimming in the river today, and _____ there tomorrow as well.

Exercise 2

Complete these questions and answers. The first one has been done for you.

1 **Is** Justine **going to** visit Leasa?   No, **she isn't**.
2 ___ you _____ go for a swim?   Yes, I ____ .
3 ___ Gerry _____ book the tickets?   Yes, he ____ .
4 ___ they _____ to help us?   No, _____ .
5 ___ your brother _____ get the food?   No, _____ .
6 ___ Morgan and Eddie _____ come?   Yes, _____ .
7 ___ Henry _____ do up the house?   Yes, _____ .
8 ___ we _____ miss the bus?   No, we _____ .

Dialogue 2

Mike and Bob are having a coffee in a café after work.

MIKE: What date is it today?
BOB: It's the fourteenth, I think.
MIKE: The fourteenth? Isn't it the twelfth?
BOB: [*looks in his diary*] No, it's definitely the fourteenth.
MIKE: Oh no! It's my mum's birthday! What time is it?
BOB: It's too late to go and buy her a card or a present, if that's what you're thinking. It's five o'clock!
MIKE: But what am I going to do? She'll think I don't care! ... [*thinks for a moment*] ... I know, I'll phone her! Can I use your mobile?

BOB: [*hands him the mobile*] Go for it! It's important to keep your mum happy!

> **Idiom**
>
> We use **Go for it!** to encourage someone to do something they're *thinking* of doing.
>
> | | |
> |---|---|
> | **Shall I apply for this job?** | – **Go for it!** |
> | **I wonder if I should ask her out** | – **Go for it!** |
> | **I feel like giving up my job.** | – **Go for it!** |

Language point 42 – empty 'it'

When we are talking about the time and date we use **it** as an *empty subject* (because in English complete sentences usually need a subject expressed) – the EMPTY IT. So, when Mike wants to know the date, he asks Bob:

        What date is it today?
not   'What date is today?'

and Bob replies:

        It's the fourteenth
not   'Is the fourteenth'

Then Mike asks:

   What time is it?

and Bob replies:

   It's five o'clock

We also use an empty **it** when we talk about the weather:

   It's raining
   Is it sunny today?
   It isn't cold this morning

and we use it with ADJECTIVES + TO-FORM of the verb:

It's important <u>to keep</u> your mum happy
It's too late <u>to go</u> now
Is <u>it</u> easy <u>to speak</u> English?
It's illegal <u>to park</u> on double yellow lines

Look at the difference in meaning between a 'real' **it** and an empty **it**:

(a) **I can't drink this coffee – <u>it</u>'s too hot**
(b) **I can't work outside today – <u>it</u>'s too hot**

The **it** in sentence (a) is a 'real' **it** – it refers to a real object (the coffee). The **it** in sentence (b) is an empty **it** – we cannot find any word in the sentence that it specifically refers to.

Exercise 3

Turn these sentences into 'empty **it**' sentences – the first one has been done for you.

1. Parking on double yellow lines is illegal.
   It's illegal to park on double yellow lines.

2. Learning Chinese is difficult.
   _____ .

3. Being friendly to your neighbours is important.
   _____ .

4. Asking for things in English is easy.
   _____ .

5. Setting fire to your nose is stupid.
   _____ .

6. Learning Vietnamese is very hard for English people.
   _____ .

7. Eating biscuits in front of the TV is nice.
   _____ .

8. Jumping off high buildings is very dangerous.
   _____ .

9. Watching French films is fun.
   _____ .

10. Reading long books is exhausting.
    _____ .

Morning

Afternoon

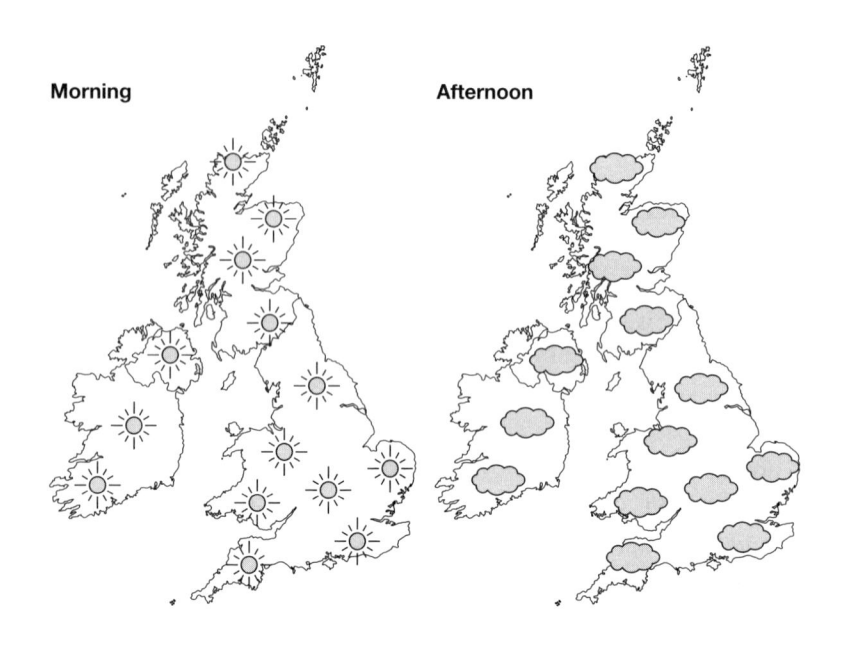

Dialogue 3

Hannah and Simon are planning a picnic with Abigail and Gary, but Hannah's a bit worried about the weather.

HANNAH:	Will it rain later, do you think?
SIMON:	[*looks in the paper*] The forecast says it'll be sunny till lunchtime.
HANNAH:	What about this afternoon?
SIMON:	[*looks in the paper again*] Clouds and wind will come in from the west.
HANNAH:	So it won't rain today, then?
SIMON:	I don't think so – but it'll be chilly for a picnic.
HANNAH:	Let's put it off till tomorrow, shall we?
SIMON:	OK. Will you phone Abigail and Gary to let them know?
HANNAH:	I'll do that right now.

Language point 43 – 'will' future

There are a number of ways of talking about the FUTURE in English. In Language point 37 we used the PRESENT SIMPLE after words like **when**, and in Language point 41 we saw two more ways: the PRESENT CONTINUOUS and **be going to**.

We can also talk about the future using the AUXILIARY **will** + BASE-FORM of the verb. This auxiliary (as with most auxiliaries in English) *doesn't* change for different persons:

I will
you will
he will   *not* 'he wills'

In colloquial English **will** is usually shortened to **'ll**, and there are the following pronunciations, which you should learn:

I'll	/aɪl/	**we'll**	/wiːl/
you'll	/juːl/	**they'll**	/ðɛɪl/
he'll	/hiːl/	**Peter'll**	/ˈpiːtərəl/
she'll	/ʃiːl/	**Jane'll**	/ˈʤɛɪnəl/

But in questions we *always* use the full form **will**, *not* **'ll**:

Will it rain?   *not* ''ll it rain?'

and we *always* use the full form in tags:

Yes, it will   *not* 'Yes, it'll'

As with all auxiliaries, we form the negative by adding **not** – but in colloquial English we have a special short form for **will not**: **won't** /wəʊnt/.

We use the will-future in two main situations:

(1) to talk about things we *know* or *expect* will happen:

The next train <u>will leave</u> at eight o'clock
China <u>will win</u> the international swimming competition
The children <u>will enjoy</u> the trip to the cinema

(2) to express *intention* to do something *in the near future*:

> **I'll phone you at about six**
> **We'll book the tickets today**
> **I'll go upstairs and tell James**

We also use **will** in the phrase **Will you ...?** + BASE-FORM:

> **Will you phone Dave and Pete?**

When Alex says this, she is *not* asking about the future – she's making a *request* (asking someone to do something). This is the normal way of making requests in English – here are some more examples:

> **Will you open the door for me?**
> **Will you help me with my homework?**
> **Will you check the oil in the car, please?**

And we use **won't** when we *refuse* to do something:

> **I won't help him because I don't like him**

Exercise 4

Rewrite these future sentences using **going to** or **will/won't** – the first one has been done for you.

1. I'll phone him tomorrow.   **I'm going to phone him tomorrow.**
2. Is Amanda going to stay here?   _____ ?
3. They're not going to wait for us.   _____ .
4. Will Dave be here tomorrow?   _____ ?
5. We'll show you the sights.   _____ .
6. The weather is going to get better.   _____ .
7. James won't forget, will he?   _____ , _____ ?
8. I won't do my homework yet.   _____ .
9. Suzie isn't going to be there.   _____ .
10. Is Fred going to read that book?   _____ ?

Exercise 5

Correct the following sentences. Be careful – *two* of them *don't* need correcting.

1 Do you go to phone them?
2 Is Justine going to doing the shopping?
3 Are Kath going to buy the tickets?
4 We're not going to meet them after all.
5 The trains go to be late all day today.
6 Does he going to be late again?
7 Do we going to be in time?
8 My brother's going to do the cooking.
9 I'll going to phone them tomorrow.
10 Be Henry going to wash the car?

Dialogue 4

James rings Dave to change plans.

JAMES: Hello Dave.
DAVE: James! How's things?
JAMES: Fine. But listen, Dave – something's come up, and I have to visit my family in Scotland. But I know we were going to get together tomorrow over lunch to discuss business, weren't we?
DAVE: Yes – do you want to put it off?
JAMES: Would you mind?
DAVE: No problem! How about later in the week?
JAMES: Would Thursday fit in with you?
DAVE: Thursday's fine. I'll put you down for twelve o'clock.

Language point 44 – more about phrasal verbs

As we saw in Language point 20 in Unit 3, PHRASAL VERBS are an important and common feature of colloquial English. And we have to be careful when we use them with PRONOUNS.
In Dialogue 4 Dave says:

I'll put you down for twelve o'clock

and he puts the OBJECT pronoun **you** *before* the second part of the phrasal verb. He *doesn't* say:

> 'I'll put down you for twelve o'clock'

When we use PRONOUNS as the objects of phrasal verbs, we *must* put them between the verb and the adverb. More examples:

> **Please <u>write</u> *it* <u>down</u> for me**
not 'Please write down it for me'

> **The radio's been on all day – why don't you <u>turn</u> *it* <u>off</u>?**
not 'why don't you switch off it?'

But with NOUN objects, we can put them either before or after the adverb:

> **Why don't you <u>turn</u> *the radio* <u>off</u>?**
or **Why don't you <u>turn off</u> *the radio*?**

> **I've got to <u>pay</u> *this cheque* <u>in</u>.**
or **I've got to <u>pay in</u> *this cheque*.**

Exercise 6

Change these phrasal verb sentences by replacing the noun with a pronoun, as in the first example.

1. I'm going to pay in this cheque.   **I'm going to pay it in**.
2. Henry's going to do up the house.   _____ .
3. Could you turn off the radio?   _____ ?
4. I need to look up these words.   _____ .
5. Could you write down the address?   _____ ?
6. Will you fill in these forms?   _____ ?
7. We're going to send back the letters.   _____ .
8. They're going to knock down this building.   _____ .
9. Tom's trying to start up the engine.   _____ .
10. Switch off the lights, please.   _____ .

Dialogue 5

Su asks Neil if he's coming to a concert.

SU: Are you going to come with us to see the Stones?
NEIL: Well, I was going to, but it looks like I can't make it.
SU: Oh dear – why not?
NEIL: It's on the twenty-fifth, isn't it?
SU: Yes. Is that a problem?
NEIL: Don't you remember? It's our wedding anniversary, and I'm going to take Fiona out somewhere to celebrate.
SU: Where are you going to take her?
NEIL: I don't know yet. I want to surprise her.
SU: Well, why don't you bring her to see the Stones?
NEIL: Fiona hates the Stones.
SU: Then it'll be a real surprise for her, won't it?

Idioms

- **it looks like** means 'it seems that . . .' or 'it's probable that . . .'

    It looks like it'll rain later
    It looks like we're going to miss the bus

- **I can't make it** means 'I won't be able to keep the appointment' or 'I won't be able to do what we planned'.

- We use **Oh dear** to show that we are *disappointed* about something, or *unhappy* about something:

    James has broken his leg.
    – Oh dear, has he?

    Oh dear, we're going to be late for the concert.

    The coffee machine's broken today, I'm afraid
    – Oh dear.

Dialogue 6

Kelly's not happy about the milk she's just bought, so she asks Di what she thinks.

KELLY: This milk doesn't seem very fresh, does it?
DI: What do you mean?
KELLY: [*Offers Di the bottle*] Have a smell.
[*Di has a smell*] What do you think?
DI: Hmm – you're right, it smells off. Take it back, I expect they'll give you your money back.
KELLY: I hope so!

Language point 45 – state verbs

Most verbs in English are ACTION VERBS – they describe an action that lasts a short period of time and has a beginning and an end. Here are some examples of action verbs:

say	write	switch on
eat	run	go out
read	phone	look for

But some verbs are *not* action but STATE VERBS – they describe:

- feelings
- states of mind
- situations that continue over a period of time

Here are some examples of state verbs:

know	remember	prefer	hope
see	feel	contain	taste
have	forget	mean	expect
belong	love	want	smell
think	hate	seem	like

State verbs work differently from action verbs in English – in particular, they *do not normally have a present continuous*. Compare these two sentences:

action		**Harry's looking for a newspaper**
state		**Harry wants a newspaper**
	not	'~~Harry's wanting a newspaper~~'

In the first sentence, **look for** describes an action, and we use the PRESENT CONTINUOUS to show that the action is happening *now* – go back and review Language point 21 if you need to remind yourself about this. In the second sentence, **want** is a *state of mind* not an action, and so we use the PRESENT SIMPLE.

In the same way, present tense questions and negatives are different for actions and states:

action	**Is Harry looking for a newspaper?**
state	**Does Harry want a newspaper?**
action	**Harry isn't looking for a newspaper.**
state	**Harry doesn't want a newspaper.**

because the present continuous uses **be** as its AUXILIARY, while the present simple uses **do**. It is *wrong* to say:

'~~Is Harry wanting a newspaper?~~'
'~~Harry isn't wanting a newspaper.~~'

⚠️ **Be careful!** Some state verbs have *secondary* meanings which are actions – for example, **expect** means 'think (something will happen)' (state), but it also means 'wait for' (action):

I expect Suzie'll be late	(state)
I'm expecting a parcel today	(action)

Another example – **see** (state) means 'understand', but **see** (action) means 'visit':

I see why you're upset	(state)
I'm seeing my family at the weekend	(action)

Exercise 7

Make the correct choice from the brackets to complete the sentences – you will need to think about whether the verbs are state or action.

1 I (want/'m wanting) to see the new film.
2 James (goes/is going) to the cinema this evening.
3 Brian (isn't liking/doesn't like) vegetables.
4 (Is this book belonging/Does this book belong) to you?
5 My diary (contains/is containing) important information.
6 Adrian (doesn't read/isn't reading) the paper at the moment.
7 (Do you know/Are you knowing) John Smith?
8 Shamira (sees/'s seeing) her family this evening.
9 I (don't expect/'m not expecting) any post today.
10 (Do you see/Are you seeing) what I'm saying?

Language point 46 – 'bring' and 'take'

Bring and **take** are DIRECTION VERBS, like **come** and **go**:

come	means:	move *towards* the speaker
bring	means:	carry (a thing) or lead (a person) *towards* the speaker
go	means:	move *away* from the speaker
take	means:	carry (a thing) or lead (a person) *away* from the speaker

In Dialogue 5, Su says to Neil:

Why don't you bring her to see the Stones?

This shows that Su will be at the Stones concert herself, and she is imagining Neil and Fiona coming to join her there – otherwise she would have said:

Why don't you take her to see the Stones?

Then Neil says to Su:

I'm going to take Fiona out somewhere

because he is imagining himself *going* with Fiona somewhere.

The important thing with **bring** and **take** is the *attitude* or *viewpoint* of the person speaking. In the following examples, Fiona is the person speaking, so it is her position relative to the kitchen (where the plates are going) that decides whether she uses **bring** or **take**:

(Fiona is in the kitchen, Neil is in the living room)
Neil, could you bring the plates into the kitchen?

(Fiona and Neil are both in the living room)
Neil, could you take the plates into the kitchen?

Bring and **take** also form a number of very common PHRASAL VERBS (Language point 44):

bring in	**take away**
bring out	**take off**
bring up	**take over**
bring round	**take out**
bring over	**take on**

Some of these have obvious meanings – **take away**, for example – but others are less easy to work out and should be learnt:

The plane is going to take off in ten minutes	(leave the ground)
Jane's bringing up the children on her own	(raise)
Babies often bring up their food	(vomit)
I'm going to bring that point up at the next meeting	(raise)
Simon's taking on too much work	(undertake)

Exercise 8

Decide whether to use **bring** or **take** in the following sentences.

1 Could you (bring/take) those bags over here?
2 We're going to (bring/take) the children on holiday to Orlando.
3 Shall I (bring/take) a curry back with me when I come home?

4 Bert and Fiona are coming, and they're (bringing/taking) the kids.
 5 (Bring/Take) those keys over to me.
 6 The food's already here – who's (bringing/taking) the drinks?
 7 Shall we (bring/take) some wine to the party?
 8 Would you like me to (bring/take) you home?
 9 I want you to (bring/take) these papers over to Henry.
10 Please (bring/take) your computer off my desk.

Exercise 9

We've seen *ordinal* numbers in some of the dialogues in this unit – **first** (1st), **second** (2nd) and **third** (3rd) are irregular, but the others are easy to recognise and end in **-th**. See if you can spot them in this exercise. Listen to the audio of these different people telling you their names and their birthdays. Then match the names to the dates.

Liam	10 May
Sally	20 March
Adam	1 October
Edward	2 November
Monica	17 July
Keith	8 February
Anthea	7 December
Greg	22 September
Susan	10 November
Carl	17 June

Phrasal verbs

come up – when we say **Something's come up**, we mean that something *unexpected* has happened which will have an effect on our plans.

do up – 'redecorate'. When we do things up, we improve them or make them look better or newer. It *doesn't* mean **tidy up** – if you say **I'm doing up the living room**, you mean that you're making *permanent* changes to the room.

get together – 'meet by arrangement'. **We must get together soon** means 'We must arrange to meet soon'.

knock down – 'demolish', 'destroy'. We use this phrasal verb mostly about *buildings* – things which are standing and which fall *down* when they are destroyed.

look up – when we look for a word in a dictionary, we say that we're **looking the word up**.
put down (for) – when you put someone down for a specific time, it means that you make an *appointment* for them at that time: **I'll put you down for ten o'clock**.
start up – we sometimes use **start up** when we talk about starting engines or other machinery; it means that we switch it on to make it start.
turn off – 'switch off' (Unit 6).
turn on – 'switch on' (Unit 6).

Life and living – seasons and weather

In Dialogue 3 we saw Hannah and Simon doing what a lot of people do in Britain a lot of the time – talking about the weather!

Because of their **geographical position** on the north-western edge of the **continent** of Europe, the **British Isles** experience a wide **variety** of types of weather, with weather systems **constantly** blowing in off the Atlantic and bringing **meteorological conditions** that are not only **changeable** but often also **dramatic**. In addition, there are four **well-defined** seasons, each with its own typical weather **patterns**.

Winter is usually cold, especially in the north of England and in Scotland, and you can expect snow, sometimes heavy, at any time from December to February. Southern areas **tend to get** less snow, sometimes none at all, but snow is very **unpredictable** and even the south can **wake up to** a white **landscape**. Spring **is characterised by milder** temperatures, windy weather and **showers** all over the country, with more rain in the west than in the east generally. Summer can be quite hot and sunny, especially in July and August, with **record temperatures** during long **spells** of **fine weather**. At the end of September the summer heat **abates** and autumn arrives, with its **misty** weather and the changing colours of the leaves on the trees **signalling** the **approach of winter** once more.

Of course, the day-to-day picture is much more complicated than that in a country like Britain, and its probably not surprising that we have a lot of weather words. Rain can come as showers, **drizzle** or a **downpour**, for example; and snow can appear as **flurries** or a **blizzard** or in **drifts** (and don't forget **hail** and **sleet!**). One day you can experience a **heatwave**, and the next day can be watching the **spectacle** of a violent **thunderstorm**.

But whatever the weather when you're in Britain, you'll always have something to talk about. And don't forget your **umbrella**!

Glossary

geographical position – where something is in the world
continent – large body of land, like Europe or Asia
British Isles – the main islands of Britain and Ireland, with all the outlying small islands that belong to them
variety – different kinds
constantly – all the time, again and again
meteorological conditions – types of weather
changeable – likely to change a lot
dramatic – noticeable, impressive, surprising
well-defined – easy to distinguish, obviously different
patterns – a regular way in which something happens
tend to get – usually get
unpredictable – coming without warning
wake up to – see or find as soon as you wake up
landscape – what the land around you looks like
is characterised by – typically or usually has
milder – less cold
showers – short periods of rain
record temperatures – very high (or very low) temperatures
spells – periods
fine weather – sunny, calm weather
abates – goes down, gets less
misty – where there is a lot of mist (wet cloud at ground level)
signalling – giving a sign that something will happen
approach of winter – that winter is coming
drizzle – very light but steady rain
downpour – very heavy rain
flurries – light snow blowing in the wind
blizzard – heavy snowstorm
drifts – lying snow
hail – frozen rain
sleet – a mixture of rain and snow; wet snow
heatwave – a long period of very hot weather
spectacle – something you see that is strange or impressive
thunderstorm – an electrical storm with thunder and lightning
umbrella – something for protecting you from the rain

8 Can I make an appointment?

In this unit you will learn:

- how to make appointments over the phone
- how to use 'can', 'could' and 'should'
- how to use two verbs together
- more about state verbs

Dialogue 1

Gerry's not feeling very well, so he phones the doctor's surgery.

RECEPTIONIST:	Surgery. Good morning.
GERRY:	Good morning. Can I make an appointment to see the doctor today?
RECEPTIONIST:	We're very busy this morning, I'm afraid. May I ask what the problem is?
GERRY:	I've got a bad cold. Do you think I could see one of the doctors just for five minutes?
RECEPTIONIST:	Hold on a moment . . . yes, Dr Smith is free at ten – will that do?
GERRY:	Great. Thanks a lot.
RECEPTIONIST:	Not at all. See you at ten.
GERRY:	Bye.

Idioms

- **hold on** means 'wait'
- **Will that do?** means 'Is that convenient for you?'

Dialogue 2

Maria has also been to see the doctor. She's prescribing her some green tablets and some red ones.

MARIA: Now, how often should I take these?
DOCTOR: I want you to take a green one each morning, and a red one at night.
MARIA: How long for?
DOCTOR: Keep taking them every day until you feel better, or until you run out.
MARIA: What if I run out and I still don't feel any better?
DOCTOR: Then you'd better come back and see me.

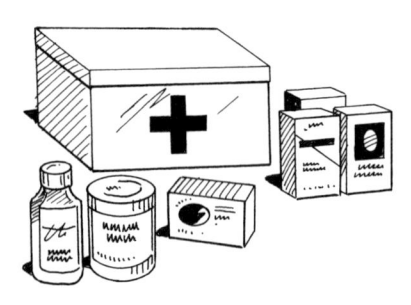

Dialogue 3

Later, Maria gets home and Tony asks her how the visit to the doctor's went.

MARIA: I've got some green pills and some red ones.
TONY: When are you supposed to take them?
MARIA: The red ones every morning, and the green ones ... oh, no, wait a minute ... Is that right?
[*Maria thinks for a moment*]
No, I'm supposed to take these green ones in the morning, and the red ones at night.
TONY: Are you sure? You ought to check if you're not. Why don't you phone the surgery and ask?
MARIA: You're right – I'd better phone and ask to speak to the doctor again.

Language point 47 – 'can', 'could' and 'should'

In Language point 18 we saw the AUXILIARY **could** /kʊd/ used with the BASE-FORM to ask someone to do something:

Could you help me?
Could you tell me where the bank is?

In Dialogue 1 Gerry uses **could** to ask *permission*:

Do you think I could see one of the doctors?

And in Dialogue 2 Maria asks the doctor to do something:

Do you think you could write that down for me?

These last two examples are just longer ways of saying

Could I see one of the doctors?
Could you write that down for me?

Gerry also uses another auxiliary **can** when he says:

Can I make an appointment?

Can I . . .? is really the same as **Could I . . .?** in this sense – in colloquial English you can ask permission using either:

Can/Could I speak to the manager?
Can/Could I see the menu?
Can/Could I offer you a lift?

But the *main* meaning of **can** is **be able to**:

Can you swim?	=	Are you able to swim?
I can speak English.	=	I am able to speak English.
Dave can ride a bike.	=	Dave is able to ride a bike.

Note that:

1. **can** *doesn't* change for **he/she** – so *not* '~~Dave cans ride~~'.
2. We use the BASE-FORM, *not* the to-form, after **can** and **could** – so *not* '~~Dave can to ride a bike~~'.

3   We *don't* use the **do** auxiliary to make questions with **can** and **could** – we simply reverse the word order, just as we do with the verb **be**:

> **He is late**   →   **Is he late?**   *not* '~~Does he be late?~~'
> **He can ride**   →   **Can he ride?**   *not* '~~Does he can ride?~~'

In Dialogue 2 we see another auxiliary: **should** /ʃʊd/. This word works in exactly the same way as **can** and **could**, and is used to talk about *obligation* – you can tell someone that you think it's a *good idea* for them to go, or that it's the *right thing* for them to go, by saying **you should go**.

The negative forms of **can**, **could**, and **should** have special SHORT FORMS that you should learn:

> **can't** /kɑːnt/   **couldn't** /'kʊdnt/   **shouldn't** /'ʃʊdnt/

Finally, when the doctor in Dialogue 2 says:

> **You'd better come back ...**

he means:

> 'it would be a good thing for you to come back ...'
> *or* 'I think you should come back ...'

... 'd better works like the other auxiliaries in this Language point – it's followed by the BASE-FORM, and it *doesn't* change for **he/she**. More examples:

> **You'd better phone her**
> **We'd better leave now**
> **I'd better do my homework**

The negative simply adds **not**:

> **You look ill – you'd better not go to work tomorrow**

The doctor also says:

> **I want you to take a green one ...**

We can say what we want someone else to do (or not do) by using:

I want
I'd like   **you** + to-form
I don't want

Exercise 1

Change these sentences to **can** or **be able** – the first one has been done for you.

1   Julie can swim.   **Julie is able to swim.**
2   Can they speak English?   _____ ?
3   Dave isn't able to come.   _____ .
4   Can you see the screen?   _____ ?
5   Are they able to walk?   _____ ?
6   Suzie's not able to make the
    appointment.   _____ .
7   I can't advise you on this.   _____ .
8   Can Julie and Simon come
    tonight?   _____ ?

Exercise 2

Write what *you* would say in these situations, using **'d better (not)** – the first one has been done for you.

1   You and Fiona are late for an appointment.   (hurry up)
    We'd better hurry up.

2   Suzie is carrying an expensive vase very carelessly.   (drop)
    _____

3   Someone is coming to buy your car. But it's
    very dirty.   (clean)
    _____

4   Barry's late, but you and Jenny don't want to go
    without him.   (wait for)
    _____

5   You're trying to read, but it's getting dark. (turn on)
    _____

6   Someone's broken into Henry's house.   (phone)
    _____

Language point 48 – 'what if . . . ?'

In Language point 41 we saw how the PRESENT CONTINUOUS is often used in English to mean the FUTURE. Sometimes we use the PRESENT SIMPLE in the same way, as for example when Maria says in Dialogue 2:

What if I <u>run</u> out . . . ?

She is talking about something that might happen *in the future*. We use the present simple after **What if . . . ?** to ask about something that we think is possible in the near future. Here are some more examples:

What if <u>we arrive</u> late?
What if Dave <u>doesn't want</u> to come with us?
What if the bus <u>is</u> late?
What if the guests <u>don't like</u> the food?

This is a short way of saying:

What shall we do if . . . ?

We *don't* usually use the present continuous or the future after **What if . . . ?**

       What if we arrive late?
not   '~~What if we're arriving late?~~'
not   '~~What if we'll arrive late?~~'

Exercise 3

You're having a very pessimistic day. Respond *negatively* to each of Brenda's suggestions with a **What if . . . ?** question. The first one has been done for you.

1   Let's go to the cinema!
     (We won't like the film)   **What if we don't like the film?**
2   Let's go shopping in town!
     (The shops will be shut)   _____?
3   Let's go for a ride in the car!
     (The car will break down)   _____?

4 Let's listen to my new CD!
   (The neighbours will complain) _____ ?
5 Let's go to a club!
   (The doorman won't let us in) _____ ?
6 Let's order some Vietnamese food!
   (The waiter won't understand
      us) _____ ?
7 Let's paint the house
   (The neighbours won't like
      the colour) _____ ?
8 Let's phone Ozzy Osbourne!
   (He won't answer) _____ ?

Dialogue 4

Jane is expecting to meet Debbie and Sarah for coffee, but only Sarah arrives.

JANE: There you are, Sarah – hello!
SARAH: Hi. Sorry I'm a bit late.
JANE: Where's Debbie? She normally comes for coffee with you.
SARAH: Not today, I'm afraid. She's not feeling very well.
JANE: What's wrong with her?
SARAH: She's got a headache and she's feeling a bit sick.
JANE: Has she seen the doctor?
SARAH: She's seeing him later on.

Dialogue 5

Scott is having trouble persuading Justine to go out for the evening.

SCOTT: Do you fancy going out tonight?
JUSTINE: OK – where do you want to go?
SCOTT: How about a film? I can't wait to see the new Johnny Depp film.
JUSTINE: I hate watching action movies – they always seem to be the same. Can't you arrange to see it with someone else another time?

SCOTT:	OK, OK. Well . . . we could go to Maria's party.
JUSTINE:	That's fine, but only if you promise to be nice to her.
SCOTT:	I'll try, but it's very difficult. I just can't help laughing at her pictures.
JUSTINE:	You'll have to avoid looking at them, or pretend to like them. If you can't manage to do either of those, then I'm not coming.
SCOTT:	You're really putting me off going now, Justine.
JUSTINE:	OK, what else could we do?
SCOTT:	Well, why don't we just decide to stay in? I don't mind ordering a pizza for us. Besides, Maria's parties are usually pretty useless, aren't they?
JUSTINE:	True.

Idiom

- **pretty useless** means 'not very good' or even 'quite bad'

Language point 49 – more about state verbs

In Language point 45 in the last unit we saw that state verbs in English describe a situation that *exists permanently or for a long time*, and that these verbs usually *don't* appear in the present continuous:

> **I like curry** *not* 'I'm liking curry'
> **This book belongs to me** *not* 'This book's belonging to me'

See and **feel** are on the list of state verbs in Language point 45, but in Dialogue 4 of this unit Sarah uses both of them in the present continuous:

> **She's not feeling very well**
> **She's seeing him later on**

In the first sentence Sarah is talking about a *temporary situation* – a situation that *won't* last long; so the usual STATE meaning of **feel** doesn't work here and we can use the present continuous.

Now look at the second example.

Some state verbs in English have *secondary* meanings which describe *actions*. Here are some examples:

(state)	**have**	=	possess
(action)	**have**	=	receive; eat food
(state)	**think**	=	believe; have an opinion
(action)	**think**	=	think about something; turn something over in your mind
(state)	**look**	=	have appearance
(action)	**look**	=	use your eyes to see
(state)	**see**	=	understand
(action)	**see**	=	visit

So when Sarah says:

She's seeing him later on

she's using the *action* meaning of **see** ('visit'), and so the present continuous is correct.

Here are other examples using the verbs above:

Adrian has a yellow car	(possess)
Adrian's having eggs for lunch	(eat food)
I think this book's wonderful	(opinion)
Be quiet – I'm thinking	(think about something)
Candace looks cross	(has appearance)
Candace is looking at her desk	(use eyes to see)

Exercise 4

Decide between the two choices in the brackets – you will have to consider whether the verb is used in its *action* meaning or its *state* meaning.

1   I ('m thinking/think) hard about that question.
2   (Are we having/Do we have) eggs for breakfast this morning?
3   You (look/'re looking) very like your sister.
4   Tom (thinks/'s thinking) Indian food's good for you.

5 What's that book you (look/'re looking) at?
6 I (don't see/'m not seeing) what he means.
7 Simon (has/'s having) a second-hand Ferrari.
8 Dave (doesn't see/isn't seeing) his girlfriend this weekend.

Language point 50 – -ing and to-forms after verbs

In colloquial English there are different ways of joining two verbs together. In Dialogue 5 Scott says:

I can't wait to see the new Johnny Depp film
but **I can't help laughing at her pictures**

Some verbs are followed by the TO-FORM of the second verb, while others are followed by the ING-FORM, and it's important to learn which is correct with each verb – if you get them wrong it will *sound* wrong!

I can't wait to see you   *not* 'I can't wait seeing you'
I can't help laughing   *not* 'I can't help to laugh'

Here are some common verbs and verb phrases followed by **-ing** or **to**:

Do you fancy			**promise**	
Do you feel like			**arrange**	
I can't help			**seem**	
avoid	+ -ing		**pretend**	+ to
put off			**decide**	
I don't mind			**I can't wait**	
I hate				

- **Do you fancy doing ...?** and **Do you feel like doing ...?** both mean **Would you like to do ...?**

- **I can't wait to do ...** means **I'm very keen/impatient to do ...**

- **I don't mind doing ...** means **I'm happy to do ...**

When you **put** someone **off doing** something, you persuade them *not* to do something.

Good learners' dictionaries will always tell you whether to use **-ing** or **to** after a verb or verb phrase.

Exercise 5

This exercise is to give you *dictionary practice* – you will need a good learners' dictionary of English. Decide whether to use the TO-FORM or the ING-FORM in the following sentences. The first one has been done for you.

1. I can't wait (see) the new film.
   I can't wait to see the new film.

2. Don't forget (order) the tickets.
   _____ .

3. She promises (come) back later.
   _____ .

4. The government is offering (help) with the costs.
   _____ .

5. I always enjoy (have) dinner with Julie.
   _____ .

6. Remember (lock) the door.
   _____ .

7. Suzie hates (do) the shopping.
   _____ .

8. We're going (swim) this afternoon.
   _____ .

9. I don't want (offend) him.
   _____ .

10. Why don't you give up (smoke)?
    _____ ?

11. We can't avoid (see) them.
    _____ .

12. Will Brenda decide (apply) for that job?
    _____ ?

13. I don't mind (pay) the bill.
    _____ .

14 Do you fancy (learn) yoga?
    _____ ?

15 You don't happen (know) where he is, do you?
    _____ ?

16 Dave doesn't really like (cook).
    _____ .

17 I'd better pretend (be) ill.
    _____ .

18 James needs (fly) to Australia next week.
    _____ .

19 We hope (see) you all again soon.
    _____ .

20 We'd better put off (see) them till next week.
    _____ .

Language point 51 – 'else'

Else means 'other'; but it's only used with:

1 PRONOUNS ending in **-one**, **-body** and **-thing**, for example:

   anyone else   (= any other person)
   nobody else   (= no other person)
   nothing else   (= no other thing)
   someone else   (= some other person)

2 the place adverbs **somewhere**, **anywhere** and **nowhere**:

   somewhere else   (= in some other place)
   nowhere else   (= in no other place)
   anywhere else   (= in any other place)

3 question words:

   who else?
   what else?
   where else?   (= in what other place?)
   why else?   (= for what other reason?)
   how else?   (= in what other way?)
   when else?   (= at what other time?)

You *must* use **else** rather than **other** with these words:

> **Shall we invite anyone else?**

not 'Shall we invite anyone other?'
not 'Shall we invite any other person?'

But **what else** (pronoun) becomes **what other** when used as an adjective with a following noun:

> **What else do you want to buy?**

not 'What other do you want to buy?'

but **What other books do you want to buy?**
not 'What else books do you want to buy?'

And it is *wrong* to use **else** with nouns:

> **The other books**

not 'The books else'

> **Shall we have another drink?**

not 'Shall we have a drink else?'

Exercise 6

Decide which of these sentences are correct, and which are wrong. Correct the wrong ones.

1. What else food shall we buy?
2. The people else will be here later.
3. Where are the others?
4. Who else is coming tonight?
5. Where other place would you like to go?
6. Can I have an else cream cake?
7. I like this coat, but the else one's better.
8. I know you, but I don't know anybody else here.
9. I need another cup of tea.
10. Would you like anything other, or is that all?

Dialogue 6

Shamira is grumbling to Kath.

SHAMIRA: Every time we come here we have to wait!
KATH: Never mind – it won't be long now.
SHAMIRA: We've been here the whole morning, practically.
KATH: [*looks at her watch*] Well ... we've only been here twenty minutes, actually.
SHAMIRA: It's really annoying, and I'm fed up!
KATH: It's no use being annoyed, Shamira. Either we can wait here and be patient, or we can come back later.
SHAMIRA: Why does everyone else decide to come here just when I want to?
KATH: Calm down. All the assistants are busy, but ...
SHAMIRA: You mean 'both the assistants'! There are only two of them! They should employ more assistants so people don't have to wait.
KATH: Look, we're in town all day today – let's come back when they're not so rushed off their feet.
SHAMIRA: I'm not budging!

Idioms

- **practically** means 'almost' or 'nearly'
- We sometimes use **actually** to *correct* what someone else has said:

    Suzie's eighteen.
    – She's nineteen, actually.

    Are you looking for ward to the party?
    – Actually I'm not coming.

- **rushed off their feet** means 'very busy'
- **I'm not budging** means 'I'm not moving from here' or 'I'm staying right where I am'

Language point 52 – 'annoyed' and 'annoying'

Shamira says:

> It's really **annoyed**!

and Kath tells her:

> It's no use being **annoyed**

In English we have **-ing** and **-ed** adjectives formed from verbs – it is important to know the difference in meaning between them. Shamira calls the *situation* **annoying**, while Kath talks about *Shamira* being **annoyed**. So:

> *cause* of situation: **-ing**
> *person affected* by situation: **-ed**

Let's look at some more pairs of examples:

> Kath is **interested** in her magazine
> because her magazine is **interesting**

> Brenda is stuck in traffic – she's **annoyed**
> because being in a traffic jam is **annoying**

> When something **surprising** happens
> everyone is **surprised**

> When we see an **amazing** film
> we are **amazed**

> ⚠️ **Be careful!** The **-ing** adjectives can come *either* after the verb **be** *or* before the noun:
>
> > **This book is interesting**
> > **This is an interesting book**
>
> but the **-ed** adjectives *don't* usually come before the noun:
>
> > **This person is annoyed**
>
> but *not*   '~~This is an annoyed person~~'

Exercise 7

Choose the correct word from the brackets for each sentence.

1 Gerry's (disappointed/disappointing) that the game's cancelled.
2 Are you (interested/interesting) in tropical fish?
3 Andy gets very (excited/exciting) when he plays computer games.
4 It's really (annoyed/annoying) to miss the bus.
5 We want to have an (excited/exciting) holiday in New Zealand.
6 This long heavy book is very (bored/boring).
7 Suzie gets rather (annoyed/annoying) when the kids are noisy.
8 Turn the TV off! I'm (bored/boring) with this programme!
9 It's very (relaxed/relaxing) to sit in a bath at the end of the day.
10 I'm (surprised/surprising) to hear your news.

Exercise 8

Complete the sentences using the words from the box. You'll need to use each word *twice*, and you'll have to decide whether it should end in **-ed** or **-ing**.

1 Janet's very _____ with her poor exam results.
2 I really don't like my job – it's dull and _____ .
3 It's _____ that I can't come your birthday party.
4 This book is very _____ – I think you'll enjoy it.
5 I'm very _____ because I've got nothing to do.
6 The noise from your bedroom is very _____ – I can't work!
7 It's raining hard, so it's _____ that so many people are here.
8 Is Tim _____ in large boats?
9 Are you _____ at Brian's good performance today?
10 I'm very _____ that the bus is late again!

annoy	disappoint	bore	interest	surprise

Phrasal verbs

calm down – 'become calm'. When we tell someone to calm down, we want them stop being nervous or agitated, and to relax.
fed up – when you are fed up, you are unhappy about something, or bored with something, or rather angry about something. **I'm fed up with this homework** means 'I've had enough of this homework' or 'I don't want to do this homework any more'.
hold on – 'wait'; **hang on** means the same thing.
put off – we saw this phrasal verb in Unit 6, meaning 'postpone'; but it has another meaning: when we put someone off doing something, we discourage them from doing it – we convince them that they shouldn't do it.
run out (of) – when we run out of something, we use the last of it and we haven't got any left. Notice that we can say *either* **We've run out of milk** *or* **The milk's run out** – both mean that there's no milk left.

Life and living – sport

If you don't want to have to visit the doctor like the people at the start of this unit, you need to keep fit – and a good way to do that is to play sport! The British take their sport very seriously, and there are two games that have a special place in their hearts. Football is **regarded as** the national game, at least in England and Scotland, and is played at all levels, both **professionally** and among **amateurs**, every weekend from autumn to spring. The best football clubs attract thousands of supporters and **spectators** to the **grounds** to watch the **action**. Millions more watch the **matches live** on television, either at home or on large screens in pubs. Many football **fans** have a particular club that they support – ask them **What team do you support?** and they'll tell you. They might even be wearing their team's **strip**, in which case you probably won't need to ask!

England (along with other English-speaking countries and members of the **Commonwealth**, such as Australia, New Zealand, South Africa, India, Pakistan and the **West Indies**) also has a *summer* game: cricket. It's played between two teams, one of which **bats** while the other fields. The batsmen (two **at a time**) try and hit the ball and run between the **wickets** when they succeed. The fielders try to get them **out** (of the game) by knocking down the wicket, or by catching the ball when it's been hit . . . or in several other ways. Yes, it's all rather **mysterious** and sounds very complicated to the **uninitiated**, but, like most things in life, it's easy when you know how. There are plenty of books in the shops that'll explain the rules of cricket in detail (sometimes far too much detail) – and there are plenty of people around who'll save you the money by doing the job themselves.

Cricket is a summer game in the UK, but it's played all year round now, because during the football season the national cricket team goes to play the national teams of the other countries in warmer parts of the world. So being a professional cricketer for your country has now become a full-time year-round job!

Glossary

regarded as – thought of as, considered
professionally – in return for payment
amateur – without being paid
spectator – someone who watches a game
ground – the field (or stadium) where a game is played
action – what's happening on the field
match – a game between two teams
live – at the time that it happens, *not* recorded and shown later
fan – supporter
strip – the uniform that a team wears when they are playing
Commonwealth – a federation of countries with historical and cultural links to the UK
West Indies – the island nations of the Caribbean
bats – uses a bat (a wooden thing for hitting a ball)
at a time – simultaneously
wicket – three sticks in the ground (don't ask – just buy a book on cricket)
out – out of the game
mysterious – hard to understand
uninitiated – someone who hasn't been told the rules

9 I've lost my passport!

> **In this unit you will learn how to:**
> - talk about things that have happened recently
> - talk about a a sequence of events
> - ask people about events that have already happened
> - form and use the past simple
> - form and use the present perfect
> - use some time adverbs

Dialogue 1

Shamira and Liz are at the supermarket checkout.

LIZ: Have we bought everything we need?
SHAMIRA: I think so – I've crossed everything off the shopping list and I don't think we've forgotten anything.

[*The checkout assistant greets them*]

C/ASSISTANT: Hello. Have you got a dividend card?
SHAMIRA: Yes – hang on ... it's in my bag.

[*Shamira looks in her bag for her card, and notices her passport is missing!*]

... Liz! I think I've lost my passport!
LIZ: What? Oh no – are you sure you brought it with you?
SHAMIRA: Yes, quite sure – it was in my bag when I left the house, and now it's gone!
LIZ: Have you dropped it somewhere in the shop here?
SHAMIRA: I don't think so – I've only just opened my bag.

Liz: OK. Don't panic. Let me pay for all this, and then we'll go to the police station and report it lost.
Shamira: Yes. Maybe someone's found it somewhere and handed it in.

Language point 53 – present perfect

This is a very important form of the verb in English – it is used for talking about things that have *recently happened* (happened a short time ago) – so it is a *past* tense.

In Dialogue 1 Liz asks:

Have we bought everything?

She uses:

- the PRESENT tense of **have**

    +

- the PAST PARTICIPLE of the main verb **buy**

to form the PRESENT PERFECT.

We already know the present tense of **have** – go back to Language point 25 in Unit 4 if you want to remind yourself. Now we need to know how to form the PAST PARTICIPLE:

- REGULAR verbs add **-ed** to the BASE-FORM. For example:

Base-form	*Past participle*
laugh	**laughed**
open	**opened**
hand in	**handed in**
cross off	**crossed off**

Spelling rules

- when the base-form of a regular verb ends in **-e**, we simply add **-d**:

    close   **closed**

- when it ends in a SINGLE VOWEL + SINGLE CONSONANT, we *double* the consonant before adding **-ed**:

    drop   **dropped** *not* '~~droped~~'

- when it ends in CONSONANT + **y** we drop the **y** and add **-ied**:

	try	**tried**
	cry	**cried**
but	**play**	**played** (VOWEL + **y**)

Pronunciation

The **-ed** ending is pronounced:

/ɪd/	after **-d** and **-t**:	**handed** /ˈhændɪd/
/d/	after vowel sounds and VOICED consonants:	**opened** /ˈəʊpənd/
/t/	after UNVOICED consonants:	**kicked** /kɪkt/

- For IRREGULAR VERBS, we have to *learn* the past participle with every verb. So, for example, the past participle of **buy** is *not* '~~buyed~~' but **bought**. Here are some more example of irregular past participles.

see	seen
fly	flown
lose	lost
find	found

At the end of this book you will find a list of all common irregular verbs with their past participles.

With all verbs, regular and irregular, we form questions in the present perfect by simply reversing the position of the SUBJECT and **have**:

Statement	*Question*
I've lost	**Have I lost?**
Dave's arrived	**Has Dave arrived?**
They've phoned	**Have they phoned?**

And we form negatives by adding **not** to **have/has**:

Statement	*Negative*
I've lost	**I haven't lost**
Dave's arrived	**Dave hasn't arrived**
They've phoned	**They haven't phoned**

Remember that we normally use SHORT FORMS of **have** in statements, and **n't** instead of **not** in negatives – and that we *must* use the FULL FORMS **have** and **has** in questions.

> **THE PAST PARTICIPLE *NEVER* CHANGES IN ANY WAY**

Exercise 1

Rewrite these sentences in the present perfect – the first one has been done for you.

1 Leasa's washing the car. **Leasa's washed the car.**
2 Justine's painting the door. _____ .
3 Andy and Bob are closing the shop. _____ .
4 We're not playing football today. _____ .
5 We're organising a party for her. _____ .
6 Are you watching the film? _____ ?
7 Is Julie opening the window? _____ ?
8 Dave isn't waiting for us. _____ .

Exercise 2

Now rewrite these present perfect sentences in the present continuous.

1. They haven't ordered any food. — **They're not ordering any food.**
2. Simon's used the computer. — _____ .
3. Su and Kath have refused to come. — _____ .
4. Have you looked for the paper? — _____ ?
5. Has Rosemary left? — _____ ?
6. Have the children come in? — _____ ?
7. Has anyone used this cup? — _____ ?
8. I haven't bought any food. — _____ .
9. Ann's sold her house. — _____ .
10. Has Jenny phoned the office? — _____ ?

Dialogue 2

Later, Shamira and Liz are at the police station, talking to the desk officer.

SHAMIRA:	Good morning. I'd like to report a lost passport.
DESK OFFICER:	I see. Could I take your name first?
SHAMIRA:	Yes – Shamira Meghani.
DESK OFFICER:	Right. And when did you lose your passport?
SHAMIRA:	I think I lost it when I was in town this morning. I'm sure I had it with me when I left the house, but I didn't have it by the time we got to the supermarket checkout.
DESK OFFICER:	Was the passport in your pocket?
SHAMIRA:	No, it wasn't. It was in my bag.
DESK OFFICER:	And did you take it out of your bag while you were in town?
SHAMIRA:	I'm not sure if I did or not. Perhaps I did, or perhaps someone stole it from my bag.
DESK OFFICER:	Which shops did you visit on your trip to town?
SHAMIRA:	Well . . . let's see now: first I went to a café to meet my friend here and we had a coffee, then we went

	to the bank to get some money, and then we both went shopping in the supermarket.
DESK OFFICER:	And did you go anywhere else?
SHAMIRA:	No – after doing the shopping and noticing the passport was missing, we came straight here.

[*Liz suddenly remembers something*]

LIZ:	You *did* take all your stuff out of your bag when we were in the bank, Shamira.
SHAMIRA:	Oh yes – so I did!
LIZ:	Maybe the passport fell out then?
SHAMIRA:	Maybe it did. Perhaps I should phone the bank and see if they've found the passport.
DESK OFFICER:	Do feel free to use my phone.
SHAMIRA:	Thanks.

Dialogue 3 🎧

Shamira phones the bank to see if they've got her passport.

BANK: MegaBank Services. Good morning.
SHAMIRA: Ah, good morning. My name is Shamira Meghani. I was in your bank earlier this morning and I'm wondering if I dropped my passport while I was there. Has anybody found a passport, by any chance?
BANK: Hold on a moment – I'll check for you. [*There is a pause*] Hello?
SHAMIRA: Hello.
BANK: Yes, one of our customers has just handed a passport in.
SHAMIRA: Oh, thank goodness for that!
BANK: When exactly did you lose your passport?
SHAMIRA: Oh, I didn't notice until about half an hour ago, but I was in the bank at about 9.30 this morning.
BANK: Have you lost anything else?
SHAMIRA: Anything else? No ... I don't think I have.

[*The bank official prompts her a bit more*]

BANK: Something you used in the bank?

[*Shamira looks again in her bag*]

SHAMIRA: Oh my God! My chequebook's gone as well!
BANK: Yes. You left your chequebook on the counter, and the passport was inside.
SHAMIRA: I'll come and pick them up when I've taken the shopping home.
BANK: That'll be fine. Remember to bring some identification with you.
SHAMIRA: OK. See you in a bit. And thanks.
BANK: See you later.

Idioms

- We say **Thank goodness**, or **Thank God**, when we are *relieved* about something (when we are worried and then find out that everything's okay)
- **in a bit** means 'soon'

Language point 54 – past simple

In Dialogue 1 Shamira and Liz were using the PRESENT PERFECT because they we talking about things that *had just happened* a short time before. For example, Shamira said:

I've lost my passport

because she had just noticed this.
But in Dialogue 2 the policeman says:

When did you lose your passport?
not '~~When have you lost your passport?~~'

He uses the PAST SIMPLE, because he is talking about an event that *happened and finished* some time in the past.

We will look in more detail at the difference in *use* between the past simple and the present perfect in Language point 55. For now, let's look at how they differ in *form*:

- with a REGULAR verb:

	Present perfect	*Past simple*
+	**she's opened**	**she opened**
?	**has she opened?**	**did she open?**
–	**she hasn't opened**	**she didn't open**

- with the IRREGULAR verbs **buy** and **see**:

	Present perfect	*Past simple*
+	**she's bought**	**she bought**
?	**has she bought?**	**did she buy?**
–	**she hasn't bought**	**she didn't buy**
+	**she's seen**	**she saw**
?	**has she seen?**	**did she see?**
–	**she hasn't seen**	**she didn't see**

There are *three* main things to notice about the past simple:

1 We use the AUXILIARY **did** + BASE-FORM to make questions and negatives.

2   We *don't* use an auxiliary in statements.
3   The statement past simple form is the *same as the past participle* in REGULAR verbs (**-ed**), but with IRREGULAR verbs it is *sometimes* the same (**bought, bought**) and *sometimes* different (**seen, saw**). This means that for all irregular verbs (there aren't too many of them, but they *are* used very frequently), you have to *learn* the past simple form *and* the past participle. You'll find a list at the end of this book.

Did you notice a difference between the PRESENT SIMPLE and the PAST SIMPLE?

Present simple	*Past simple*	
I buy	**I bought**	
she buys	**she bought**	*not* 'she boughts'

We *don't* add **-s** for **he/she** in the past simple, *only* in the present simple!

Exercise 3

Complete these sentences by writing the verbs in the past simple – the first one has been done for you.

 1 Sandra **broke** her leg last week.   (break)
 2 James _____ off a ladder yesterday.   (fall)
 3 That man _____ my wallet!   (steal)
 4 I _____ yesterday but no one _____ .   (phone) (answer)
 5 Suzie _____ last night.   (call)
 6 I _____ my bag at the office.   (leave)
 7 She _____ to me at the end of the meeting.   (speak)
 8 Who _____ that ball?   (throw)
 9 We all _____ TV after dinner.   (watch)
10 My sister _____ to Italy last month.   (go)

Exercise 4

Change these past simple sentences into positive, question or negative as indicated. The first one has been done for you.

1 Candace travelled by bus.   [?]   **Did Candace travel by bus?**
2 Did they help him?   [–]   _____

3   Did she open the window?   [+]   _____
4   Terry didn't wash the car. [+]   _____
5   Henry walked to college
    today.   [?]   _____
6   Suzie cleaned her teeth.   [–]   _____
7   The others arrived late.   [?]   _____
8   Sandra played the piano.   [?]   _____

Language point 55 – more about the past simple

In Dialogue 3 both PAST SIMPLE and PRESENT PERFECT tenses are used – it's important in English to use them correctly and to understand the differences; they are *both* past tenses, but they are *not* interchangeable!
   The bank employee says:

  One of our customers <u>has</u> just <u>handed</u> a passport in

He uses the PRESENT PERFECT because it happened *a very short time ago* – a few minutes, perhaps. But then he asks:

  When exactly <u>did you lose</u> your passport?

He uses the PAST SIMPLE here because he's talking about an event that happened *further back in the past* – earlier that day.

Let's look at these two sentences using **go**:

a **Anne's gone to the bank**   (present perfect)
b **Anne went to the bank yesterday**   (past simple)

Sentence (a) means that Anne was here a short while ago, but she isn't here now. Sentence (b) simply states what happened yesterday.
   Another way of looking at this difference is to imagine that we are in a room where Anne works. If someone comes in and asks for Anne, then we can only say (a) if Anne isn't in the room (because she's gone); but we could say (b) *even if Anne is in the room with us*, because the past simple describes a *completed action in the past* with no reference to the present.

It is sometimes difficult for students of English to decide whether to use the present perfect or the past simple when talking about the past – but here are two helpful rules:

1. if something has happened a very short time ago: PRESENT PERFECT
2. if there is a word that indicates *when* something happened: PAST SIMPLE

So:

Is Kath here?

– She's gone out to get a coffee – she'll be back in a minute (1)
– She went out <u>half an hour ago</u> – I don't know where she is (2)

Back in Dialogue 2, Liz makes a statement and says:

You <u>did take</u> all your stuff out of your bag

She *could* have said:

You <u>took</u> all your stuff out of your bag

This would be the normal past simple statement – but here she uses the auxiliary **did** (which we usually find only in past simple questions and negatives) to *emphasise* the action. And then Shamira uses **did** as a tag response:

Oh yes – so I did!

Then she does the same thing again. Liz says:

Maybe the passport fell out then?

and Shamira replies:

Maybe it did

We also use **did** to make QUESTION TAGS in the past simple:

We went to Italy last year.	**– Did you?**
Stuart hurt his knee at football today.	**– Oh dear, did he?**

Look at the difference between past simple and present perfect tags:

Helen has gone.	**– Has she?**
Helen went yesterday.	**– Did she?**
You haven't seen Brenda, have you?	**– No, I haven't.**
You didn't see Brenda yesterday, did you?	**– No, I didn't.**
Candace hasn't come back yet, has she?	**– No, she hasn't.**
Candace didn't come back yesterday, did she?	**– No, she didn't.**

Finally, notice another use of **do** as an AUXILIARY – the policeman in Dialogue 2 says:

Do feel free to use my phone

He puts **Do** before the COMMAND FORM (which is the same as the BASE-FORM – Language point 17) to change it from a command to a friendly invitation. Here are some more examples:

Do sit down!
Do have a cup of tea!
Do remember to write!

Exercise 5

Decide whether to use the past simple or present perfect from the brackets.

1 Come and look, everyone – Henry (fell/'s fallen) in the water!
2 The manager (went/'s gone) out an hour ago.
3 (Did you see/Have you seen) that new film yet?
4 It's getting late – (did you finish/have you finished) your drink?
5 Dave (phoned/'s phoned) yesterday.
6 (Did you see/Have you seen) that French film on TV last week?
7 I (invited/'ve invited) Fiona round – she'll be here in a few minutes.
8 Where (did my passport go/'s my passport gone)? It was here just now!

9   It's very quiet next door – (did they turn/have they turned) the TV off at last?
10 (Have you spoken/Did you speak) French on your holiday to France?

Language point 56 – past simple: 'be' and 'have'

The verb **have** is easy in the past simple: **had** /hæd/; and questions and answers are done in the usual way:

+   **I had an apple**
?   **Did I have an apple?**
–   **I didn't have an apple**

But **be** is unusual – first of all, it has *two* past simple forms: **was** /wɔz/ and **were** /wɜːʳ/:

I was
you were
he/she was
we were
they were

But it's *also* unusual in how we form past simple questions and negatives:

+   **Leasa was in the shop**
?   **Was Leasa in the shop?**
    not '~~Did Leasa be in the shop?~~'
–   **Leasa wasn't in the shop**
    not '~~Leasa didn't be in the shop~~'

We *don't* use the auxiliary **did** with the past simple of **be**.

You will notice, as you get more familiar with colloquial English, that **be** and **have** are much more frequently used in the past simple than in the present perfect. The same is true for some other common verbs, for example **said** /sɛd/ (past simple of **say**) and **thought** /θɔːt/ (past simple of **think**).

Exercise 6

Turn these sentences into statement, question or negative as indicated.

1	Fred wasn't at home.	[?]	**Was Fred at home?**
2	I didn't have breakfast today.	[+]	_____
3	You were late for the meeting.	[?]	_____
4	Was James ready?	[–]	_____
5	Did they have any money?	[–]	_____
6	The children weren't happy.	[+]	_____
7	Was Fiona in town today?	[+]	_____
8	My brother had the money.	[–]	_____

Dialogue 4

Jenny has some news to tell Candace.

JENNY: Guess who I saw in town today!
CANDACE: Who?
JENNY: Johnny Depp!
CANDACE: You're joking!
JENNY: No, I really did see him. I was walking down the High Street and all of a sudden I saw Johnny!
CANDACE: What was he doing?
JENNY: He was sitting in a café reading a newspaper. I saw him through the window.
CANDACE: So what did you do?
JENNY: What do you think I did? I knew it was him, so I walked straight in and asked him for his autograph.
CANDACE: And did he give you it?
JENNY: Yes, and while he was signing my T-shirt I invited him round for coffee this afternoon.
CANDACE: What? Johnny Depp is coming round for coffee?
JENNY: Of course not, silly. He's far too busy filming.
CANDACE: What a relief – I don't have to tidy the house.
JENNY: Oh yes you do – Brad Pitt was with him in the café, and he's finished filming for the day.
CANDACE: What!!?
JENNY: Better get tidying, Candace. We're expecting him at eleven.

> **Idioms**
>
> - We use **guess** to ask the other person a question, especially when we think they'll be surprised at the answer:
>
>   **Guess who's coming to the party tonight**
>   **Guess what's in this bag**
>   **Guess why I've phoned you**
>
> - **All of a sudden** means 'suddenly'.
>
> - **Better get (tidying)** means 'It would be a good idea if you started tidying immediately'.

Language point 57 – past continuous

In Language point 21 we saw how the PRESENT CONTINUOUS is made by using the PRESENT of **be** with the ING-FORM of the verb:

He's sitting in the café

and that this tense is used to describe *continuing action in the present*, something happening now.

In Dialogue 4 Jenny says about Johnny Depp:

He was sitting in a café

She uses the PAST SIMPLE of **be** + ING-FORM of the verb to describe a *continuing action* in the *past*. Now look at these two sentences:

PAST CONTINUOUS	**Pete was writing a letter**
PAST SIMPLE	**Pete wrote a letter**

In the first of these, we focus on the *ongoing action* of Pete writing his letter; in the second we think about Pete *finishing* his letter – it is a *completed* action in the past.

PAST CONTINUOUS	ongoing or continuous action in the past
PAST SIMPLE	completed action in the past

So when Jenny says:

I <u>was walking</u> down the High Street and I <u>saw</u> Johnny

we can see the continuous action (**walking**) and the single event (**saw**).

> ⚠ **Be careful!** Do you remember that STATE VERBS *aren't* normally used in the present continuous?
>   **I know him**   *not* '~~I'm knowing him~~'
> (Look again at Language point 45 if you're not sure about this.)
>
> State verbs *don't* like being used with continuous tenses generally, so the same is true with the PAST continuous:
>   **I knew him**   *not* '~~I was knowing him~~'

Exercise 7

Rewrite these sentences using the past continuous tense. The first one has been done for you.

1. I watched a TV programme.
   I was watching a TV programme.
2. Did you work?
   _____ ?
3. We didn't watch the film.
   _____ .
4. Dave didn't answer his phone today.
   _____ .
5. Su looked after the children.
   _____ .
6. Did you speak to the teacher?
   _____ ?
7. The bus came round the corner.
   _____ .
8. Did you listen to your new CD?
   _____ ?

9 The kids played in the garden.
   _____ .

10 Henry didn't do his work.
   _____ .

Exercise 8

Write the verbs in these sentences in the correct tenses. Be careful – some verbs will need to go in the past simple, and some will need to go in the past continuous. The first one has been done for you.

1 I (walk) down the road when I (meet) Brenda.
   was walking   **met**
2 I (take) a photo when a bird (land) on me!
3 Stuart (break) his leg when he (play) football.
4 An apple (fall) on Nigel when he (stand) under a tree.
5 Justine (see) me as I (queue) for tickets.
6 Jenny (do) the washing-up when she (drop) a cup.
7 Sandra (cut) her finger when she (cut) the bread.
8 I (look) at the moon when I (see) a shooting star.

Dialogue 5

Kevin and Geoff are both changing addresses.

KEVIN: Have you moved house yet?
GEOFF: No, we haven't moved yet, but it won't be long. We've already signed all the documents, but we're still waiting for the bank to clear the money. Anyway, what about you? Are you still living in the flat over the curry house?
KEVIN: Yes, but not for much longer.
GEOFF: Really? How come?
KEVIN: I've just bought a house by the beach.
GEOFF: Why haven't you moved in yet, then?
KEVIN: It's not ready. I've started decorating it, but it still needs quite a bit of work before I can move in.
GEOFF: Have you ever decorated a house before?
KEVIN: Never. But I'm already getting the hang of it.
GEOFF: When you've finished, you can come and do ours!

Idiom

- **quite a bit of** means 'a lot of'
- **How come?** means 'Why?' or 'What's the reason for that?'
- **I'm getting the hang of it** means 'I'm slowly learning how to do it'

Language point 58 – time words

Some 'time words' are often found with particular tenses. For example, **while** (= 'during the time that . . .') is very common with the PAST CONTINUOUS:

While I was sitting in the café, a friend walked by

And we often use it with the PRESENT CONTINUOUS:

Why don't you have a cup of tea while you're waiting?

Still often appears with the PRESENT CONTINUOUS:

I'm still waiting for a letter from her

or with the PRESENT SIMPLE:

I still see Fiona every month at the judo club

Just, **yet**, **already** and **ever** are often used with the PRESENT PERFECT:

James has just sold his house
Have you phoned your brother yet?

I've already paid for the tickets
Have you ever visited the National Gallery in London?

The *position* of these words in relation to the verb is important – if you place them wrongly it sounds strange.

- **just**, **already** and **ever** come before the past participle
- **still** comes before the **ing**-form, or before the present simple
- **yet** usually comes at the end of the sentence
- **already** comes before the past participle or the **ing**-form.

Exercise 9

Pick the correct sentence from each pair.

1. a I'm still looking for a new job.
   b I still look for a new job.
2. a Did you already pay for the tickets?
   b Have you already paid for the tickets?
3. a We still wait for a bus.
   b We're still waiting for a bus.
4. a I sat on the bus when I was seeing Kath.
   b I was sitting on the bus when I saw Kath.
5. a Were they already ordering the food?
   b Have they already ordered the food?
6. a Has your brother phoned you back yet?
   b Did your brother phone you back yet?

Exercise 10

Put the time words in their correct place in the sentences.

1. We've seen Brenda in the coffee shop.   (just)
2. I'm working in the local supermarket.   (still)
3. Rosemary has worked in the supermarket.   (never)
4. Have you finished your homework?   (yet)
5. The students have passed their exams.   (already)
6. I want to visit the museum.   (still)
7. Do you go to the opera?   (ever)
8. Have you been to New Zealand?   (ever)
9. Is your sister back from university?   (yet)
10. I've explained that to you.   (already)

Exercise 11

Follow the instructions for this exercise on the audio.

Phrasal verbs

bring along – if you ask someone to bring something along, it means that you want them to bring it *with them*; it's a bit like **come along** (Unit 5).

drop by – 'visit at home'; if you want to invite someone to call on you at home next week, you can say **Why don't you drop by next week?**

hand in – if we find someone's wallet in the street and we take it to the police station, we call this **handing** something **in**.

invite round – 'invite to your home'.

pick up – 'collect'. We use this phrasal verb for both things and people – **We can pick up the food on the way back; Can you pick me up from the station?**

10 Which do you prefer?

> **In this unit you will learn how to:**
> - compare things
> - express preferences
> - compare and contrast what people do
> - use adverbs of degree

Dialogue 1

Rosemary and Stuart are discussing preferences.

STUART: Which do you prefer – Indian or Chinese food?
ROSEMARY: Well, I really like both.

[*thinks for a moment*]

I suppose I prefer Chinese when it's a takeaway, but I'd rather have Indian when I go out. What about you?
STUART: Indian is my favourite. And I don't like Italian food at all.
ROSEMARY: Neither do I.

Dialogue 2

Hannah and Natalie are trying on clothes in an expensive shop.

HANNAH: What do you think of this jumper?
NATALIE: You can't afford that – it's £60!

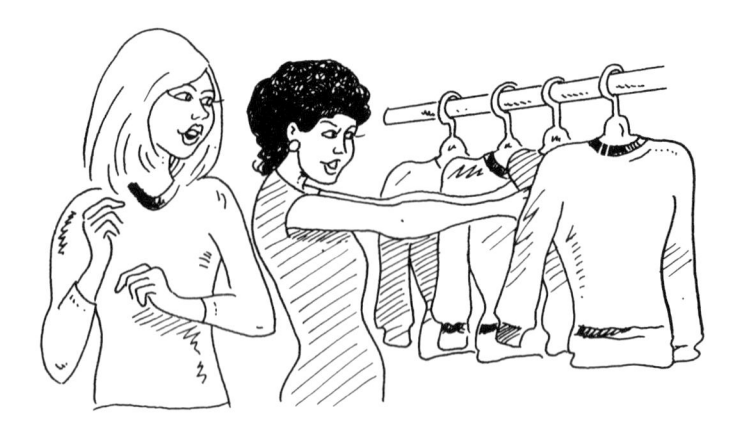

HANNAH: I know. But what do you think of it?
NATALIE: I prefer the red one.
HANNAH: You're just saying that because it's cheaper.
NATALIE: No I'm not! I really think it's better.
HANNAH: That's fine, then – you buy the cheap one, and I'll buy the nice one.

Idioms

- We use **I suppose** to show that we are not quite certain about the statement we're going to make. **I suppose I prefer Chinese food** means 'I *think* I prefer Chinese food, but I'm not quite sure'. See also Language point 89.

- **at all** after a NEGATIVE verb means 'completely' – **I don't like Italian food at all** means 'I *really dislike* Italian food'.

- **favourite** means '(the one) I like *best*' – you can use it as a NOUN:

    Curry is my favourite

    or as an ADJECTIVE:

    Curry is my favourite food

- **can't afford** means 'haven't got enough money for . . .'

Language point 59 – comparatives and superlatives

When we compare two things we can use the COMPARATIVE form of the ADJECTIVE. Here are some examples:

cheap	These shoes are <u>cheaper</u> than those
heavy	Steel is <u>heavier</u> than aluminium
comfortable	My new armchair is <u>more comfortable</u> than my old one
good	I think brown bread is <u>better</u> than white

There are *two* ways of forming comparatives of regular adjectives:

1. with *short* adjectives, we add **-er** (so **cheap** → **cheaper**)

Spelling rules

- When the adjective ends in **-e**, we add **-r**:

    fine → **fine<u>r</u>**
    blue → **blue<u>r</u>**

- When the adjective ends in a single vowel + single consonant, we *double* the consonant:

    big → **big<u>g</u>er**
    hot → **hot<u>t</u>er**

- When the adjective ends in CONSONANT + **y**, we *change* **-y** to **-ier**:

    happy → **happ<u>ier</u>**
    heavy → **heav<u>ier</u>**

2 with *longer* adjectives (more than two syllables) we simply put **more** *before* the adjective:

| **comfortable** | → | **more comfortable** |
| **expensive** | → | **more expensive** |

Notice that you *can't* use **-er** with longer words, and you *can't* use **more** with short words:

| **comfortable** | → | **more comfortable** | *not* 'comfortabler' |
| **cheap** | → | **cheaper** | *not* 'more cheap' |

There are also some IRREGULAR comparatives that you simply have to learn:

| **good** | → | **better** |
| **bad** | → | **worse** /wɜːs/ |

We use **than** /ðæn/, WEAK FORM /ðən/, between the comparative and the second thing compared:

London is bigger than Paris
James is taller than Ben

And when we compare *three or more* things or people, we use the SUPERLATIVE – you can form it directly from the COMPARATIVE that we've just seen:

- change **-er** to **-est**: **cheaper → cheapest**
  hotter → hottest
  heavier → heaviest

- change **more** to **most**: **more comfortable → most comfortable**
  more expensive → most expensive

- irregular: **better → best**
  worse → worst /wɜːst/

Unlike the comparative, the superlative is *always* used with **the**:

The blue shirt is cheaper than the red one
The white shirt is the cheapest (of them all)

Exercise 1

Complete these sentences using the correct adjective from the box. Remember to use the correct comparative form.

1. Leasa's _____ than Justine.
2. A sofa's _____ than a wooden chair.
3. Gold is _____ than silver.
4. This suitcase feels _____ than that one.
5. My car's _____ than yours.
6. This film's much _____ than the one last night.
7. Australia's _____ than New Zealand.
8. A trip from the UK to New Zealand's _____ than one to France.
9. Wolves are _____ than hamsters.
10. Swords are _____ than hammers.

> interesting   intelligent   tall   expensive   fast
> sharp   heavy   valuable   comfortable   big

Exercise 2

Complete the sentences using the correct comparative form. Use a dictionary if you need to. The first one is done for you.

1. This bag is too heavy. Can I have a **lighter** one?
2. These toys are expensive now, but they'll be _____ after Christmas.
3. The exam was very easy. I was expecting it to be _____ .
4. Could you put some more sugar in this? I prefer _____ tea.
5. What a boring programme. I though it was going to be _____ .
6. We arrived late. We should have taken an _____ train.
7. This coat is too big for me – have you got a _____ one?
8. This CD's far too noisy – put on a _____ one, will you?
9. Henry's room is a real mess, but Tom's is much _____ .
10. This road's very narrow – I though it was _____ , didn't you?

Language point 60 – 'which'

We use **which** /wɪtʃ/ to ask about a *choice* of options or possibilities – it can be a PRONOUN:

Which do you prefer?   (= 'Which one . . .?')

or an ADJECTIVE with a noun:

Which shirt do you prefer?

It's often used with verbs of *liking*, *wanting*, etc. Here are some examples. Notice that we can use **one**, **ones** with **which** if we want to:

Which one do you want?   **Which would you like?**
Which would you prefer?   **Which ones do you like best?**

And sometimes we use **which** with a following to-form of a verb:

I don't know which one to choose

I'm not sure which to have

We need to decide which CD to buy for Stuart

Dialogue 3

Su's brought Jenny along to the phone shop to help her choose a new mobile.

SU: I can't decide which of these two mobiles to have.
JENNY: Well, you could have either. Which one do you like more?
SU: Hmmm . . . well, this blue one is nicer, but it's more expensive.
JENNY: And what about the black one?
SU: The black one's cheaper, but it's more basic.

[Jenny picks both mobiles up]

JENNY: And heavier.
SU: Yes. And it's less elegant as well, don't you think?
JENNY: Looks like you *have* decided after all!
SU: Yes – I think I'll be a lot happier with the blue one. Actually, I don't really like the black one.
JENNY: I don't either.

Language point 61 – 'either'

When Su is trying to decide between two mobile phones, and Jenny says:

You could have either

she means that it doesn't matter which one Su has – she could have the blue one *or* the black one.

Either /ˈaɪðəʳ/ or /ˈiːðəʳ/ is rather like a statement equivalent of the question word **which**:

Which would you like? – **I'll have either**

> ⚠ **Be careful!** We can only use **either** when we are talking about *two* things. Compare these two sentences:
>
> There are two mobile phones here – you can have **either.**
>
> There are three mobile phones here – you can have **any** (one) of them.

We also use **either** in a completely different way at the *end of a negative sentence*. Su says:

I don't really like the black one

and Jenny replies:

I don't either

She means: 'Su doesn't like it, and <u>she</u> <u>also</u> doesn't like it'.

Here are some more examples:

Fred doesn't speak Russian, and Charlie doesn't either
We don't buy a Sunday paper, and our neighbours don't either

I'm not working tomorrow, and my wife isn't either
Candace isn't coming to the meeting. – No, and I'm not either!

In this meaning **either** in negative sentences corresponds to **as well** or **so** in statements:

+ Diane reads Latin poetry, and Gary does <u>as well</u>
+ Diane reads Latin poetry, and <u>so</u> does Gary
− Diane doesn't read junk mail, and Gary doesn't <u>either</u>.

Exercise 3

Look at the information in the box about what languages Jack speaks, and what languages Jill speaks. Then say who speaks what, using **(not) either**, **and**, **but**, **so** and **as well** – the first two have been done for you.

1 Jack **doesn't speak** Italian, **and** Jill **doesn't either**.
2 Jack **doesn't speak** Chinese **but** Jill **does**.
3 Jack _____ Swedish ___ Jill _____ .
4 Jack _____ German ___ Jill _____ .
5 Jack _____ Arabic ___ Jill _____ .
6 Jack _____ Welsh ___ Jill _____ .
7 Jack _____ Klingon ___ Jill _____ .
8 Jack _____ French ___ Jill _____ .
9 Jack _____ Hindi ___ Jill _____ .
10 Jack _____ Spanish ___ Jill _____ .

Language	*Jack*	*Jill*
French	yes	yes
German	no	yes
Spanish	yes	no
~~Italian~~	~~no~~	~~no~~
Swedish	yes	yes
~~Chinese~~	~~no~~	~~yes~~
Arabic	no	no
Hindi	no	yes
Welsh	yes	yes
Klingon	no	no

Dialogue 4

Helen takes an item of clothing back to the shop where she bought it.

HELEN:	Can I change this top? It was too small for me. Here's the receipt.
ASSISTANT:	Unfortunately the next size up is sold out. Would you like your money back or would you prefer to choose something else?
HELEN:	Have you got any other tops in a bigger size?
ASSISTANT:	Certainly. Try some of these.

[*Helen holds them up against herself*]

HELEN:	These are all quite nice. Which one do you think looks best?
ASSISTANT:	That green one really suits you.
HELEN:	Better than the blue one?
ASSISTANT:	Oh yes, very nice – green is definitely your colour!
HELEN:	Are you quite sure?
ASSISTANT:	Of course I am! Look in the mirror!
HELEN:	OK – I'll take the green one. How much is it?
ASSISTANT:	It's the same as the one you brought back.
HELEN:	Perfect!

Language point 62 – 'quite', 'very' and 'too'

When we use adjectives to describe things, there are special words we can put *before* the adjective to show different degrees of the quality described:

	too	**hot**	highest degree
	very	**hot**	
This tea is		**hot**	
	quite	**hot**	
	not very	**hot**	
	not	**hot**	lowest degree

> **⚠ Be careful!** We *can* use **a** and **the** before **very**, but *not* before **quite** and **too**:
>
> | | |
> |---|---|
> | **This shirt is small** | – it's <u>a small</u> shirt |
> | **This shirt is very small** | – it's <u>a very</u> small shirt |
> | **This shirt is quite small** | – 'it's a quite small shirt' |
>
> (but we *can* say – **it's <u>quite a</u> small shirt**)
>
> **This shirt is too small** – 'it's a too small shirt'

Quite has two *different* meanings. When Helen says:

These are all quite nice

she means that they are 'medium-nice' – not *very* nice, but nice enough. But when she then asks the shop assistant:

Are you quite sure?

she means 'Are you <u>completely</u> sure?'.

quite	=	[medium degree]
quite	=	completely

But **not quite** *always* means 'not completely':

I'm <u>not quite</u> sure where to go
The food <u>isn't quite</u> ready
I'm <u>not quite</u> convinced that this is the right thing to do

You will come across other DEGREE WORDS in colloquial English. Here they are in approximate order:

High degree:	**completely**	**quite** (= **completely**)	**absolutely**
	extremely		
	really	**awfully**	**terribly**
	very		
Medium degree:	**pretty**		
	quite	**fairly**	

Medium to low degree:	**rather** (usually with bad or negative meanings)
Low degree:	**not very** **a bit** **slightly**

Here are some examples of these:

This book is really boring
John's absolutely certain he left his wallet on the table

I'm fairly sure that's our bus
This film is pretty good, isn't it?   – Yes, it's quite entertaining

This house is rather ugly
This food's not very nice, is it?

My watch is slightly slow
I felt a bit sick on the way home after the party

Exercise 4

In Jim & Kate's Coffee Shop they only sell one type of coffee, but at different temperatures. Can you put them in order, starting with the *coldest* and finishing with the *hottest*? Here's the menu.

Froth Fantasy	quite hot
Coffee Crikey	very hot
BEAN BONANZA	not very hot
Radical Roast	extremely hot
Gorgeous Grind	not hot at all
PERCOLATOR II	too hot
Cafetiere Combo	rather hot
Steam Surprise	terribly hot

Language point 63 – 'some' and 'one'

Some (and **any**) can be used with both UNCOUNTABLE nouns and PLURAL COUNTABLE nouns – review Language point 23 in Unit 4 if you need to remind yourself of these.

UNCOUNTABLE	Have you got <u>any</u> money? – Yes, I think I've got <u>some</u> in my pocket
PLURAL COUNTABLE	Have you got <u>any</u> pens? – Yes, I think I've got <u>some</u> in my desk

You can see from these examples that we can use them to avoid repeating a noun that has already been mentioned. More examples:

UNCOUNTABLE	We've run out of milk! – It's OK, I'll get <u>some</u> when I'm out
PLURAL COUNTABLE	Will we need sandwiches? – Yes, I'll bring <u>some</u> tomorrow
UNCOUNTABLE	Do you like Christmas pudding? – I don't know. I'd better try <u>some</u>
PLURAL COUNTABLE	I can't find <u>any</u> biscuits – I think there are <u>some</u> in the cupboard

With SINGULAR COUNTABLE nouns we use **one**, not **some**:

I want a biscuit!	– I think there's <u>one</u> in the cupboard
Would you like a sandwich?	– Yes, have you got <u>one</u>?

And we also use **one** with ADJECTIVES to take the place of a noun. Helen and the shop assistant are talking about tops; the assistant says:

That green <u>one</u> really suits you

and Helen asks:

Better than the blue <u>one</u>?

When we use **a**, **the**, **this**, **that**, **these** or **those** + ADJECTIVE but *without* the noun, we have to use **one** (singular) or **ones** (plural) instead:

this blue shirt	**this blue one**
	not 'this blue'
a green shirt	**a green one**
	not 'a green'
blue shirts	**blue ones**
	not 'blue', *not* 'blues'
these red shirts	**these red ones**
	not 'these red', *not* 'these reds'

> ⚠ **Be careful!** We use **ones**, *not* **some**, *after* adjectives:
>
> **those red ones**   *not* 'those red some'
>
> But we *can* use **some** *before* adjectives:
>
> **some red ones**   *not* 'some red some'

Exercise 5

Answer these questions using the adjectives given. You'll have to decide whether to use **one** or **ones**. You may also need to add **the**.

1   Do you want the red tie or the blue tie?
    I want the blue one.   (blue)

2   Which knife shall we use for this?
    Let's _____ .   (long)

3   Which bananas would you like?
    _____ .   (ripe)

4   Which car is yours?
    _____ .   (big red)

5   Shall I wear the brown shoes or the black shoes?
    Why don't you_____ ?   (black)

6   What size drink would you like with your meal?
    _____ .   (large)

7   What kind of lenses have you got?
    _____ .   (plastic)

8   Do you want a hot drink or a cold drink?
    _____ .   (hot)

Exercise 6

Complete this conversation between Keith and Carl with **one** or **ones**.

CARL: Hello, Keith. I like your motorbike. I'd like to get (1) _____ like that myself.
KEITH: That's not all – I've got another (2) _____ in the garage. Do you like my boots?
CARL: Well, I think leather (3) _____ suit you better, like the (4) _____ I'm wearing.
KEITH: Where did you buy them?
CARL: In a shop on the High Street – the (5) _____ next to the music shop.
KEITH: Oh, I know. It's called 'Boots & Suits'.
CARL: No, that's the wrong (6) _____ . That (7) _____ is further down the road. The (8) _____ I mean is called 'Neat Feet'.

Dialogue 5

Vicki and Leasa have been clubbing.

VICKI: Come one, Leasa – we can get a bus at the end of the road.
LEASA: A bus? Look at the time, Vicki!!
VICKI: [*looks with difficulty at her watch*]

Midnight – what's the big deal?
LEASA: We'll never get a bus at this time of night. We'd be better off phoning for a taxi.
VICKI: A taxi? That'll cost a small fortune – don't you remember where we live?
LEASA: Listen Vicki, we can split the fare and at least we'll get home in one piece. Now phone, will you?
VICKI: All right, all right . . .

[*phones on her mobile*]

. . . I didn't feel like waiting for a bus anyway.

Idiom

- **What's the big deal?** means 'Don't get so worried about something that isn't important'
- **cost a small fortune** means 'cost a lot of money'
- **split** means 'share the cost of . . .'
- **in one piece** means 'safe' or 'unharmed'

Language point 64 – more phrases with '-ing'

In Dialogue 5 Leasa says:

We'd be better off phoning for a taxi

| I you he/she we they | 'd be better off | + | -ing |

This is a common way in colloquial English of saying

| It's better for | me you him/her us them | to | (do something) |

More examples:

Julie'd be better off staying with us tonight
I'd be better off paying for this by credit card
**You'd be better off going to Brighton by train today –
the roads will be bad**

And Vicki uses another **-ing** phrase when she says:

I didn't feel like waiting for a bus

> doesn't/don't   feel like   +   -ing
> didn't

is a colloquial way of saying that someone doesn't *want* to do something. More examples:

I don't feel like watching TV tonight – there's nothing good on
Henry doesn't feel like coming out with us this evening
Gerry didn't feel like cleaning the car this weekend

And you can use the question form:

> **Do you feel like**   +   **-ing?**

to ask someone if they *would like to* do something:

Do you feel like going to the cinema this evening?
= **Would you like to go to the cinema this evening?**

Exercise 7

Answer the questions using **better off**. The first one has been done for you.

1 Will James go by train?
   He'd be better off going by car.   (car)

2 Will Anna come today?
   _____.   (tomorrow)

3 Will Fiona do the work one her own?
   _____.   (with Suzie)

4 Are Andy and Bob drinking whisky again?
   _____.   (mineral water)

5 Shall we phone them?
   _____.   (write a letter)

6   Will your sister sit next to Henry?
    _____.   (Gerry)
7   Will Jenny do the cooking tonight?
    _____.   (eat out)
8   Shall we go to the cinema tonight?
    _____.   (watch TV)
9   Shall I shut the door?
    _____.   (window)
10 Shall we visit Dave and Rhoda today?
    _____.   (tomorrow)

Exercise 8

Rewrite the sentences using **feel like** – the first one has been done for you.

1   Would you like to come out with us tonight?
    Do you feel like coming out with us tonight?
2   Would you like to see a film in town?
    _____?
3   Would you like to fly to the South of France for the weekend?
    _____?
4   Would you like to invite some friends round?
    _____?
5   Would you like to run in the London Marathon this year?
    _____?
6   Would you like to lend me ten pounds?
    _____?
7   Would you like to order us a pizza?
    _____?
8   Would you like to hire a rowing boat for the afternoon?
    _____?

Exercise 9

Follow the instructions on the audio to do this exercise.

Dialogue 6

Justine arrives late at Helen's house.

HELEN: You look cold!
JUSTINE: I'm freezing!
HELEN: Haven't you got a coat?
JUSTINE: No, I didn't plan on needing one. I came in the car, but it broke down halfway here. And it's colder than I expected.
HELEN: [*hands Justine a jumper*] Here – put this jumper on. And you'd better sit down in front of the fire and warm up.
JUSTINE: Thanks, Helen.
HELEN: Can I get you anything else?
JUSTINE: I could do with a hot drink.
HELEN: Coming right up!

Idioms

- **I could do with** means 'I need'
- **Coming right up!** means 'I'll bring it straight away'

Phrasal verbs

break down – 'stop working' (machines). We use this phrasal verb when things stop working unexpectedly for some reason.

pick up – 'lift with your hand or hands'; when we use our hands to lift something from the floor or the table, we say that we're **picking** it **up**.

put on – we use this when talking about clothes; if you want to wear something, you first have to put it on. When you want to *stop* wearing something, you **take** it **off**.

sit down – 'move from a standing position to a sitting position'. The opposite is **stand up**.

warm up – when we say that we want to warm up, we mean that we want to get warmer.

Life and living – television

In this unit we've been talking about preferences and choices, and you'll certainly have plenty of choices to make if you turn the TV on in the UK. To begin with, there are five main **terrestrial** channels: BBC1, BBC2, ITV, Channel 4 and Channel 5. The BBC (British Broadcasting Corporation) is a government-**funded** broadcasting **agency**, paid for through **taxes** – every **household** that uses a television (even if they never watch the BBC!) has to pay for a TV **licence** every year (it costs about £120). Because they're funded in this way, the BBC channels don't need to carry **adverts** (or **commercials**) during and between programmes (though they *do* advertise their own programmes, so you still get **commercial breaks** between programmes – but they're all for the same company!). ITV and Channel 4 *aren't* publicly funded, and **finance** themselves primarily by carrying advertising. In the past, the five terrestrial channels were very **distinct**, but many **viewers** now see them all as quite **similar**, particularly BBC1 and ITV, which are **increasingly in competition with** each other.

These days there are also many **additional** channels available **via satellite** and **cable** – you can **subscribe** to a service, and for a monthly **fee** you can have a **dish** fitted to your house so that you can **pick up** a wide **range** of channels, not only in English but in many other languages as well.

You can buy TV guides every week, which list all the programmes on all terrestrial and main satellite channels. The weekend newspapers also publish their own guides for the week. But if you want to *ask* someone what programmes are **scheduled**, you can simply say 'What's on tonight?'. And if you don't like what you're watching, you can use the **remote** to 'turn over' (phrasal verb = 'change channels') or even 'turn off' (*another* phrasal verb! = 'switch off') and do something else instead – there's always the radio (five main BBC **stations** and lots of independent and local stations, including new digital radio channels). Or you could get out of the house for a bit and get some **exercise**!

Glossary

terrestrial – transmitted by television masts rather than satellite
fund (something) – provide the money to pay (for something)
agency – organisation

taxes – money we pay to the state for the government to use
household – group of people sharing a home
licence – a piece of paper you have to buy from the government to be allowed to do something
adverts – short films designed to encourage you to buy things
commercial breaks – interruptions during and between programmes to show adverts
finance – fund
distinct – visibly or noticeably different from each other
viewers – people who watch television
similar – looking almost the same as each other, having almost the same appearance
increasingly – more and more
in competition with – trying to be or do better than
additional – extra, more
via – through
satellite – machine that orbits the earth and relays TV and radio signals
cable – an underground electronic bundle of wires that feeds television signals into homes
subscribe – pay a regular amount of money to have a continual service
fee – the payment you make to subscribe to a service
dish – piece of equipment to receive satellite signals
pick up – receive (television and radio signals)
range – selection, choice
scheduled – planned to be shown, set down in the TV guide
remote – device for controlling your television at a distance, so you don't have to get out of your chair to change channels
station – channel (but we say **channel** for TV and **station** for radio)
exercise – physical activity to keep yourself fit

11 I'll see you at half past five!

> **In this unit you will learn how to:**
> - make arrangements with people
> - tell the time
> - use other time expressions
> - buy tickets for public transport
> - use prepositions in wh-questions

Dialogue 1

Adrian's buying a train ticket over the phone.

ADRIAN: Could I have a return ticket to Glasgow for tomorrow?
CLERK: Certainly. Where are you travelling from?
ADRIAN: From Brighton.
CLERK: And when do you want to arrive?
ADRIAN: I've got a meeting at twelve. Will the seven o'clock train get me there in time?
CLERK: Yes, but unfortunately you've left it too late – there are no seats left on that train. I can book you onto the nine-thirty, but you'll be late for your meeting.
ADRIAN: I can't miss the meeting. What about the sleeper train tonight?
CLERK: Hold on – I'll check to see if there are any seats left.

[*checks on her computer*]

Yes, you're in luck. There are a few left. Shall I make the reservation?

ADRIAN: Yes please. What time does it leave this evening?
CLERK: Eight o'clock. And you'll be in Glasgow by seven o'clock tomorrow morning.
ADRIAN: That'll give me bags of time to get to the meeting, won't it? It *will* arrive on time, won't it?
CLERK: Yes – and make sure you get here by eight evening ... all our trains *leave* on time as well!

Idioms

- **in time** means 'before the latest time possible'
- **on time** means 'at the scheduled time' or 'punctually'
- **bags of time** means 'a lot of time' or 'plenty of time'

Language point 65 – telling the time

Telling the time is easy in English. We've seen the numbers in Unit 4 – here are the other words you will need:

o'clock	/əˈklɔk/	it's
past		just coming up to
to		just gone
half	/hɑːf /	exactly
a quarter	/əˈkwɔːtə/	
at		
at about		
by		

To tell someone what the time is, we use **it's ...**:

What time is it? – **It's ten o'clock**

To say *when* something happens, we use **at**:

I'll meet you both at ten o'clock

To give the *latest* time when something should happen, we use **by**:

I'll be back home by ten o'clock   (perhaps earlier)

When we are not sure of the *exact* time, we use **about**:

It's <u>about</u> ten o'clock

Now let's have a look at the clock:

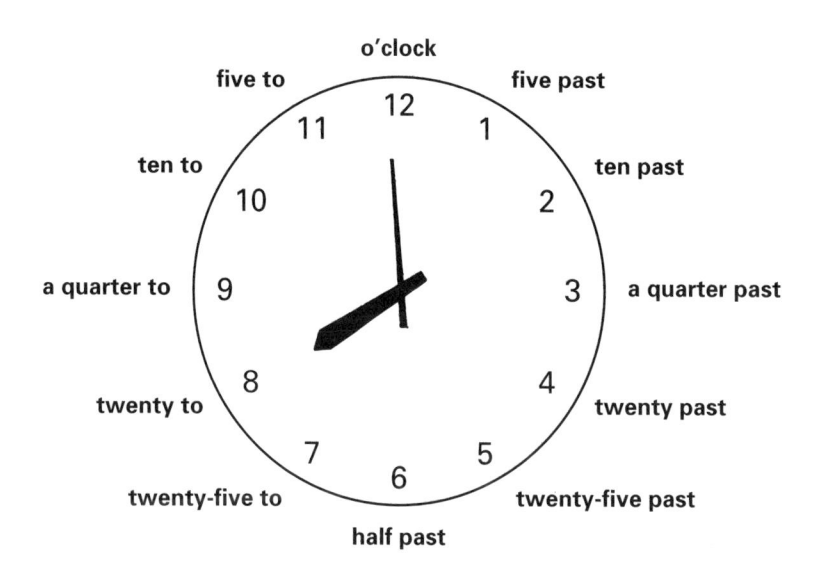

```
                    o'clock
          five to           five past
                  12
             11        1
      ten to                    ten past
           10          2
a quarter to  9            3   a quarter past
            8          4
      twenty to                 twenty past
              7   6   5
   twenty-five to             twenty-five past
                  half past
```

Notice that:

- we say <u>**a** quarter</u>, but **half** (*not* '~~a half~~')
- we usually say **ten past** (etc.), *not* '~~ten minutes past~~' which sounds rather formal
- we *always* say **half past**, *never* '~~half to~~'
- in colloquial English we often say just **ten** instead of **ten o'clock**:

    I'll meet you at ten

- in colloquial English we often say **half ten** instead of **half past ten**

    I'll meet you at half ten

    half ten and **half past ten** *both* mean 10.30!

- we have special words for 12.00 at night (**midnight**) and 12.00 in the day (**midday** or **noon**).

We use **just gone** and **just coming up to** to deal with times *between* the five-minute intervals on the clock face:

just gone = a short time after
just coming up to = a short time before

So:

10.16 **it's just gone a quarter past ten**
10.19 **it's just coming up to twenty past ten**

For very precise times, such as railway timetables and schedules, we use the 24-hour clock, giving two numbers:

10.56 **ten fifty-six**
13.12 **thirteen twelve**

Notice:

12.00 **twelve hundred**
12.07 **twelve oh seven**

> ⚠ **Be careful!** The 24-hour clock is common in official uses of English where precise times are important, but it is *not* used in ordinary situations in colloquial English:
>
> I'll see you at a quarter past five
> *not* 'I'll see you at seventeen fifteen'

Exercise 1

Give the 12-hour clock equivalents for these 24-hour clock times – the first one has been done for you.

1 1316 **It's just gone a quarter past one.**
2 1544
3 0940
4 2359
5 0710
6 1754
7 1602
8 1435
9 2226
10 0330

Exercise 2

Write the times shown on the clock faces in the normal 12-hour system.

1 It's _____
2 It's _____
3 It's _____
4 It's _____
5 It's _____
6 It's _____

Dialogue 2

Candace and Jenny are about to go into the art gallery, but Jenny stops at the door.

CANDACE: What are you looking for, Jenny?
JENNY: My money, of course. Oh God, I can't find it!
CANDACE: What are you worrying about? We don't need to pay for tickets here – it's free!

[*Candace points at a sign over the door saying ADMISSION FREE*]

JENNY: So it is! Great – we can look at loads of wonderful paintings for nothing!

> **Idioms**
>
> - When something is **free** you *don't* have to pay any money for it.
> - **Great!** means 'Wonderful!' or 'That's good!'.
> - **loads of** means 'a lot of' (COUNTABLE nouns); for UNCOUNTABLE nouns we use **a load of**.

Language point 66 – 'where . . . from?', 'where . . . to?'

In Dialogue 1 the assistant asks Adrian:

Where are you travelling **from**?

And in Dialogue 2 Candace asks Jenny:

What are you looking **for**?

and

What are you worrying **about**?

These are sentences that contain a PREPOSITION used with a WH-WORD. In colloquial English we do *not* usually put any word *before* the wh-word (although formal English does). If there is a wh-word, we prefer it to be the *first word* in the sentence. So we *don't* say:

'From where are you travelling?'
'For what are you looking?'
'About what are you worrying?'

We move the preposition to the *end* of the sentence, leaving the wh-word to *start* the sentence. Here are some more examples:

      Who were you talking to?
not 'To who were you talking?'

      What shall I pay for this with?
not 'With what shall I pay for this?'

      What is she looking at?
not 'At what is she looking?'

When shall I get these to you by?
not 'By when shall I get these to you?'

> ⚠ **Be careful!** You may see prepositions in front of wh-words at the start of sentences in formal written English, but you *won't* usually hear this in normal conversations and speech.
>
> Remember that it is CORRECT to *end* a sentence with a PREPOSITION in English!

Exercise 3

Aunt Aggie is rather deaf – every time you tell her something, she misses part of the information and asks a question. Write out her questions – the first one has been done for you.

1. YOU: Gerry's looking for a new house.
   AUNT AGGIE: **What is Gerry looking for?**

2. YOU: I'm writing a letter to Liz.
   AUNT AGGIE: Wh_____?

3. YOU: The cat's looking at some birds in the garden.
   AUNT AGGIE: Wh_____?

4. YOU: Suzie's worried about her exams.
   AUNT AGGIE: Wh_____?

5. YOU: I'm going to the party with Hannah.
   AUNT AGGIE: Wh_____?

6. YOU: Stuart plays football for England.
   AUNT AGGIE: Wh_____?

7. YOU: Miranda works for a film company.
   AUNT AGGIE: Wh_____?

8. YOU: Otto comes from Austria.
   AUNT AGGIE: Wh_____?

9. YOU: Terry and June live next door to the Simpsons.
   AUNT AGGIE: Wh_____?

10. YOU: I've got to be home by ten.
    AUNT AGGIE: Wh_____?

Dialogue 3

Gerry spots Sophie sitting on her own in the coffee shop, looking at her watch.

GERRY: Hello Sophie – who are you waiting for?
SOPHIE: Leasa. We were meant to meet up here at one, but I got here late. I've been waiting for about half an hour, but I'm wondering if I've missed her, or if she just didn't show up. You haven't seen her, have you?
GERRY: Not since yesterday, no.

[*Suddenly Leasa arrives*]

LEASA: Hi, you two! Sorry I'm so late, Sophie. I've been stuck in a traffic jam since a quarter to one. Have you been sitting here for ages?
SOPHIE: No, it's all right – I haven't been here long. I got here late myself, so I've only been here about twenty minutes. And I had Gerry here to talk to.
LEASA: Let me buy us all coffee and some cakes!

Idioms

- **on her own** means 'alone' – we change the middle word according to the person: **on my own**, **on his own**, etc.
- **we were meant** /mɛnt/ **to** means 'we had arranged to' or 'we had expected to'
- **stuck** means 'unable to move' or 'unable to get out/away'

Language point 67 – 'for' and 'since'

When we talk about the *length of time* that we have been doing something, we use **since** or **for** – they mean different things:

- **since** is used with a *point* in time (or a *block* of time) in the past
- **for** is used with a *period* of time *from past to present*

Compare what Sophie and Leasa say in Dialogue 3:

SOPHIE: I've been waiting <u>for</u> about half an hour
LEASA: I've been stuck in a traffic jam <u>since</u> a quarter to one

Half an hour is a *period* of time; **a quarter to one** is a *point* in time.

Here are examples of words and phrases used with **for**:

an hour	three minutes
a week	**ages** (= 'a very long time')
a month	a long time
six years	a short while

And here are the types of words and phrases we find with **since**:

1953	half past three
last Tuesday	the end of the war
February 14th	Christmas
yesterday	the summer holidays

Since and **for** are used with the PRESENT PERFECT (Language point 53):

John and Fiona <u>have lived</u> here <u>since</u> June 2001
John and Fiona <u>have lived</u> here <u>for</u> three years

or with the PRESENT PERFECT CONTINUOUS – this is formed as follows:

have/has been	+	-ing

I've been waiting here for an hour
I've been waiting here since ten o'clock

Suzie's been working in the garden for three hours
Suzie's been working in the garden since early this morning

Notice that we *don't* say:

~~'I am waiting here since ten o'clock'~~
~~'Suzie works in the garden since early this morning'~~

- We always use the PRESENT PERFECT or the PRESENT PERFECT CONTINUOUS with **since**, *not* the present or present continuous.
- With **for** we use the PRESENT PERFECT or PRESENT PERFECT CONTINUOUS, *or* the PAST SIMPLE – but there is a difference in meaning:

    (a) **Dave's lived in Brighton for three years**
    (and he still lives there now)

    (b) **Dave lived in Brighton for three years**
    (some time in the past – he doesn't live there now)

Sentence (a) uses the present perfect, because it describes a period of time that started in the past but has continued to the present and has *not finished*. Sentence (b) uses the past simple, because it describes a period of time that started *and finished* in the past.

Exercise 4

Complete these sentences using **for** or **since**.

1 Dave's lived in Heathfield ____ last July.
2 We haven't see Gerry ____ at least two years.
3 Justine's been at the dentist's ____ ages.
4 My car's been in the garage ____ a week.
5 These people have been waiting ____ four o'clock
6 This parcel's been here ____ last week.
7 We've been coming here every year ____ 1997.
8 I've waited here ____ an hour, and now I'm leaving!
9 This place has changed a lot ____ we were here last.
10 I've been learning English ____ a long time.

Exercise 5

Choose the correct verb from the brackets for each sentence – the first one has been done for you.

1 We (live/'ve lived) here since December 1999.
2 I (lived/'ve lived) in Italy for three months in 1988.
3 Suzie ('s been learning/'s learnt) French since last year.

4 How long (have you been working/have you worked) in the garden today?
5 We (haven't seen/didn't see) Fiona since yesterday.
6 (Have you been/Are you) waiting here long?
7 I (learn/'ve been learning) English for five years.
8 The kids (are/have been) playing football since ten o'clock.

Dialogue 4

Niels, Dave and Julie are talking about the last time Niels came over from Denmark to visit.

NIELS: Do you remember when I came over to visit last year?
DAVE: Of course I do! You arrived in the evening after coming over on the ferry and driving straight here. When exactly was it?
NIELS: I think it was in April, wasn't it? It was definitely some time in spring.
JULIE: Yes, you're right. It was Eli's birthday while you were here, and that's on the 9th of April, so it was in the Easter holiday.
NIELS: And then I went upstairs and slept for a bit to recover from the journey ...
DAVE: ... and while you were asleep Julie phoned up Ronnie and Fifi and invited them round ...
JULIE: ... and then an hour later when Ronnie and Fifi turned up I woke you up, and we stayed up with them till the early hours drinking wine.
DAVE: And we ended up singing rude songs.
NIELS: *You* all did – I was asleep again by the time you all started singing.
JULIE: Just as well you were – they were *very* rude songs.
DAVE: I know – why don't I ask Ronnie and Fifi round again tonight?
NIELS: Why not? And this time I'll try and stay awake!

> **Idioms**
>
> - **for a bit** means 'for a short period of time'
> - **till the early hours** means 'until early in the morning, but while it is still dark'
> - **just as well** means 'it was a good thing' or 'it was lucky'

Language point 68 – more time expressions

We met a lot of time expressions in Language point 39, using general words such as **day**, **night** and **year**. We also use months, seasons and festivals to talk about when things happen. Be careful with the different PREPOSITIONS:

<u>in</u>	**April**
	winter
	the Christmas holidays
	the evening
<u>at</u>	**Christmas**
	the end of April
	the weekend
	the beginning of (the) winter
(no preposition)	**next Christmas**
	last April
	an hour later
	this summer

We will look at months, seasons and festivals at the end of this unit.

Exercise 6

Fill in the blanks in Henry's account of past and future holidays, using the words from the box. You can only use each word once.

_____ April we went _____ holiday to the Caribbean. We often go _____ the end _____ the spring because the

weather's just right over there _____ that time of the year.
We arrived _____ the airport and _____ hour later we were
_____ our villa in the mountains. In the evening we went
_____ and had a Caribbean meal. We had a lovely time _____
the sun, and we're going to go again _____ summer.

Next year we're going _____ New Zealand, _____ the
Christmas holidays. We'll have to leave _____ the middle
_____ the night to get to the airport, and the trip'll last _____
twenty-four hours. I'm looking forward _____ seeing my
relatives _____ Wellington. We'll probably stay _____ several
weeks – I expect we'll come back to the UK _____ the end
of January.

in	next	in	nearly	at
of	an	on	out	at
in	at	for	to	of
in	at	last	in	to

Language point 69 – a-adjectives

We learnt about STATE VERBS in Language point 45 – go back and look at this again if you need to before reading through this Language point.

In English we also have a small number of ADJECTIVES that describe physical and mental STATES. They all have an **a-** prefix, and are stressed on the second syllable:

asleep	/əˈsliːp/	**aware**	/əˈwɛəʳ/
awake	/əˈweɪk/	**alive**	/əˈlaɪv/
afraid	/əˈfreɪd/	**alike**	/əˈlaɪk/
alone	/əˈləʊn/	**ashamed**	/əˈʃeɪmd/

Here's what they mean:

be asleep	=	be sleeping
be awake	=	not be sleeping
be afraid (of something)	=	fear something; feel fear

be alone	=	be on your own; not be with anyone
be aware (of something)	=	know about something; sense something
be alive	=	be living; not be dead
be alike	=	be similar; look similar; be the same
be ashamed (of something)	=	feel guilty about something you've done

Here are some examples:

Are you <u>aware of</u> any problems with this car?

I'm <u>alone</u> in the office tomorrow – everyone else is on holiday.

James is <u>afraid of</u> spiders.

Queen Victoria was still <u>alive</u> in 1900.

**These two girls are very <u>alike</u>, aren't they?
– Yes, they're sisters.**

⚠️ **Be careful!** Most adjectives can be used *before* a noun:

The shirt is blue   **The blue shirt**

but you *can't* use these special STATE adjectives before a noun:

The cat is asleep   but *not* 'the asleep cat'
The girl is afraid   but *not* 'an afraid girl'
I feel rather alone   but *not* 'an alone person'

Exercise 7

Put the correct **a**-adjective in each sentence.

1 Leasa's very quiet upstairs – is she _____ ?
2 Dave won't go bungee-jumping – he's _____ of heights.
3 We need water to keep us _____ .
4 Other people disturb me, so I prefer working _____ .

5   I couldn't see in the dark, but I was _____ of someone else in the room.
6   This film is so boring, I can't stay _____!
7   Twins that are exactly _____ are called identical twins.
8   The burglar was _____ of his crimes.

Dialogue 5

Henry is asking Suzie about her plans after university.

HENRY: What are you planning to do after you finish university, Suzie?
SUZIE: I'm taking a year out to travel, and when I come back I'm going to look for a job in advertising.
HENRY: Don't you think you should sort out a job before you go abroad?
SUZIE: No – when I'm enjoying myself travelling round the world I don't want to be thinking about work! I'll find something easily enough when I get back.

Language point 70 – 'when', 'after', 'before' + present

We've seen the PRESENT used in English to refer to the FUTURE – in Language point 41 we saw the PRESENT CONTINUOUS used in this way:

We're going to Ibiza next month

and in Language point 48 we saw the PRESENT SIMPLE after **What if . . .?**:

What if the bus arrives late?

In Dialogue 5 we can see the present simple again used to express the future, after the time words **when**, **after** and **before**:

after you finish university
when I come back
before you go abroad

Notice that you *must* use the present simple for the future in these types of sentences – you *can't* use the will-future or the present continuous. So it's *wrong* to say:

> 'after you'll finish university'
> 'after you're finishing university'

But you *can* use the present continuous after **when**, as Suzie does when she says:

> **when I'm enjoying myself**

when you are making a GENERAL STATEMENT and *not* referring to the future. Here Suzie is simply talking about something that is a fact – she doesn't like thinking about work when she's enjoying herself – and is *not* referring to a future event.

Exercise 8

Choose between **when** and **before** to complete the sentences.

1 Don't forget to phone us ____ you get home.
2 I'll have a word with Henry ____ I see him.
3 Hide Ann's birthday present ____ she comes in!
4 Do you think Dave'll be surprised ____ he sees us?
5 We'll need to show our passports ____ we fly.
6 It'll be quieter in the town centre ____ the shops shut.
7 Gerry'll show us his holiday photos ____ he gets back.
8 We've got to buy some milk ____ the shops shut!

Exercise 9

Listen to the audio and match the times and places to the people.

	Time	Place
ADRIAN	**7.30**	**pub**
SAMANTHA	____	____
SU AND SHAMIRA	____	____
STUART	____	____
HELEN	____	____
GERRY	____	____

cinema	7.00	~~pub~~	7.45
football match	6.30	vegan restaurant	~~7.30~~
Indian restaurant	6.45	theatre	7.15

Phrasal verbs

ask round – 'invite to your home'.
come over – we say, for example, **When are you coming over?** if we want to know when someone is arriving at our home for a visit – it can be from far away, or from next door. In the same way, **Come over tomorrow** means 'Come and visit us at home tomorrow'.
end up – in Unit 5 we saw that we can use this phrasal verb to talk about the last in a series of visits to *places*; in this unit it is used to talk about the last in a series of *actions*.
show up – 'arrive, appear'.
sort out – 'arrange'.
turn up – 'arrive, appear' (same as **show up**).
wake up – 'stop sleeping'; 'wake from sleep'.

Life and living – holidays

If you're going **on holiday**, you need to be able to say when you're going. Here are the names of the **months** in English, with the number of days each one has:

January (31)   **July** (31)
February (28 or 29)   **August** (31)
March (31)   **September** (30)
April (30)   **October** (31)
May (31)   **November** (30)
June (30)   **December** (31)

February usually has 28 days, but has an **extra day** every fourth year, which we call a **leap year**.

We say **in January** but **on January the third** (or **on the third of January**).

And here are the names of the four **seasons** that we have in Britain:

spring   **autumn** /ˈɔːtəm/
summer   **winter**

We say **in spring** or **in the spring**, and we say **last spring**, **this spring**, **next spring** and **during the spring**.

Holiday /ˈhɒlɪdeɪ/ means 'a time when we don't work', but there are different kinds of holiday.

Many people have a holiday every year (or more than once a year if they can **afford** it) when they go away from home for a period of perhaps one to three weeks, usually in the summer. You can ask someone:

Where are you going on holiday this year?
or **Where are you going on/for your holidays this year?**

We say **on holiday**, but we say either **on your holidays** or **for your holidays**.

The schools in Britain have three **sets** of holidays:

the Christmas holidays   (late December to early January)
the Easter holidays   (late March or early April)
the summer holidays   (late July to early September)

These are periods when the schools close. Of these, the summer holidays are the longest, with schoolchildren having about six weeks **off**. Sometimes they will have single days off during **term**-time – we call these **days off** rather than holidays.

We also have bank holidays in Britain – these are one-day holidays (usually a Monday) when banks and **government departments** don't open and certain **services** either don't **operate** or operate at a **reduced** level. Small shops often don't open either on bank holidays, but large **supermarkets** and **department stores** usually do nowadays.

Glossary

afford – have enough money to buy
off – away from work or school
term – each of the three periods in the year when the schools are open and schoolchildren must attend

government departments – offices run by the government rather than by private companies
services – trains, buses, rubbish collection – things we pay for with our taxes
operate – work, function
reduced – lower
supermarket – large shop selling all kinds of food and sometimes other things as well
department store – a very large shop, often on many floors, that sells all kinds of things, including clothes, kitchen equipment, food, toys

12 You can't be serious!

In this unit you will learn how to:

- talk about what you and others have to do
- say that you're not sure about something
- talk about possibilities and probabilities
- use the TO-FORM after different types of word

Dialogue 1

Tim and Paul are getting ready to go to Henry's birthday party.

TIM: Can we stop at the shop on the way, Tim?
PAUL: Do we have to? We've got to get there by eight, and it's a quarter to already.
TIM: I have to get him a present – a bottle of wine or something.
PAUL: I've already bought him a present.
TIM: Well you must be more organised than me, then, mustn't you?

Dialogue 2

Tim and Paul are at a party, trying to identify people.

TIM: Is that Fiona over there?
PAUL: It can't be – she had to go to London this weekend.
TIM: Well who is it, then?
PAUL: It might be Suzie – she looks a bit like Fiona at a distance.
TIM: No – I've just seen Suzie in the bar.

PAUL: Well it must be someone else, then, mustn't it?
TIM: Shall we go and introduce ourselves?
PAUL: Can't do any harm, can it?

> **Idioms**
>
> - **a bit like** means 'quite similar'
> - **at a distance** means 'not near'
> - **(It) can't do any harm** means 'Nothing bad will happen if we do it'

Dialogue 3

Everyone's in the pub, but Mike's leaving early.

MIKE: OK, everyone – I'm off!
PAUL: Off? You can't be serious – it's not even eight o'clock!
MIKE: I told you earlier – I'm expecting a phone call from my sister in Australia, and she may call tonight.
PAUL: [*looks at his watch and does some mental arithmetic*] But it must be the middle of the night down there!
MIKE: No, it's early morning. She might phone before she goes to work. See you all tomorrow.
PAUL: See you, Mike.

> **Idioms**
>
> - **I'm off** means 'I'm going now'

Language point 71 – obligation

There are three ways of talking about obligation (when someone *must* do something) in colloquial English:

have to
have got to
must

Here are some examples using all of these:

I	have to 've got to must	do the shopping
Dave	has to 's got to must	work all day tomorrow
we	have to 've got to must	go home now

Must is *not* so common in colloquial English – **have to** and **have got to** are more usual.

Notice that, if we use **have to**, we *never* use the SHORT FORM:

We have to go now   *not* 'We've to go now'
Pete has to go now   *not* 'Pete's to go now'

but if we use **have got to** we *don't* normally use the LONG FORM in statements:

We've got to go now   *not* 'We have got to go now'
Pete's got to go now   *not* 'Pete has got to go now'

Pronunciation

have to is always pronounced /ˈhæftə/
(*or* /ˈhæftʊ/ before vowels)

has to is always pronounced /ˈhæstə/
(*or* /ˈhæstʊ/ before vowels)

The past tense of *both* **have to** *and* **have got to** is **had to** /ˈhættə/ or /ˈhættʊ/:

PRESENT	**I have to phone my brother later**
PRESENT	**I've got to phone my brother later**
PAST	**I had to phone my brother yesterday**
	not 'I had got to phone my brother yesterday'

And here's how we make questions:

	Statement		Question
PRESENT	You have to phone.	→	Do you have to phone?
	He has to phone.	→	Does he have to phone?
	You've got to phone.	→	Have you got to phone?
	He's got to phone.	→	Has he got to phone?
PAST	You had to phone.	→	Did you have to phone?
	He had to phone.	→	Did he have to phone?

But notice that at the end of Dialogue 1 Tim *does* use **must**:

> **You must be more organised than me**
> *not* 'You have to be more organised than me'

Here, **must** is correct, and **have to/have got to** is *wrong*, because Tim is *not* talking about obligation – he's using **must** to show that he *assumes* something is true, or that he is *fairly certain* that something is true. We will learn more about this in Language point 72.

Exercise 1

Match the two halves of each sentence – the first one has been done for you.

1 **The car's broken down so I've**   a   have to speak louder.
2 There's a power cut so we   b   has to wait.
3 The train's late so everybody   c   **got to phone the garage.**
4 Dave's run out of money so he   d   have to do it again.
5 We're late so we   e   got to walk to work.
6 I can't hear you so you   f   have to use candles.
7 The buses are on strike so I've   g   have to hurry up.
8 Their homework is wrong so they   h   has to go to the bank.

Exercise 2

Change the statements into questions, and vice versa. The first one has been done for you.

1. Dave's got to go now.
   Has Dave got to go now?
2. We had to show our passports.
   _____ ?
3. I've got to sign the form.
   _____ ?
4. Do the children have to pay?
   _____ .
5. Did they have to pay by cheque?
   _____
6. Greg had to do the work.
   _____ ?
7. Have Keith and Carl got to play a song?
   _____ .
8. I have to have my picture taken.
   _____ ?
9. We've got to leave early.
   _____ ?
10. Did Gerry have to work late?
    _____ .

Language point 72 – possibility and certainty

We use the AUXILIARIES **can**, **might** and **must** to say how 'certain' (or not) we are of something. In Dialogue 1 Phil says:

it can't be	= it <u>isn't</u> possible
it might be	= it <u>is</u> possible
it must be	= it is <u>fairly certain</u>

And in Dialogue 2 Paul and Mike use these auxiliaries in longer sentences:

You can't be serious
= 'it isn't possible that you are serious'

She might phone
= 'it is possible that she'll phone'

It must be the middle of the night
= 'I'm fairly certain that it's the middle of the night'

Might /maɪt/ can be used with the BASE-FORM of any verb to show that it is *possible* that something will happen. Here are some more examples:

James might come with us
Your sister might help you with your homework
We might arrive late at the party

And we can add **not** to show that it's possible that something *won't* happen:

James might not come with us
= 'it's possible that James won't come'
Your sister might not want to help
We might not be in time

And instead of **might** we can use **may** /meɪ/ or **could** /kʊd/:

James may come with us
We could arrive late

⚠️ **Be careful!** We *don't* use **can** to mean possibility:
  James can come with us
  = 'James is able to come with us'
  not 'it's possible that James will come'

So, for example:

'It's possible that it's too late'

It might be too late
It may be too late
It could be too late

but not 'It can be too late'

Exercise 3

Use **can't**, **might** and **must** to make these sentences more colloquial – the first one has been done for you.

1 It isn't possible that he's late. → **He can't be late**
2 It's possible that James is ill. →
3 It isn't possible that you're right. →
4 It's fairly certain that you're joking! →
5 It's possible that it'll snow tonight. →
6 It's fairly certain that they like Indian food. →
7 It isn't possible that this is true. →
8 It's possible that Terry will come later. →
9 It's possible that the rain will stop soon. →
10 It isn't possible that Pete thinks that. →

Exercise 4

Correct the following sentences. Be careful – one of them *doesn't* need correcting.

1 You don't can be serious!
2 I might to phone Julie after dinner.
3 It musts be very hot in Australia in the summer.
4 We're having got to do the shopping.
5 Did Adrian got to work late yesterday?
6 Did you had to light the fire yourself?
7 Gerry might call in later on.
8 I've get to got some money from the bank.

Dialogue 4

Jane comes in to find Henry at the computer. He doesn't look very happy.

HENRY: I'm never doing *this* again!
JANE: What, dear?
HENRY: Writing a novel on the computer.
JANE: Why? What's wrong?
HENRY: The bloody thing's packed up on me!
JANE: You're joking! How's that happened?
HENRY: The hard drive must have crashed, or something.
JANE: But you can't have lost the whole novel!

HENRY: I don't know. I may be able to retrieve it if I can get the computer up and running again.
JANE: But you must have kept a back-up, surely?
HENRY: If only!

Idioms

- **bloody** /ˈblʌdɪ/ is an ADJECTIVE that we use in *informal* situations with NOUNS, or an ADVERB that we use with adjectives, to add emphasis when we are angry or frustrated. It's a *bit* rude, but not very.

    this bloody computer
    bloody stupid

- **up and running** means 'functioning properly and without problems'

- **If only!** means 'I wish what you just said was true, but it's not!'

Language point 73 – 'must have'

When Henry says in Dialogue 4:

The hard drive <u>must have</u> crashed

he uses **must** (*not* **have to/have got to**) + **have** + PAST PARTICIPLE to say what he *thinks has happened*. This might be a good time to look again at Language point 53 if you want to remind yourself about how to form the past participle.

More examples:

> There's milk on the floor – the cat <u>must have knocked</u> the bottle over
> The front door is open – someone <u>must have broken</u> into the house!
> My passport's not in my bag – I <u>must have left</u> it at the post office
> Gerry's not at his desk – he <u>must have gone</u> home early

But when we want to say what we think *hasn't* happened, we *don't* use **mustn't have**. Look what Jane says:

> You <u>can't have lost</u> the whole novel
> *not* 'You mustn't have lost the whole novel'

She means 'It isn't possible that you've lost the whole novel'.

This fits with what we saw about **must be** and **can't be** in Language point 72 – let's remind ourselves:

+	It <u>must</u> be ten o'clock	= 'I think that it's ten o'clock'
–	It <u>can't</u> be ten o'clock	= 'I <u>don't</u> think it's ten o'clock'
+	He <u>must have</u> gone home	= 'I think that he's gone home'
–	He <u>can't have</u> gone home	= 'I <u>don't</u> think that he's gone home'

Exercise 5

Fill in the blanks using **must have** or **can't have** – the first one has been done for you.

1. The front door's open – I **must have left** it unlocked! (leave)
2. Dom and Sarah are very late – the car _____ down. (break)
3. This kettle doesn't work – you _____ it up properly. (wire)
4. Candace _____ – there's no message on the answer machine. (ring)

5 The window's smashed – someone _____ a brick
   through it.   (throw)
6 Jane looks very happy – Henry _____ her the
   good news.   (tell)
7 Fred's looking guilty – he _____ his
   homework.   (do)
8 The lights are off in that shop – they _____
   early today.   (close)
9 Helen doesn't look very well – she _____
   a cold.   (catch)
10 The students all gave the wrong answer – they
   _____ the question.   (understand)

Dialogue 5

Dave's showing off his latest acquisition to Paul.

DAVE: How do you like my new home cinema system?
PAUL: Very impressive. Is it easy to use?
DAVE: Yes, it came with full instructions and it was dead easy to set up.
PAUL: Was it expensive?
DAVE: I'll say! It was the most expensive one in the shop. But I arranged to pay for it over five years.
PAUL: Are you glad you decided to buy it?
DAVE: Yes, there's just one problem to sort out.
PAUL: What's that?
DAVE: I can't find out how to switch it on.

Idioms

- **dead easy** means 'really easy' or 'extremely easy'
- **I'll say!** /ˈaɪlseɪ/ is a way of strongly *confirming* what the other person has just said, or of giving a strong 'yes' to a question:

    This place is packed out!   – I'll say!
    Is Henry very rich?   – I'll say!

Language point 74 – more about the to-form

The TO-FORM of the verb is very important because it's used in so many situations and with so many other types of word. Let's see what combinations there are in Dialogue 5:

- ADJECTIVE + to-form: Is it <u>easy to use</u>?
  It was dead <u>easy to set up</u>

ADJECTIVE + to-form phrases are usually easy to understand:

The computer is easy to use
  means 'Using the computer is easy'

It was hard to find so much money
  means 'Finding so much money was hard'

Some adjectives describing a *state of mind* are *always* followed by the to-form:

pleased:	I'm <u>pleased to see</u> you
happy:	We're so <u>happy to be</u> here
keen:	I'm <u>keen to visit</u> the new art gallery
eager:	Dave is <u>eager to get</u> started at his new job

- NOUN + to-form: There's just one <u>problem to sort out</u>

This means 'There's just one problem <u>that has to be sorted out</u>'.

But the NOUN + to-form structure can have other meanings as well. Here are some examples:

Can I have a <u>book to read</u>?
= 'Can I have a book <u>that I can read</u>?'

That is a difficult <u>question to answer</u>
'= Answering that question is difficult'

- VERB + to-form: I <u>arranged to pay</u> for it
  you <u>decided to buy</u> it

In Language point 50 we saw the ING-FORM is used after some verbs, and the TO-FORM after others. You have to *learn* what form to use with each verb – good learners' dictionaries will tell you. Here are some more that are followed by the to-form:

agree:	Brian <u>agreed to change</u> the schedule
ask:	Shall we <u>ask</u> them <u>to come back</u> later?
(can't) afford:	I can't <u>afford to miss</u> this lecture
expect:	We're <u>expecting to see</u> the family at Christmas
fail:	Suzie <u>failed to get</u> the results she needed
help:	Will you <u>help</u> me <u>to tidy</u> the room
offer:	Shall we <u>offer to do</u> the washing-up?
refuse:	I <u>refuse to listen</u> to this nonsense!
want:	What do you <u>want to do</u>?

- WH-WORD + to-form: **I can't find out <u>how to switch</u> it on**

We can use most question words with a to-form after verbs describing:

knowing
understanding
thinking
finding out
deciding
saying
telling

Here are some more examples:

I don't know <u>where to park</u>
= I don't know where I should park

Pete told me <u>what to write down</u>
I can't decide <u>who to invite</u>
They didn't say <u>when to come</u>
I need to know <u>how many to order</u>

But we *can't* use **why** with a to-form:

~~'He doesn't know why to do it'~~
He doesn't know why he should do it

Exercise 6

Rewrite the ing-sentences as to-sentences, and vice versa. The first one has been done for you.

1. Speaking Vietnamese is hard. → **It's hard to speak Vietnamese**
2. Eating chocolate is nice. →
3. It's unpleasant to have injections. →
4. It's annoying to get phone bills. →
5. Swimming underwater is fun. →
6. It's nice to get birthday presents. →
7. It's easy to speak colloquial English. →
8. Writing thank you letters is polite. →
9. Painting pictures is relaxing. →
10. Drinking the water here isn't safe. →

Exercise 7

Complete these sentences using the correct WH-WORD. The first one is done for you.

1. I don't know **how** to get to the cinema.
2. Can you tell me ____ to do?
3. I don't know ____ to buy her.
4. We need to decide ____ to invite.
5. Do you know ____ to drive?
6. I'm not sure ____ to park the car.
7. Can you tell me ____ to do it?
8. Terry doesn't know ____ to put the luggage.
9. We'd better find out ____ to ask.
10. I don't know ____ to say to them.

Exercise 8

Complete these sentences by adding a WH-WORD and one of the verbs from the box. Use each verb only *once*. The first one has been done for you.

1. I've written a letter telling people **what to bring** on the trip.
2. I've no idea _____ to the airport on time.
3. Do the children know _____ the video?
4. Let's discuss _____ on holiday this year.

5 Can someone tell me _____ this form?
6 I've told everyone _____ at the station.
7 Tom isn't sure _____ the roses this year.
8 I'll show you _____ your bags.

| to be | to put | to get | to work |
| to fill in | to plant | ~~to bring~~ | to go |

Phrasal verbs

find out – 'discover'; we often use this phrasal verb with wh-words.

pack up – 'stop working (machines)'; this phrasal verb is similar to **break down** that we saw in Unit 10 – but it's often used about smaller machines, such as computers: we say **The car's broken down**, but **The computer's packed up**. We also use **pack up** to talk about *people* stopping work: **When are you packing up today?** means 'What time are you stopping work today?'.

set up – when we talk about setting up a home cinema system (for example), we mean doing all the things necessary to make it work and placing all the component parts (e.g. the screen, the DVD-player, the speakers) in the right places.

Life and living – computers

You're never very far away from a computer in the UK – everyone seems to have one these days, either at home or at work (or both!). They're very **versatile**, of course, and quite **user-friendly**. We call the machine itself and its **associated equipment** the hardware. Hardware includes things like the **monitor**, the **keyboard**, the **printer**, the **hard disk** and the **floppy disks** – all things that you can *touch*. The **programs** that make the computer work by giving it **instructions** and so allow you to use it in different ways are called the **software**. The most popular and widely used programs are for **word-processing**, **spreadsheets** and games. And of course you can always use your computer to **access** the Internet. On the World Wide Web you can visit a huge number of **websites** representing and dealing with **every** subject and **field** of interest **under the sun**, and you can use special websites called search engines to help you **navigate** your way to particular sites – just type in a few **keywords** and let the search engine do the rest. Alternatively, you can just **surf** the Web, following your own path from **link** to link to see where you end up.

But perhaps the most frequent and **ubiquitous** use for Internet access is email (electronic mail) – you can send someone a message **instantaneously** anywhere in the world, and it's both cheap and convenient. You'd better watch out for **viruses**, though!

Glossary

versatile – able to be used for many different purposes
user-friendly – easy for anyone to use
associated equipment – machine used in conjunction with the computer
monitor – the screen you look at
keyboard – the thing you type with
printer – the machine that prints out your documents onto paper
hard disk – the computer's built-in memory
floppy disk – a portable memory device for transferring information
program – a set of instructions to allow a computer to perform a task
instruction – command
word-processing – writing and editing documents
spreadsheet – program for handling varied types of data
access – get access to
every ... under the sun – every kind you can think of
field – area
navigate – find your way
keywords – important words
link – pointers on a website that take you automatically to other websites
ubiquitous – existing everywhere
instantaneously – immediately, at once
virus – a program designed to find its way into a computer's hard disk and damage it

13 The people we met were fantastic!

In this unit you will learn how to:

- how to use **who** and **that** in longer sentences
- use prepositions in longer sentences
- use more adverbs

Dialogue 1

Su is showing James some of her holiday photos.

JAMES: Who's this bloke?[1]
SU: That's the man who helped us when the car broke down. And next to him is the woman who was staying in the room below us.
JAMES: And what's this place?
SU: That's the building that used to be the National Library. Now it's a drama school for people who want to be actors. And then ...

[*she shows another photo ...*]

... this is one of the students who showed us round the place.

[*... and another one ...*]

JAMES: And this must be the driver who drove you around.
SU: Yes. We had two drivers – a man who didn't speak any English, and a young woman who really did speak excellent English.

[... *and another* ...]

... And this is the plane that brought us back home.

[... *and another* ...]

... And this is the taxi driver that met us at the airport to bring us back to Brighton.

JAMES: Looks like you had a great holiday!

SU: Oh yes! The places we saw were amazing, the food we ate was delicious and the people we met were fantastic.

JAMES: What about the money you spent?

SU: None left!

1 **bloke** is a colloquial word for 'man'

Dialogue 2

Helen and Justine are discussing clothes.

HELEN: That's a nice top, Justine.

JUSTINE: Do you like it? I got it in a great little shop I found when I was doing the shopping in Brighton the other week.

HELEN: It really suits you. So ... where's this shop then? I can picture myself in something like that.

JUSTINE: Right – you know the Indian restaurant on London Road that does vegan dishes?

HELEN: The one we went to on Stuart's birthday?

JUSTINE: The one we got thrown out of after Stuart made himself sick, yes. Well, behind it there's a public garden that most people don't know about. And at the other end there's a little bakery that makes banana doughnuts. You go past there ...

HELEN: Oh God, Justine – can't you just take me there?

JUSTINE: OK – we'll go and see if we can find something you like.

Idioms

- **the other week** means ' two or three or a few weeks ago' (*not* 'last week'); we can also say **the other day** (= 'two or three or a few days ago'), and **the other morning/afternoon/evening/night**
- **this** (**shop**) means 'the (shop) you've just been talking about'
- **oh God**: we use this expression in informal situations if we are annoyed, or worried, about something. It's *not* rude, and it *won't* offend people you are on informal terms with – it's really a very gentle little phrase!

Language point 75 – relative clauses: 'who' and 'that'

Look at these two sentences:

a **That's the man**
b **He helped us with the car**

We can join these together to make *one sentence* by using **who** /huː/ weak form /hʊ/ instead of **he** in sentence (b):

That's the man <u>who</u> helped us with the car

Now look at these two sentences:

a **That's the building**
b **It houses the nation's modern art collection**

Because **building** is a *thing* and not a person, we use **that** (/ðæt/, weak form /ðət/), *not* **who**, to join the sentences together:

That's the building <u>that</u> houses the nation's modern art collection

But did you notice that, later in Dialogue 1, Su says:

And this is the taxi driver <u>that</u> met us at the airport

With *things* we *have* to use **that**, but with *people* we can use *either* **who** *or* **that**:

The woman who lives next door
The woman that lives next door

'The building who stands opposite the bank'
The building that stands opposite the bank

In more formal English **which** can be used instead of **that** for things:

The building which stands opposite the bank

This word is *not* normally used to join sentences in colloquial English, although it *is* okay in colloquial English as a question word – see Language point 60.
   At the end of the dialogue Su says:

The food we ate was delicious
The people we met were fantastic

She *could* have said:

The food that we ate was delicious
The people who we met were fantastic

but she *leaves the joining words out*. We can do this in English when the word *before* the joining word is the OBJECT in the sentence, and the word *following* it is the SUBJECT. But we *can't* leave out the joining word when the word *before* it is the SUBJECT. Compare these two sentences:

	Object	*Subject*
	The people who	we saw
=	'The people	we saw'

	Subject	*Object*
	The people who saw	us
not	'The people saw	us'

Exercise 1

Match the pairs of sentences, then join them using **who** or **that**.

1 I'm looking for a man
2 I need a pencil
3 I can see the bridge
4 This is the road
5 This is the door
6 I'm looking for a shop
7 Those are the children
8 That's the pilot

a It leads to the garden.
b It leads to the town centre.
c They broke the window.
d It sells cheap chocolate.
e He flew us home.
f He can mend cars.
g It has a sharp point.
h It crosses the river.

Exercise 2

Join the two sentences using **who** or **that** – the first one has been done for you.

1 The men ran away. (They robbed the bank)
   The men who robbed the bank ran away.

2 The restaurant won a prize. (It did the best food)
   _____

3 The students are very clever. (They're learning Russian)
   _____

4 The woman phoned the police. (She lost her passport)
   _____

5 The train was very full. (It was late)
   _____

6 The newsreader lost her job. (She sneezed on camera)
   _____

7 The artist refused to take any money. (He painted the Queen)
   _____

8 The tree is big. (It fell on our house)
   _____

9 The fish are pretty. (They live in the garden pond)
   _____

10 The ship was enormous. (It took us to the Caribbean)
   _____

Exercise 3

Decide which of these sentences can have the **who** or **that** *removed*.

1 The film that I saw was exciting.
2 The house that we bought was very old.
3 The man who showed us round was very polite.
4 The instruction manual that came with the video was useless.
5 The policeman who we asked was helpful.
6 The computer that my brother bought was expensive.
7 The people that we met were fantastic.
8 The fireworks that they set off were stupendous.
9 The computer that sits on my desk is rather noisy.
10 The children who live next door are very friendly.

Language point 76 – relative clauses with prepositions

We saw in Language point 75 that we can change:

We phoned the restaurant

into

The restaurant (that) we phoned

Now look what happens when we add a PREPOSITION:

We went to the restaurant
→ **The restaurant (that) we went to**

The preposition goes to the *end* when we turn the sentence into a relative. This happens even when we leave out the joining word **who** or **that**, as when Justine and Helen say in Dialogue 2:

(We went to the restaurant)
The one we went to

(We got thrown out of the restaurant)
The one we got thrown out of

Here are some more examples:

(James was talking to the woman)
The woman James was talking to

(The children are playing with the ball)
The ball the children are playing with

And here's another example from the Dialogue:

(Most people don't know about the public garden)
A public garden that most people don't know about

In more formal English the preposition *doesn't* move, and **which** is added to it. But remember from the last Language point that we *don't* use **which** in RELATIVE CLAUSES in colloquial English:

~~'A public garden about which most people don't know'~~

Exercise 4

Complete the sentences by filling in the first blank with a phrase from the first box, and the second blank with a phrase from the second box. Use each phrase only once. The first one has been done for you.

1 The woman **who I helped** was **very grateful**.
2 The programme _____ was _____ .
3 The patient _____ has _____ .
4 The music _____ was _____ .
5 The trousers _____ were _____ .
6 The chair _____ was _____ .
7 The rubbish _____ was _____ .
8 The meal _____ was _____ .

that I saw	that we were listening to
that Dave bought	that I was sitting on
that Henry cooked	that we threw away
~~who I helped~~	who was in hospital
very uncomfortable	rather boring
got better now	too short for him
very loud	really delicious
~~very grateful~~	rather smelly

Exercise 5

Join the pairs of sentences together *without* **who** and **that**. Be careful where you put the PREPOSITIONS. The first one has been done for you.

1. Nobody knows about this shop.
   → **This is the shop nobody knows about.**

2. Justine works in this office.
   → _____.

3. I was sitting in that chair.
   → _____.

4. We've been listening to this music all morning.
   → _____.

5. I wrote the message on this piece of paper.
   → _____.

6. We lived in this town for five years.
   → _____.

7. Andy comes from this town.
   → _____.

8. I told you about these people.
   → _____.

9. I got my DVD-player from this shop.
   → _____.

10. I came with these students.
    → _____.

Dialogue 3

Fiona has been stopped in the street by a market researcher, who is asking her what she likes on TV.

MARKET RESEARCHER: Now, first of all, could you tell me how much time you spend every day watching TV?

FIONA: Goodness! Let me think – well, on weekdays I'm usually back from work at about 5.30, and I generally switch the television on as soon as I come in.

M/RESEARCHER: Do you always leave the TV on all evening?
FIONA: I usually do, yes. I probably have it on too much, actually, because I'm certainly not always watching it.
M/RESEARCHER: Now – what kind of programme do you like best?
FIONA: Well, I like drama and nature programmes a lot. And I often watch the soaps.
M/RESEARCHER: I see. And what about the late news bulletins?
FIONA: I've usually gone to bed by then!
M/RESEARCHER: Do you watch morning TV at all?
FIONA: I never watch TV in the mornings because I'm never in the house. During the week I always leave very early for work, and I have yoga classes every weekend on both Saturday and Sunday mornings.
M/RESEARCHER: And finally, what do you think about the amount of TV you watch every week?
FIONA: I definitely watch too much, but I find it really relaxing after a day's work, so I probably won't change!
M/RESEARCHER: Thanks for your time and your help.
FIONA: Not at all.

Idiom

- We use **Not at all** as a polite response when someone has *thanked* us.

Dialogue 4

Candace calls in on Brenda, who's been a bit unwell.

CANDACE: Hello, Brenda – I just thought I'd call in and see how you are.
BRENDA: Hi – I'm still a bit iffy, but I'm definitely feeling better than I was.
CANDACE: You certainly look a lot better. Still, you probably don't want to come swimming today.
BRENDA: I know we always do that on Wednesdays, but I probably shouldn't. I don't feel sick any more, but I'm still feeling a bit weak.
CANDACE: [*suddenly concerned*] Shall I make you a cup of tea?
BRENDA: No thanks, Candace – I've already had three this morning, and it's only ten o'clock!

Idiom

When Brenda says she's still **a bit iffy** she's using a colloquial word to describe how she's feeling – **iffy** comes from **if**, one of the words we've been looking at in this unit, and it means **uncertain** or **not completely OK**. Here, she's telling Candace that she's still a bit uncertain about her health. More examples:

I'm not eating this – it smells iffy!
(it doesn't smell right)

This car looks a bit iffy
(there's something wrong with it)

Language point 77 – 'do' and 'make'

We've seen **do** a lot in this book as an AUXILIARY – **do**, **don't**, **did**, **didn't** – in questions in the PRESENT SIMPLE and PAST SIMPLE, and in negatives, and in tags. But **do** is also a verb with a real meaning. In Dialogue 2 we see another verb as well: **make**.

These two verbs have similar meanings and it is easy for learners of English to confuse them. Let's see how Justine uses them in Dialogue 2:

I was doing the shopping
The bakery that makes banana doughnuts

Now, let's imagine that Justine has given us a list of all the things she does in a day – if we arrange them into *two* lists, we will be able to see the difference between **do** and **make**:

Justine

<u>does</u>	<u>makes</u>
the shopping	a cup of tea
the household finances	a shopping list
some yoga	an evening meal
the washing-up	a loaf of bread
the gardening	some paper aeroplanes

Can you see the difference?

do	=	perform an action
make	=	produce or create something

Do also has many *special meanings* – look in a dictionary and see how many! In the Dialogue, Justine talks about:

the restaurant that <u>does</u> vegan dishes

Here **do** = serve.

Here are some more special meanings of **do**:

Liz is <u>doing</u> Law at university	(study)
The local theatre company's <u>doing</u> Hamlet this week	(perform)
That will <u>do</u> for today	(be enough)
This car <u>does</u> 150 mile per hour	(travels at a speed of)
I'm <u>done</u> for today	(finished)

Finally, remember that most forms of **do** have unusual pronunciations:

do	/duː/
does	/dʌz/
don't	/dəʊnt/
done	/dʌn/

Exercise 6

Choose between the verbs in brackets for each sentence.

1 Have you (done/made) your homework yet?
2 Kath's (doing/making) bread rolls for the picnic.
3 I can't (do/make) this Maths problem.
4 Will you (do/make) the washing-up for me?
5 I'm thinking of (doing/making) the London Marathon this year.
6 This restaurant doesn't (do/make) curry.
7 They've (done/made) a film of this book.
8 When the weather gets better I'll (do/make) the gardening.

Exercise 7

Correct these sentences. Be careful – one of them *doesn't* need correcting.

1 What have you did with my trousers?
2 The children made a lot of noise at the party.
3 I done my homework already.
4 Suzie's made an important decision.
5 Let's be careful – we don't want to do a mistake, do we?
6 James dids a good job.
7 Has Lucy doed her yoga exercises?
8 Let's make the rest of the work later.

Dialogue 5

Andy and Brian are on their way to the pub, moaning about money as usual.

ANDY: Oh, it's always the same!
BRIAN: What?
ANDY: I never have any money on me when I go out. Every week I carefully plan my spending, but by Friday it's all gone.
BRIAN: Never mind. Surely there's a bank nearby. You definitely *have* got money in the bank, haven't you?
ANDY: We'll soon find out. I was still in the black last week, but I'm often overdrawn by the end of the month.

BRIAN: I really hate being overdrawn, don't you?
ANDY: I often get rude letters form the bank about it, so they obviously don't like it either.
BRIAN: They certainly don't.

Idioms

- **on me** means 'with me' or 'in my possession' particularly when talking about money. **Have you got any money on you?** is the normal way in colloquial English of asking someone if they have money in their pocket on in their wallet or purse.
- **I was in the black** means 'I had money in the bank'; **in the black** means 'in credit with the bank', **in the red** means 'in debt to the bank'.

Language point 78 – adverb position

In Language point 58 we saw that the *position of adverbs* is important in colloquial English. In Dialogue 3 we see some more – we can divide them into two groups according to the position they occupy in the sentence:

every day **every weekend** **on Saturday**	time
(not) at all **a lot**	degree

These adverbs usually come at the *end* of the sentence:

I buy a newspaper <u>every morning</u>	✓
'~~I buy every morning a newspaper~~'	✗
I don't like lemon tea <u>at all</u>	✓
'~~I don't like at all lemon tea~~'	✗
We'll phone you <u>on Saturday</u>	✓
'~~We'll on Saturday phone you~~'	✗

The *time* expressions can also come at the *start* of the sentences:

Every morning I buy a newspaper	✓

always **never** **often** **usually** **generally**	frequency
definitely **probably**	

These adverbs come:

1. after the first AUXILIARY:

    I've usually gone to bed

2. after **be** if there is no other verb or auxiliary:

    I'm usually back from work
    I'm never in the house

3. before the *main verb* when there is no auxiliary:

    I often watch the soaps

Notice what happens in questions:

> **Do you always leave the TV on?**
> **Have you often visited Italy?**

– the adverb comes after the SUBJECT.

Exercise 8

Decide which of these sentences have the adverb in the wrong position, and correct them. Some of the sentences are okay.

1. Simon reads often in the evenings.
2. You probably'll miss the bus.
3. Does Gerry usually drive to work?
4. They'll definitely want to come with us.
5. Suzie likes a lot Indian food.
6. Is often the weather wet in this part of the country?
7. Barry doesn't like at all Indian food.
8. We every Saturday go to watch a football match.
9. Every evening I have a bath.
10. I have a bath every evening.

Exercise 9

Turn these statements into questions – watch out for the adverbs.

1. Henry's often in the local library.
2. James is always working in the Internet café.
3. Tom's brother and his wife have often visited France.
4. You usually go to the restaurant next door.
5. He often has to go abroad.
6. George goes to the pub every Friday evening.

Phrasal verbs

drive (around) – 'drive to lots of different places'; we can drive around, or we can drive *people* around. **Let me drive you around** means 'Let me take you to different places in the car and tell you about them'.

show (a)round – 'show someone lots of different places'; **Will you show us round?** means 'Will you take us to different places and tell us about them?'. You can show someone round a town or city, or you can show them round your house! When people come to look at your house to see if they want to buy it, we say **Let me show you round**.

Life and living – people and population

There's a lot of talk about people in this unit, and in the United Kingdom there's certainly no **shortage** of people. Nearly sixty million people live in the four **constituent countries** of the UK – by far the **majority** (48 million) live in England, with 6 million living in Scotland, 3 million in Wales and 2 million in Northern Ireland. Also part of the British Isles, but not part of the UK, is the Republic of Ireland with over 3.5 million people.

Britain is famous for the **multicultural** nature of its population. Particularly in the cities – not just London but other cities such as Birmingham (Britain's second city), Bristol and Brighton (where Helen and Justine in Dialogue 2 come from) – you'll meet people from all parts of the world. Just walk down the street and you'll **encounter** British citizens whose family **links** go back to Africa, India, China and **just about** anywhere else in the world you can think of. Many of these people speak languages in addition to English – for example, in London there are over 200 languages spoken among the 8 million **inhabitants** of the city! If you want to **broaden** your experience of this side of things, you can buy books in the same series as this one to help you learn: Chinese, Cantonese,

Hindi, Urdu, Panjabi, Gujarati, Somali, for example, **as well as** two language which, like English, are **indigenous** to the UK: Welsh and Scottish Gaelic.

This cultural and linguistic **diversity** is what many people think makes Britain a very special place to live and work, and of course a **great** country to visit!

Glossary

shortage – not many (so **no shortage** means 'a lot')
constituent countries – the countries that together form the UK
majority – most, the greatest number
multicultural – having people from many cultural backgrounds
encounter – meet
links – connections
just about – almost, very nearly
inhabitants – people who live in a place
broaden – widen, make more broad
as well as – and also
indigenous – something or someone that arose or was born in a place rather than being imported or coming from somewhere else
diversity – variety, having many different aspects
great – wonderful, very good

14 What would you do?

> **In this unit you will learn how to:**
> - talk about things that haven't happened
> - talk about what might happen
> - discuss possibilities
> - identify and use the two main types of conditional in English

Dialogue 1

Justine and Ann are in town. Suddenly Justine sees a newsagent's and remembers something she has to do.

JUSTINE: Hang on a minute, Ann! I need to go into the newsagent's.
ANN: What for? We've already got a newspaper.
JUSTINE: I need to buy a lottery ticket.
ANN: A lottery ticket? I'm surprised at you, Justine – *really* I am! What a waste of money!
JUSTINE: What do you mean, a waste of money? If I play, I might win!
ANN: Like hell! But anyway, even if you *did* win, what would you do with the money?
JUSTINE: If I won I'd do lots of things – I'd go on a trip round the world, for a start. And I'd buy my Mum and Dad a new house. And I'd give money to charity. And ...
ANN: I bet you wouldn't be happy, though.
JUSTINE: [*snorts*] I bet I would! If *you* won the lottery, *you'd* be happy, wouldn't you?
ANN: I wouldn't play in the first place, so it wouldn't happen, would it?

JUSTINE:	But if you *did*. You'd find plenty of things to spend the money on, wouldn't you?
ANN:	Well, yes . . . I suppose I would. But . . .
JUSTINE:	Well there you are then! Wait here while I go in and buy a ticket.
ANN:	You'll be wasting your money.
JUSTINE:	You won't say that if I win.
	[*Justine goes in, but Ann calls after her*]
ANN:	Justine!
JUSTINE:	Yes, what is it *now*?
ANN:	Get me a ticket as well, would you?

Language point 79 – conditionals

CONDITIONALS are forms of the verb that describe actions or events that have not happened, but *could* happen – things that are possible. Conditional sentences have two parts: a MAIN CLAUSE and an IF-CLAUSE. There are *two* main types of conditional in English – **C1** and **C2** – and we are going to look at both of them in this unit. So – let's look at the following similar, but different, sentences:

[C1] **If I have time, I'll help you with the washing-up**
[C2] **If I had time, I'd help you with the washing-up**

You can see that these sentences are the same *except for the verbs*. Now let's look at the meanings:

- in the **C1** sentence, I am saying that it is *possible* that I'll have time to help, but that I don't know for sure – so it's *possible* that I'll be helping with the washing-up;
- in the **C2** sentence I am saying that I *haven't* got the time, so I *won't* be helping with the washing-up at all.

You can see the difference in Dialogue 1, where Justine uses both C1 and C2 conditionals – she says **if I win** (C1) because she thinks it's a possibility, but when talking about Ann she says **if you won** (C2) because Ann doesn't do the lottery and so it won't happen and is therefore unreal.

We'll look at C2 conditionals later in this unit, but first we'll concentrate on C1.

The normal verb pattern for C1 conditionals is:

> **if**-clause PRESENT SIMPLE – main clause WILL-FUTURE

Here are some examples showing both statements and negatives:

If she stays, I'll stay too
If she doesn't stay, I won't stay either
If I stay, she won't
If I don't stay, she will

This is usually all we need to know to form C1 conditionals. But there *are* other tenses that can be used in C1 conditionals, and especially the MODAL AUXILIARIES. For example, in Dialogue 1 Justine says **If I play I might win**; we saw the **might** /mait/ in Unit 13 (Language point 72) – it indicates that the speaker thinks the action or event described *could* happen, so it fits well in a conditional sentence. Here are some more examples with modals:

If it's fine tomorrow, we could take the boat out on the river
If you don't get the job, you could apply for another one

If the students don't do their homework tonight, they can't go swimming tomorrow
If we don't take the car, we must carry the shopping home

If Helen is late, we should start without her
If the bus is full, we might not get a seat

Exercise 1

Look at these conditional sentences and simply decide whether each one is **possible** or **unreal** – the first one has been done for you. Be careful with no. 4.

1	I'll buy the drinks if you order the food	possible / ~~unreal~~
2	If Dave broke the window, he'd have to buy new one	possible / unreal
3	If we hurry we'll catch the bus	possible / unreal
4	The food would keep longer if we put it in the fridge	possible / unreal
5	If you give me the money, I'll take care of it	possible / unreal

6 We'd miss you if you went away   possible / unreal
7 If it rains we'll get very wet   possible / unreal
8 If it started to snow now the kids would
   be excited   possible / unreal

Exercise 2

Match the actions on the left to their results on the right – the first one has been done for you.

1	**If you cut your finger,**	a	your eyes close.
2	If you heat glass,	b	it burns.
3	If you sneeze,	c	it turns to ice.
4	If you freeze water,	d	you get wet.
5	If you go out in the rain	e	**it bleeds.**
6	If you light a candle,	f	it melts.

Exercise 3

Rewrite the verbs in these sentences in the correct tenses – the first one has been done for you.

1 If he (go) to Finland next week, he (need) a passport.   **goes**   **'ll need**
2 If Gerry (be) late, we (leave) without him.   _____   _____
3 If you (stand) in the rain, you (get) wet.   _____   _____
4 If the TV (break down), James (repair) it.   _____   _____
5 If I (not see) you tonight, I (phone) you in the morning.   _____   _____
6 If Suzi (not hurry), she (miss) the bus.   _____   _____
7 Mike (be) pleased if he (get) the job.   _____   _____
8 This microwave (not work) if you (not plug) it in.   _____   _____

Exercise 4

Match the **if**-clauses and main clauses to make complete sentences – the first one has been done for you.

1. **If it rains,**
2. If you write the essay,
3. If the sun gets too hot,
4. If you bend this too much,
5. If you don't leave now,
6. If Simon orders the drinks,
7. If you don't practise,
8. If the bus is late,

a you'll have to wear a hat.
b I'll pay for them.
c it will break.
d we'll miss the concert.
e you won't improve.
f **we won't have a picnic.**
g you'll miss your train.
h I'll check the spelling.

Language point 80 – 'if' and 'when'

We use **if** to talk about things that *may* happen, but that we are not sure about. If we *know* for certain that something *will* happen, then we must use **when**. Compare:

If it rains tomorrow, ...   *not* 'When it rains tomorrow'
When it gets dark tonight   *not* 'If it gets dark tonight'

Exercise 5

Start the clauses below with either **if** or **when** as you think right.

1. _____ this programme finishes, ...
2. _____ the sun rises, ...
3. _____ there's a thunderstorm next week, ...
4. _____ the shop is still open, ...
5. _____ it's a nice day tomorrow, ...
6. _____ you decide not to come, ...

Language point 81 – 'what for?'

What for? is another way of saying **Why?** in colloquial English, when asking about *purpose*. It can be used on its own, as in Dialogue 1, when Ann asks why Justine is going into the newsagent's, but if it's being used in a sentence it has to be split up, with **for?** going to the end of the sentence:

<u>Why</u> are you going in the shop?	=	<u>What</u> are you going in the shop <u>for</u>?
<u>Why</u> are you looking at me?	=	<u>What</u> are you looking at me <u>for</u>?
<u>Why</u> did you do that?	=	<u>What</u> did you do that <u>for</u>?
<u>Why</u> is he here?	=	<u>What</u> is he here <u>for</u>?

But **what for?** *can't* be used with negatives:

Why didn't you tell me? *not* 'What didn't you tell me for?'
Why isn't he here? *not* 'What isn't he here for?'

and it *can't* be used when the **why?** question asks about a *reason* rather than purpose:

Why are the summers getting hotter?
not 'What are the summers getting hotter for?'

Why does wood float?
not 'What does wood float for?'

Exercise 6

Some of these **why?** questions can be rewritten with **what for?** Decide which ones can, and rewrite them. The first one has been done for you.

1 Why is John carrying that brick?
   What is John carrying that brick for?

2 Why didn't you phone me?
   _____

3 Why did your sister leave early?
   _____

4 Why does the sun rise in the east?
   _____

5 Why did the Romans invade Britain?
   _____

6 Why did the Roman Empire collapse?
   _____

7 Why haven't you bought any tickets?
   _____

8 Why is English a world language?
   _____

9 Why did Sweden win the ice hockey?
   _____

10 Why are you watching the ice hockey?
   _____

> ## Idiom
>
> - **Like hell!** Justine says **If I play, I might win**, and Ann replies **Like hell!** We use this phrase to express disagreement with what's just been said. It is very informal, but is not rude. Here are some more examples:
>
> | | | |
> |---|---|---|
> | Do you think Arsenal will win tonight? | *or* | – **Like hell!**
– **Like hell they will!** |
> | We're going to get a pay rise. | *or* | – **Like hell!**
– **Like hell we are!** |
> | Simon says he paid the bill. | *or* | – **Like hell!**
– **Like hell he did!** |
> | Amy says she wasn't rude to Gerry | *or* | – **Like hell!**
– **Like hell she wasn't!** |
>
> - Be careful with this idiom when a tag is added:
>
>   **Like hell he will!** means **He won't!**
>   **Like hell we are!** means **We aren't!**
>   **Like hell she wasn't** means **She was!**
>
>   But there is also a phrase **the hell** which we use as an intensifier, particularly with question words (but *not* **whose?** or **which?**), and in this use it is usually rather rude, or at least abrupt:
>
> | | |
> |---|---|
> | Who are you? | Who the hell are you? |
> | What's wrong? | What the hell is wrong? |
> | Why are they here? | Why the hell are they here? |
> | Where are my keys? | Where the hell are my keys? |
> | How should I know? | How the hell should I know? |
>
>   It's safer *not* to use **the hell** with people you don't know, unless you *want* to be rude, of course!

Dialogue 2

Gillian finds Lauren in the canteen at work and sits down next to her.

LAUREN: Hello, Gillian. Aren't you having lunch?
GILLIAN: No – I just wanted to ask: have you seen James today?
LAUREN: No, I don't think so. Why?
GILLIAN: I need to talk to him quite urgently about something. If you see him, will you tell him to phone me?
LAUREN: I'll certainly tell him if I see him. But listen ... why don't you phone him yourself on his mobile?
GILLIAN: If I knew his mobile number, I would.
LAUREN: Ah. [*thinks for a moment*]
... Wait a minute! What about his friends?
GILLIAN: What about them?
LAUREN: Well – if you phoned one of James's friends, perhaps they could tell you his mobile number.
GILLIAN: Great idea! Good thinking, Lauren – I knew I'd get everything sorted if I sat next to you!

Idiom

- **I'd get everything sorted** means 'I'd solve all my problems'; **get something sorted** (or **sorted out**) can also mean **put right, put in order** or **arrange**. More examples:

    Have you got the dishwasher sorted out?
    = 'Have you fixed the problem with the dishwasher?'

    This room is chaos – how are we going to get it sorted?
    = 'This room is chaos – how are we going get it organised?'

    We'll need to get the tickets sorted by the weekend
    = 'We'll need to have booked the tickets by the weekend'

Language point 82 – C2 conditionals

The verb pattern for C2 conditionals is:

> **if**-clause PAST SIMPLE – main clause **would** /**'d** + BASE-FORM

You might like to review the PAST SIMPLE in Unit 9 – remember that many common verbs (the strong verbs) have irregular past simples that have to be learnt.

Let's remind ourselves of C1 and C2:

[C1] **If I <u>see</u> Amy, <u>I'll tell</u> her**
[C2] **If I <u>saw</u> Amy, <u>I'd tell</u> her**

Remember that the first example is talking about an event that is possible in the future, while the second one is talking about an event that the speaker doesn't expect to happen.

So in Dialogue 2, Gillian says to Lauren **If you <u>see</u> him ...**, because she thinks that is a possibility, but she says **If I <u>knew</u> his mobile number** because she *doesn't* know the number.

Here are some more examples:

[C1] **If the train arrives late, we'll have to get a taxi from the station**
[C2] **If the train arrived late, we'd have to get a taxi from the station**

[C1] **If I become world president, I'll stop global warming**
[C2] **If I became world president, I'd stop global warming**

The last pair of examples shows very clearly the difference between C1 and C2 – **If I become world president ...** could only be said by someone who was in the running for the office, someone who had put himself up for election; **If I became world president ...**, on the other hand, is what all the rest of us would say, because we don't expect it to happen to us.

⚠️ **Be careful!** It is *wrong* to use the conditional form **would /'d** in the **if**-clause:

    If he ate the cake, he'd be sick
not '~~If he'd eat the cake~~'

    If we left by eleven, we'd catch the last bus
not '~~If we'd leave~~'

Sometimes we can use conditionals to make suggestions – for example, when Lauren says to Gillian **If you <u>phoned</u> one of James's friends, perhaps they <u>could</u> tell you ...** Here the **if**-clause is just there to suggest to Gillian that she does something, and in this use of the conditional the rules about C1 and C2 are much looser – all of the following variants are okay:

> **If you <u>phone</u> one of James's friends, perhaps they <u>can</u> tell you ...**
> **If you <u>phone</u> one of James's friends, perhaps they <u>could</u> tell you ...**

Just as **will** is short to **'ll**, so **'d** is the short form of **would**, which is used with the BASE-FORM of the verb to make the CONDITIONAL.

Full form	Short form	Full form	Short form
I would /wʊd/	I'd /aɪd/	I would not	I wouldn't /ˈwʊdnt/
you would	you'd /juːd/	you would not	you wouldn't
he would	he'd /hiːd/	he would not	he wouldn't
she would	she'd /ʃiːd/	she would not	she wouldn't
James would	**James'd**	**James would not**	**James wouldn't**
we would	we'd /wiːd/	**we would not**	**we wouldn't**
they would	they'd /ðɛɪd/	**they would not**	**they wouldn't**

As usual, the full forms are used for questions – **would he?**, and the short forms for negative questions – **wouldn't he?**. The negative short forms (**wouldn't**) are normal in colloquial English; in statements both short forms and full forms are common.

Exercise 7

Choose the correct verb in these C2 conditional sentences. The first one has been done for you.

1   If I (win) the lottery, I (buy) a car.
    If I won the lottery, I'd buy a car

2   You (be) angry if they (come) home late.
    _____

3   If you (take) more exercise, you (feel) healthier.
    _____

4   Helen (pay) the bill if she (have) any money.

5   I (phone) the police if someone (steal) my car.

6   I (be) surprised if she (agree) to do that.

7   If we (leave) too late we (miss) the train.

8   It (be) too dark if we (wait) till ten o'clock.

Exercise 8

Correct these sentences. Be careful! One of them *doesn't need* correcting.

1   I'd buy this ring if I'd have enough money.
2   Would you prefer it if we'll come tomorrow?
3   James would help you if you did explain the problem.
4   What will you do if you won the lottery?
5   Amy would be pleased if she would get the job.
6   I'd invite Sarah if I knew her address.
7   This room looked better if you'd paint it blue.
8   If the guests will arrive late I'd be annoyed.

Language point 83 – 'I bet', 'I wish', 'if only'

In Dialogue 1 Ann says to Justine **I bet you wouldn't be happy**, and Justine answers with the tag response **I bet I would** – we can use **I bet** to express a strong opinion and invite agreement:

I bet Amy didn't pass her driving test!	– **I bet she did!**
I bet you don't know what I've got in this bag.	– **I bet I do!**
I bet they haven't seen the film yet.	– **I bet they have!**

or simply to contradict what the other person has just said:

Harry's not coming tonight.	– **I bet he is!**
It's too late now to get tickets.	– **I bet it isn't!**

I don't think Dave was interested.   – I bet he was!
Your parents wouldn't like it here.   – I bet they would!

I wish and **If only** are used with a C2 conditional (**would** /**'d**) to say that you want someone to do something even though you know they probably won't. More examples:

I wish Adrian would give up singing!
If only our employers would give us a pay rise!
If only it would rain!
I wish you wouldn't be so awkward!

Notice that **If only ...** is the *only* instance of **if** where we use **would**.

You *can't* use these phrases for making ordinary requests:

      Please open the window for me
=   **Would you open the window for me?**
=   **Could you open the window for me?**

not   'I wish you'd open the window for me'
not   'If only you'd open the window for me'

Dialogue 3

Sarah has dropped Dave at the station car park. Dave's got a train to catch, and he's late.

SARAH: You'd better get a move on, darling. If you don't hurry you'll miss the train.
DAVE: I know, I know. Could you just help me with these bags?
SARAH: Oh for goodness sake – I *told* you you'd have too much luggage! But you wouldn't listen!
DAVE: I need two bags in case one of them breaks, OK?
SARAH: OK, OK. Anyway, ...

    [*she stops to give Dave a farewell kiss at the barrier*]

    ... phone me when you get to Scotland, will you?
DAVE: I wish you'd stop fussing. I won't phone unless there are problems.
SARAH: But I'll worry if I don't hear you've arrived!

DAVE: Unless you hear from me, you'll know everything's OK, won't you?
SARAH: I'd feel better if you phoned, that's all. If only you'd just accept that, Dave.
DAVE: All right, all right – I'll phone when I get there, OK?
SARAH: Thanks, darling. I knew you'd see it my way if I explained.
DAVE: If you nagged enough, you mean.

> **Idiom**
>
> - **You'd better get a move on** means 'You'd better hurry'. We can also use this idiom in commands and requests:
>
> | Get a move on! | = | Hurry up! |
> | Could you get a move on? | = | Could you hurry up? |
> | Get a move on, will you? | = | Hurry up, will you? |

Language point 84 – 'unless' and 'in case'

Unless is another way of saying **if ... not** – Sarah says **... if I don't hear**, but Dave says **unless you hear** instead of **if you don't hear**. And Sarah *could* have said **unless I hear**.

More examples:

    I'm not going to the pub unless you're coming too
or **I'm not going to the pub if you're not coming too**

    Don't post the letter unless you've put a stamp on it
or **Don't post the letter if you haven't put a stamp on it**

Then Dave says he needs two bags **in case** one of them breaks – he's foreseeing a problem in the future and trying to avoid it; **in case** is usually followed by the PRESENT SIMPLE:

Take your swimming trunks in case there's a pool at the hotel

I'm putting the garden furniture away in case we have a storm

We've bought some candles in case we get a power cut

Exercise 9

Rewrite these **if ... not** sentences as **unless** sentences, and vice versa. The first one has been done for you.

1. I'm leaving if she doesn't say sorry.
   I'm leaving unless she says sorry.

2. You won't pass your English exam unless you study hard.
   _____ .

3. You can't send an email if you haven't got a computer.
   _____ .

4. We'll go swimming this afternoon if it doesn't rain.
   _____ .

5. Start without me unless I phone.
   _____ .

6   I'm going if he doesn't come in the next ten minutes.
    _____.

7   You can't come in unless you're a member.
    _____.

8   You can't eat here if you're not wearing a tie.
    _____.

Exercise 10

Match the clauses on the left with those on the right to make complete sentences. The first one has been done for you.

1   **I'll throw you out**   a   I won't be friends with him
2   Unless I get something to eat   b   unless you need it yourself
3   I'm not going to listen to you   c   unless they are watered
4   If he doesn't say sorry   d   unless it's raining outside
5   I'll borrow your book   e   **if you don't start behaving**
6   I'm going to go for a walk   f   if the referee isn't ready
7   We can't start the game   g   I'm going to starve
8   The plants will die   h   unless you stop shouting

15 I said you'd phone back later

In this unit you will learn how to:

- report what other people have said
- distinguish between direct and reported speech
- use verbs of saying, reporting and thinking
- form and use the past perfect tense
- recognise the passive

Dialogue 1

Julie comes back from work. Pete's already taken a phone call for her.

PETE: Karen phoned while you were out.
JULIE: What did she want?
PETE: She said she'd bought the three tickets for the concert tonight.
JULIE: Oh good. I was afraid they might be sold out. Did she say anything else?
PETE: She asked if you'd arranged to pick up Fiona on the way. I said I didn't know and that you'd phone back when you got in.
JULIE: OK, I'll do that now.

Dialogue 2

Paul and Mike have met up outside the cinema.

PAUL: Where's Fred? He said he'd be here at eight.
MIKE: Fred told me he wasn't coming tonight after all.

PAUL: Why not? I thought he wanted to see this film.
MIKE: He does, but he phoned me earlier and said he'd broken his leg.
PAUL: Broken his leg? How did he do that?
MIKE: Fell off a ladder, I think.
PAUL: I thought he didn't like heights.
MIKE: Maybe that's why he fell off.

Language point 85 – past perfect

In Language point 53 we saw how to form the PRESENT PERFECT by using the PRESENT of **have** with the PAST PARTICIPLE. Go back and review this now if you need to.

If we use the *past* of **have** (**had** – Language point 56) with the past participle, we get the PAST PERFECT. Compare:

PRESENT PERFECT **I've bought the tickets**
PAST PERFECT **I'd bought the tickets**

(Remember that **have** and **had** are generally used in their SHORT FORMS in colloquial English).

And now compare questions:

Has he bought the tickets?
Had he bought the tickets?

And finally negatives:

We **haven't bought** the tickets
We **hadn't bought** the tickets

– short forms again!

Remember that, as with the present perfect, you need the PAST PARTICIPLE of the main verb when you use the past perfect.

REGULAR verbs: past participle = past simple (**-ed**)
IRREGULAR verbs: past participle must be learnt

Meaning – the PAST PERFECT takes the PRESENT PERFECT *one stage back into the past* (sometimes it's called 'the past in the past'):

When Dave arrived, Jenny <u>had</u> already <u>gone</u>
    (past)   (past perfect)

In this example we are talking about an event that happened in the past (**Dave arrived**), and *when* that happened, something else was *already* in the past (**Jenny had gone**).

We often use the past perfect when reporting what people have said – see next Language point.

Exercise 1

These people have all been very busy this afternoon. Use the information to make sentences saying what each of them had done by three o'clock. The first one has been done for you.

1 Candace (fall asleep)
   By three o'clock **Candace had fallen asleep**

2 Fiona (do the shopping)
   By three o'clock _____

3 James (write six letters)
   By three o'clock _____

4 Simon (mend the video)
   By three o'clock _____

5 Liz (pay all the bills)
   By three o'clock _____

6 Justine (finish her book)
   By three o'clock _____

7 Adam (do his homework)
   By three o'clock _____

8 Liam (make some rolls)
   By three o'clock _____

9 Ann (clean four cars)
   By three o'clock _____

10 Brenda (order the pizzas)
   By three o'clock _____

Exercise 2

Rewrite these sentences in the past perfect tense. The first one has been done for you.

1 Terry fell off the ladder.   **Terry had fallen off the ladder.**
2 James is going out.
3 They were watching the film.
4 He's feeding the cat.
5 Will Su buy the food?
6 I'm writing the letter.
7 The bus is leaving early.
8 I wasn't working in the office.
9 Did Henry see the doctor?
10 Are you phoning them?

Language point 86 – reported speech

When we *report* what someone said, we can either *quote* their actual words (DIRECT SPEECH):

Kath said: 'I'm not coming'

or we can incorporate the words into one sentence:

Kath said (that) she wasn't coming

This second option is called REPORTED SPEECH (or INDIRECT SPEECH).

The most common verbs to introduce reported speech are **said** sɛd and **told** /təʊld/ – and when we use these, we *change* the TENSE of the verb in the words that we're reporting:

Actual words		Reported speech
present	→	past simple
present perfect	→	past perfect
past simple	→	past perfect
future	→	conditional

Here are some examples of each of these:

Actual words	Reported speech
'We <u>live</u> in Heathfield'	They said (that) they <u>lived</u> in Heathfield
'I'<u>ve sold</u> my house'	He said (that) he'<u>d sold</u> his house
'I <u>went</u> abroad last year'	She told me (that) she'<u>d gone</u> abroad last year
'We'<u>ll phone</u> later'	They said (that) they'<u>d phone</u> later
'We <u>can</u> call a taxi'	They said (that) they <u>could</u> call a taxi

Notice that we can use **that** after **said/told** to introduce the reported speech, but we can *also*, in colloquial English, leave it out. It is more usual to leave it out.

In Dialogues 1 and 2 there are a lot of examples of reported speech – let's convert some of them back to the *actual words*:

Reported speech		Actual words
She said she'd bought ...	→	'I've bought ...'
I said I didn't know	→	'I don't know'
... that you'd phone back	→	'He'll phone back'
He said he'd be ...	→	'I'll be ...'
He said he'd broken his leg	→	'I've broken my leg'
Fred told me he wasn't coming	→	'I'm not coming'

Notice that **told** *has* to be followed by a NOUN or a PRONOUN, but **said** *mustn't* be:

      He told me he was ill
not '<s>He told he was ill</s>'

      He said he was ill
not '<s>He said me he was ill</s>'

And don't forget that you can use *other* words to introduce reported speech as well:

asked
thought
answered
replied

Exercise 3

Rewrite these sentences as reported speech – the first one has been done for you.

1	'My name is Lisa.'	She said **her name was Lisa** .
2	'I'm twenty-four years old.'	She said _____ .
3	'I live in Brighton.'	She said _____ .
4	'I've got two sisters.'	She said _____ .
5	'I'll be coming to the party.'	She said _____ .
6	'I've written a poem.'	She said _____ .
7	'I've just joined a yoga class.'	She said _____ .
8	'My favourite food is curry.'	She said _____ .
9	'I hope to see you at the party later.'	She said _____ .
10	'I'll take a taxi home.'	She said _____ .

Exercise 4

Beatrice has changed her mind about everything she told Andy. Complete Andy's replies, as in the first example.

1. BEATRICE: I'm going to the disco tonight.
   ANDY: But you said **you weren't**!
2. BEATRICE: The food in this restaurant is awful.
   ANDY: But you said _____ wonderful!
3. BEATRICE: My brother'll lend me the money for the car.
   ANDY: But you said _____ !
4. BEATRICE: We can't go to Sicily this year.
   ANDY: But you said _____ !
5. BEATRICE: Dave and Rhoda aren't coming tonight.
   ANDY: But you said _____ !

6 BEATRICE: Anna doesn't speak English.
   ANDY: But you said _____ !
7 BEATRICE: I haven't got any money at the moment.
   ANDY: But you said _____!
8 BEATRICE: It'll rain all day tomorrow.
   ANDY: But you said _____!
9 BEATRICE: We can take a taxi home later.
   ANDY: But you said _____!
10 BEATRICE: Paul's applying for that new job.
   ANDY: But you said _____!

Exercise 5

Read these sentences in reported speech and write down what was actually said – the first one is done for you.

1 The doctor told Dave he'd have to stay in bed.
   'You'll have to stay in bed.'

2 Gerry said it was too late.
   _____

3 Jenny said it would rain later.
   _____

4 Pete told Simon he could come along.
   _____

5 Henry said he'd broken his arm.
   _____

6 Julie said the box was too heavy for her to lift.
   _____

7 Keith told Brenda he wouldn't help her.
   _____

8 Nigel said he could understand why I was angry.
   _____

9 I told them I couldn't help them.
   _____

10 Shamira said her computer had broken down.
   _____

Language point 87 – 'that's why/who/what . . .'

In Dialogue 2 Paul says about Fred:

I thought he didn't like heights

and then Mike says:

Maybe <u>that's why</u> he fell off

We use **that's** + WH-WORD to refer *back* to something just mentioned. Mike means:

Maybe [the fact that Fred doesn't like heights] is why he fell off

We replace the idea in the square brackets with **that** to avoid repeating it.

> ⚠️ **Be careful!** We have seen many examples in recent Language points of the word **that** being *left out* – but when we use **that's** with a WH-WORD in this way, we *can't* leave it out!

Here are some more examples:

**I saw Stuart <u>in Birmingham</u> last week
– Maybe <u>that's where</u> he's living now**

**The waiter's brought you <u>a chicken biryani</u>!
– Of course he has – <u>that's what</u> I ordered!**

**Why have you bought <u>forty</u> bottles of beer?
– Because <u>that's how many</u> we need for the party tonight!**

I always have a hot bath <u>in the evening</u> because <u>that's when</u> I need to relax

Exercise 6

Use **that's** + WH-WORD to complete the sentences, as above.

1. I've asked James to do it for me because _____ I trust.
2. I know Brighton very well because _____ I live.
3. Don't call after ten because _____ the kids go to bed.
4. Tom always does the cooking because _____ he likes doing best.
5. Adam's a keen swordsman because _____ he relaxes.
6. I hope this room holds thirty people, because _____ I've invited.
7. Lightning struck our house last night, and _____ we haven't got a roof.
8. I know Liam likes the music shop, because _____ he spends all his money.

Dialogue 3

Stuart is looking for Terry – he asks Helen where he is.

STUART: Where's Terry? I haven't seen him since this morning.
HELEN: I don't know. Who cares, anyway? His coat's not on his chair – he must have gone home.

[*Stuart looks out of the window*]

STUART: He can't have left work – his car's still in the car park. I wonder where he is.
HELEN: I suppose he may have gone to a meeting.
STUART: He didn't tell me he was going to a meeting ... [*Stuart turns to Vicki*] ... Vicki, did Terry say he had a meeting this afternoon?
VICKI: Not to me, he didn't. I don't care, anyway.

[*Terry walks in*]

STUART: Terry! There you are!
TERRY: What's up?
STUART: We were just wondering where you'd got to.
HELEN: You mean *you* were just wondering where he'd got to, Stuart. The rest of us couldn't care less.
TERRY: Well, you needn't have worried – I'm back.
VICKI: Hooray.

> **Idioms**
>
> - **I don't care** means 'It's unimportant to me' or 'It doesn't matter to me'
> - **What's up?** means 'What's the problem?' or 'What's the matter?'
> - **I couldn't care less** means 'I don't care at all' or 'It's completely unimportant to me'
> - **where he'd got to** means 'where he'd gone'

Language point 88 – 'may have', 'needn't have'

In Language point 73 we met **can't have** with the PAST PARTICIPLE, and in Dialogue 3 in this unit Stuart uses it when he says about Terry:

> **He can't have left work**
= It isn't possible that he's left work.

Go back and review Language point 73 now if you need to.

Then Helen uses **may have** + past participle:

> **He may have gone to a meeting**
= It's possible that he's gone to a meeting

So:

> | + | **may have** + past participle | (possible) |
> | — | **can't have** + past participle | (not possible) |

Pronunciation

may have /ˈmɛijəv/ **can't have** /ˈkɑːntəv/

Here are some more examples, in + and – pairs:

> \+ **Dave may have phoned earlier**
> – **Dave can't have phoned earlier**

+ **You may have misunderstood me**
− **You can't have misunderstood me**
+ **We may have missed the bus**
− **We can't have missed the bus**

Remember (from Language point 73) that we *don't* use **can** for *possibility* in English (even though we *do* use **can't** for *impossibility*!):

> **We may have missed the bus**
> *not* 'We can have missed the bus'

At the end of the Dialogue, Terry uses another expression: **needn't have** /ˈniːdntəv/ with the past participle:

> **You needn't have worried**
> = 'It <u>wasn't necessary</u> for you to worry'

More examples:

> **She needn't have spoken to you like that**
> **You needn't have come into work so early**
> **Your sister needn't have felt embarrassed**

Exercise 7

Decide between **may have**, **can't have** and **needn't have** to complete the sentences.

1 We _____ brought the umbrella – it's not going to rain.
2 Brenda's very late – the bad weather _____ delayed her.
3 You _____ got up early this morning – it's the weekend!
4 They _____ gone out – the lights are on in the house.
5 I think we _____ paid too much for our TV – they're cheaper here.
6 James looks awfully ill – I think he _____ caught a cold.
7 He _____ caught a cold – he's only just come back from Barbados!
8 Sylvia hasn't phoned – she _____ got home yet.

Language point 89 – 'wonder' and 'suppose'

When Stuart says in Dialogue 3:

> **I wonder where she is**

he means that he is thinking about the question but doesn't know the answer. **I wonder** /ˈwʌndəʳ/ is used with WH-WORDS (and **if** as well) – we *don't* normally use it with any of the other pronouns, or with nouns. Here are some more examples:

> **I wonder what the time is**
> **I wonder who that woman is**
>
> **I wonder when they'll arrive**
> **I wonder how much they're going to pay us**

Particularly when we use it with **if**, **I wonder** invites the other person to offer an opinion:

> **I wonder if Kath and Shamira will be at the party.**
> **– I don't know, perhaps they will.**
>
> **I wonder if Adrian's missed the train.**
> **– Could be, he's very late.**

We *can* use **wonder** with the other pronouns, and with nouns, in the PAST SIMPLE and PAST CONTINUOUS:

> **We were wondering where you'd got to**
= 'We didn't know where you were (and we were thinking about it)'
> **James wondered what to do**
= 'James wasn't sure what to do'

Suppose /səˈpəʊz/ is another verb that we normally use only with **I** – when Helen says:

> **I suppose he may have gone to a meeting**

she means 'I think it's possible that he's gone to a meeting'.

Or it *can* mean something stronger:

> **I suppose you've come to collect the money**
> = 'I assume that you've come to collect the money'

I suppose is *not* used in other tenses very often.

Exercise 8

Decide between the verbs in brackets to complete each sentence.

1. I (suppose/wonder) where James is.
2. We were (supposing/wondering) where to go for coffee.
3. I (suppose/wonder) you're going to the pub, are you?
4. I (suppose/wonder) whose book this is.
5. I (suppose/wonder) Andy may have left already.
6. Kath was (supposing/wondering) what to do tomorrow.
7. I (suppose/wonder) if Gerry could come along as well.
8. I (suppose/wonder) Gerry could come along as well.

Dialogue 4

Abigail is reading a dramatic news item from the local paper to Gary.

ABIGAIL: Listen to this, Gary:
'Two men were arrested last night after a car was stolen in the town centre. Police said that the car, a blue Audi, was driven through the town at high speed, but was stopped by a roadblock just outside the supermarket. The two men have been named as Bert Shift and Ernie Dodge. They will be charged tomorrow with theft and dangerous driving, and are expected to appear in court on Monday. Their families have been informed, and a press conference will be held at ten o'clock tomorrow.

GARY: Wow!

Language point 90 – passive

The PASSIVE is *not* used much in colloquial English, but you will *hear* it quite often on the TV and radio news, and *see* it in newspapers and books.

Look at these two sentences:

ACTIVE	**The dog <u>bit</u> the postman**
PASSIVE	**The postman <u>was bitten</u> by the dog**

They *mean* the same thing. The OBJECT of the ACTIVE sentence (**the postman**) becomes the SUBJECT of the PASSIVE sentence, and the verb is changed. We use **by** to show who or what *did* the action in a passive sentence.

The passive is formed of two parts:

be + PAST PARTICIPLE

So, if you can use **be** in all tenses, and you're happy with the past participle (go back and look at Language point 53 again if you're not), then you can easily use the passive. Here are some examples:

PRESENT SIMPLE	**Dinner <u>is served</u> at eight o'clock**
PRESENT CONTINUOUS	**The game <u>is being played</u> under floodlights**
FUTURE	**A prize <u>will be awarded</u>**
PAST SIMPLE	**This book <u>was written</u> in 1948**
PAST CONTINUOUS	**Ice creams <u>were being sold</u> on the seafront**
PRESENT PERFECT	**Your car <u>has been stolen</u>**
PAST PERFECT	**The money <u>had been hidden</u> in the garden**

To make passive statements into questions, we simply put the *first verb* at the start of the sentence, and leave everything else unchanged:

<u>Was</u> this book <u>written</u> in 1948?
<u>Has</u> your car <u>been stolen</u>?

<u>Were</u> ice creams <u>being sold</u> on the seafront?
<u>Is</u> dinner <u>served</u> at eight o'clock?

And negatives simply add **not/n't** to the *first verb*:

+	−
is served	isn't served
is being played	isn't being played
had been hidden	hadn't been hidden
will be awarded	won't be awarded
	(remember **will not** → **won't**)

You *won't* need to use the passive much when speaking in normal situations, but it's important to know about it and recognise it when you come across it.

Exercise 9

Rewrite these active sentences as passives. The first one is done for you.

1. The cat chases the mouse.
   The mouse is chased by the cat.
2. The employers pay the workers. _____ .
3. Does Sarah feed the chickens? _____ ?
4. The postman delivered the letters. _____ .
5. James has broken this chair. _____ .
6. The organisers will cancel the concert. _____ .
7. Su made the tea. _____ .
8. Rich people drive big cars. _____ .
9. Henry'd do the gardening. _____ .
10. Authors write books. _____ .

Exercise 10

Complete these sentences using the future or past passive – the first one has been done for you.

1. Send the letters. **They'll be sent** tomorrow.
2. Pay the hotel bill. _____ yesterday.
3. Book the holiday. _____ last week.
4. Do the shopping. _____ tomorrow.
5. Take the rubbish out. _____ yesterday.
6. Throw the old papers out. _____ yesterday.
7. Recycle the milk bottles. _____ yesterday.
8. Buy the Christmas tree. _____ tomorrow.
9. Fill the car up. _____ tomorrow.
10. Eat the food! _____ yesterday.

Exercise 11

See if you can find all the passives in the newspaper articles below. The first is from a tabloid and the second is from a broadsheet. Which one has more?

TRAPPED NINE DAYS

By ANTHONY HARWOOD
US Editor in Mexico

DIVERS who have flown out from the UK will today try to rescue six British cavers trapped for nine days in a flooded Mexican cavern.

The men, from a military caving team, only expected to spend 36 hours underground during an adventure training mission.

But they were trapped 120ft down when torrential rain blocked their way out.

Jose Ignacio Macias, of the Civil Protection Agency, said: "This is a dangerous situation.

"People are now on their way to rescue them. It has rained and the water level has risen a lot."

The men had prepared a camp in an area that never floods in case of such an emergency and are holed up there. They stocked it with food, sleeping bags, medical supplies and a radio and laid a land telephone cable behind them as they explored the caves.

They are waiting for the waters to subside at the eight mile Alpazat complex in Cuetzalan, 110 miles north east of Mexico City. But it is still raining and the Royal Navy divers will today decide what to do.

Divers sent to rescue Britons trapped in flooded Mexican cave system

Owen Bowcott

Two experienced cave divers have been flown to Mexico by the Ministry of Defence to evacuate six Britons trapped deep in a labyrinth of partly flooded caves.

The underground team, made up of four servicemen, a retired army officer and a civilian scientist, was forced to retreat into the Alpazat cave system six days ago when flood water began rising rapidly.

Another six members of the expedition have remained on the surface near Cuetzalan, north-east of Mexico City. They are in contact with their colleagues who originally had 10 days' supply of food, as well as lighting and sleeping bags.

None of the men below the surface is injured and all were yesterday reported by the MoD to be in a state of "high morale but incredibly bored". They were said to have finished the two novels left in the emergency camp, which had been prepared in case of flooding. They have declined local offers of rescue, preferring to await the arrival of the British divers.

© *Guardian*

Life and living – reading

With this unit we've come to the end of the book – and you'll want to build on what you've learnt and practised. One good way to independently and effectively improve your English (and especially to **expand** your **vocabulary**) is to read – and there's plenty to read wherever you look.

If you go to a **newsagent's** (like the one Damian went to in Unit 6) you'll find a wide **range** of newspapers (or **papers**, as we often call them). **Daily** papers come in two **formats**: some, such as *The Times*, the *Guardian* and the *Daily Telegraph*, are broadsheets – large-format papers with quite serious **style** and **content**, and with very wide and deep **coverage** of both home news and international news. If you want to read *everything* in a broadsheet, you'll need quite a bit of time. Other papers, such as the *Mirror*, the *Daily Mail* and the *Express*, are tabloids – smaller-format papers with less serious, more popular style and language, and covering news in rather less depth. They have more pictures as well, and they sell more than the broadsheets. These days one or two of the broadsheets are also available as tabloids – same content, but smaller pages and more of them. You can also buy Sunday papers, such as the *Observer*, *The Sunday Times*, the *Independent on Sunday* and the *Sunday Telegraph*. They are bigger than the dailies, and they come in several **sections**, for example Review, Travel, Finance, Food and Sport. If you're a busy person with lots to do **apart from** reading, a Sunday paper can **last** you most of the week!

Or why not visit a bookshop and buy a book to read? Every large town has a **fair-sized** bookshop, with thousands of titles arranged by **category** or **genre**. **Fiction** is always a very large section, and it's a good place for learners of English to start. You'll find the fiction books grouped under different types, for example modern fiction (general modern novels), historical fiction (stories set in the past), science fiction (stories set in the future) and horror (ghosts, blood and axe-murderers) – pick something you like the look of and get reading!

Glossary

expand – widen
vocabulary – the words of a language
newsagent's – shop that sells newspapers

range – choice, selection
daily – appearing every day
style – general appearance and effect
content – what something contains; the articles and reports that are in a paper
coverage – treatment of the news
section – part
apart from – except; in addition to
last – be enough (for someone for a period of time)
fair-sized – medium to large
category – type
genre – type of writing
fiction – writing that isn't true; stories that have been invented by the writer

Key to exercises

Unit 1

Exercise 1

2 I'm 3 Sue's 4 Terry's 5 They're 6 Chris is 7 We're 8 Stuart's
9 My brother's 10 CD's

Exercise 2

2 isn't he? 3 isn't she? 4 aren't they? 5 isn't she? 6 isn't it? 7 aren't we?
8 isn't it? 9 aren't you? 10 isn't she?

Exercise 3

2 Is Dave off work today? 3 Is it cold outside? 4 Are we in the right place? 5 Is everyone ready? 6 Are you tired? 7 Are they in the garden?
8 Are Morgan and Eddie here? 9 Is Oliver outside? 10 Is Jenny inside?

Exercise 4

2 her 3 him 4 them 5 her 6 them

Exercise 5

1 me your 2 you his 3 I their 4 you her 5 my you 6 I me

Exercise 6

1 a 2 a 3 a 4 a 5 an 6 a 7 an 8 an 9 a 10 an

Exercise 7

2 Gerry 3 doctor 4 teacher 5 scientist 6 Nigel 7 Brian 8 Allison
9 policeman 10 journalist

Exercise 8

1 the 2 the 3 the the 4 a the 5 a the 6 a 7 the 8 a 9 the 10 the a

Unit 2

Exercise 1

2 We aren't We're not 3 I'm not (only one possible) 4 They aren't They're not 5 You aren't You're not 6 Suzie isn't Suzie's not 7 It isn't It's not 8 She isn't She's not

Exercise 2

2 Do you drink tea? 3 Does that bus go to the station? 4 Does she speak Spanish? 5 Do Pete and Sally speak Italian? 6 Where do you teach? 7 Where does this bus go? 8 Does Su live nearby? 9 When do Mick and Sandra leave? 10 When does the post arrive?

Exercise 3

2 Oliver doesn't drink coffee 3 James doesn't speak Russian 4 Jenny plays the piano 5 Stephen doesn't play the piano 6 Jenny doesn't wear glasses 7 James drinks coffee 8 Oliver wears glasses

Exercise 4

1 who 2 what 3 where 4 when 5 why 6 which 7 where 8 whose 9 what 10 what

Exercise 5

2 a person 3 a place 4 a time 5 a reason 6 an owner 7 a choice 8 a way/method

Exercise 6

1 correct 2 yours 3 hers 4 yours mine 5 my 6 mine

Exercise 7

2 that kind mother of his 3 some close friends of ours 4 a great idea of mine 5 those friends of hers 6 this stupid idea of theirs

Exercise 8

Henry: mineral water, cake; Dave: cup of tea; Su: mineral water, salad roll; Kath: cheese roll, cappuccino

Unit 3

Exercise 1

2 h 3 f 4 g 5 b 6 a 7 d 8 i 9 c 10 e

Exercise 2

1 Don't make noise here! 2 Please wait here a minute 3 Don't be rude to customers! 4 correct 5 Please don't throw litter 6 Open the door, could you? 7 Could you close the door, please? 8 Don't wait for me

Exercise 3

2 of 3 's 4 of 5 of 6 's 7 of 8 of 9 's 10 's

Exercise 4

1 removing 2 writing 3 reading 4 hurrying 5 fitting 6 opening 7 flying 8 chasing 9 paying 10 asking

Exercise 5

1 'm eating 2 reads 3 grow 4 goes 5 's reading 6 speaks

Exercise 6

2 Are they waiting for us? 3 Is Dave studying Law? 4 Are the children having breakfast? 5 Are Jack and Jill washing the car? 6 Is the weather improving? 7 Is this music disturbing them? 8 Am I driving too fast?

Exercise 7

2 I don't understand you 3 Is she asking a question? 4 Do these shoes belong to Suzie? 5 Do you understand me? 6 I'm not reading the paper 7 Gerry's reading the paper 8 We're listening

Unit 4

Exercise 1

1 c 2 uc 3 c 4 c 5 uc 6 c 7 uc 8 c 9 uc 10 c 11 uc 12 c 13 c 14 c 15 uc 16 c 17 c 18 c 19 c 20 c

Exercise 2

1 some 2 some 3 a 4 some 5 a 6 some 7 a 8 a 9 a 10 some 11 some 12 a 13 a 14 some 15 an 16 a 17 some 18 some 19 some 20 a

Exercise 3

1 did 2 do 3 do 4 did 5 do 6 did 7 did 8 do

Exercise 4

2 does 3 don't 4 didn't 5 don't 6 did 7 doesn't 8 do

Exercise 5

3 He's got time 4 I've got enough time 5 They haven't got enough money 6 Su hasn't got a car 7 Have we got the tickets? 8 Fiona's got them

Exercise 6

1 x 2 p 3 p 4 x 5 p 6 x 7 x 8 x 9 x 10 p

Exercise 7

2 I don't think my watch is working properly 3 I don't think the children are hungry 4 I don't think that's important 5 I don't think this coffee's very nice 6 I don't think we're on the right bus 7 I don't think this bus goes to the airport 8 I don't think you understand 9 I don't think Henry reads books 10 I don't think the students are listening

Exercise 8

1 can I have another one? 2 try the others 3 like another cup 4 another glass 5 prefer the other one 6 correct 7 correct 8 try the other ones 9 The other CD 10 The other car

Unit 5

Exercise 1

2 watch 3 buy 4 taking 5 catch 6 meeting 7 playing 8 phone 9 stay 10 going

Exercise 2

2 about good 3 how about no let's 4 why we OK/all right 5 I then 6 shall not 7 how about rather 8 don't we idea 9 how want 10 shall we all right

Exercise 3

2 Shall we go swimming? 3 Let's organise a party 4 Why don't we practise our English? 5 Shall we wash the car? 6 Why don't we call in on Sam and Fred? 7 How about writing some postcards home? 8 Shall we cook an Indian meal? 9 Let's invite James and Fiona to tea 10 Why don't we help with the washing-up?

Exercise 4

2 Do you like Indian food? 3 Do you like apples? 4 Would you like a cheese sandwich? 5 Would you like some soup? 6 Do you like milk in your coffee? 7 Would you like another cup of tea? 8 Would you like some more soup? 9 Do you like tea? 10 Would you like some pizza, Dave?

Exercise 5

2 Would you like some more coffee? 3 Would you like to visit the museum today? 4 Would you like to go swimming this afternoon? 5 Would you like another cake? 6 Would you like to see the menu?

Exercise 6

2 Does James like ice cream? 3 My parents don't like fish 4 Sarah likes apples 5 Does Fiona like vegetables? 6 They like fish and chips 7 Fred and Kim don't like sport 8 Does Pete like carrots?

Exercise 7

1 correct 2 Would you like some more coffee? 3 correct 4 Do you like English food? 5 James doesn't like hot weather 6 Do you like ice cream? 7 correct 8 Does your sister like oranges? 9 Would you like an orange? 10 Does Jerry like milk in his tea?

Exercise 8

2 playing 3 does sunbathing 4 would stay 5 doing 6 likes helping 7 like play 8 don't working 9 do 10 would listen

Exercise 9

positive: Yes I love it, Yes I quite like it // neutral: It's OK I suppose, I'm not bothered // negative the rest

Exercise 10

2 e 3 a 4 f 5 c 6 b

Exercise 11

2 this 3 those 4 these 5 this 6 this that 7 this 8 those 9 these 10 this that

Exercise 12

1 T 2 F 3 F 4 F 5 F 6 T

Unit 6

Exercise 1

1 c 2 f 3 a 4 b 5 h 6 d 7 e 8 g

Exercise 2

2 He's giving her 3 He's buying it 4 They use it 5 He keeps them 6 He's buying them 7 She's picking them up 8 She's giving him

Exercise 3

1 Let's wait until the rain stops 2 Phone us as soon as you get back 3 Don't forget to ring us when you arrive 4 Let's hide the presents before the children see them 5 Could you shut the door when you leave? 6 Let's buy some souvenirs before we go home

Exercise 4

2 when 3 when 4 as soon as 5 when 6 till 7 when 8 until

Exercise 5

2 Why don't you pay the bill? 3 Why don't we go to the cinema? 4 Why don't I help you with the cooking? 5 Why don't we watch TV? 6 Why don't I do the washing-up? 7 Why don't you switch channels? 8 Why don't we ask some friends round for coffee?

Exercise 6

2 next 3 next 4 this 5 all 6 today 7 tomorrow 8 on

Exercise 7

1 for 2 with 3 in 4 of 5 with 6 at 7 to 8 with 9 about 10 on

Exercise 8

2 h 3 e 4 f 5 a 6 b 7 c 8 g

Unit 7

Exercise 1

2 it's going to rain 3 I'm going to do the shopping 4 she's going to eat 5 she's going to go 6 she's going to ride 7 he's going to phone 8 they're going to wash 9 I'm going to plant 10 he's going to swim

Exercise 2

2 Are going to am 3 Is going to is 4 Are going to they aren't 5 Is going to he isn't 6 Are going to they are 7 Is going to he is 8 Are going to aren't

Exercise 3

2 It's difficult to learn Chinese 3 It's important to be friendly to your neighbours 4 It's easy to ask for things in English 5 It's stupid to set fire to your nose 6 It's very hard for English people to learn Vietnamese 7 It's nice to eat biscuits in front of the TV 8 It's very dangerous to jump off high buildings 9 It's fun to watch French films 10 It's exhausting to read long books

Exercise 4

2 Will Amanda stay here? 3 They won't wait for us 4 Is Dave going to be here tomorrow? 5 We're going to show you the sights 6 The weather will get better 7 James isn't going to forget, is he? 8 I'm not going to do my homework yet 9 Suzie won't be there 10 Will Fred read that book?

Exercise 5

1 Are you going 2 going to do the 3 Is Kath 4 correct 5 trains are going to be 6 Is he 7 Are we 8 correct 9 I'm going 10 Is Henry

Exercise 6

2 Henry's going to do it up 3 Could you turn it off? 4 I need to look them up 5 Could you write it down? 6 Will you fill them in? 7 We're going to send them back 8 They're going to knock it down 9 Tom's trying to start it up 10 Switch them off, please

Exercise 7

1 want 2 is going 3 doesn't like 4 Does this book belong 5 contains 6 isn't reading 7 Do you know 8 's seeing 9 'm not expecting 10 Do you see

Exercise 8

1 bring 2 take 3 bring 4 bringing 5 bring 6 bringing 7 take 8 take 9 take 10 take

Exercise 9

Liam: 1 October; Sally: 10 May; Adam: 7 December; Edward: 22 September; Monica: 8 February; Keith: 2 November; Anthea: 17 June; Greg: 10 November; Susan: 17 July; Carl: 20 March

Unit 8

Exercise 1

2 Are they able to speak English? 3 Dave can't come 4 Are you able to see the screen? 5 Can they walk? 6 Suzie can't make the appointment 7 I'm not able to advise you on this 8 Are Julie and Simon able to come tonight?

Exercise 2

2 You'd better not drop it 3 I'd better clean it 4 We'd better wait for him 5 I'd better turn the light on 6 I'd better phone him

Exercise 3

2 What if the shops are shut? 3 What if the car breaks down? 4 What if the neighbours complain? 5 What if the doorman doesn't let us in? 6 What if the waiter doesn't understand us? 7 What if the neighbours don't like the colour? 8 What if he doesn't answer?

Exercise 4

1 'm thinking 2 Are we having 3 look 4 thinks 5 're looking 6 don't see 7 has 8 isn't seeing

Exercise 5

2 to order 3 to come 4 to help 5 having 6 to lock 7 doing 8 swimming 9 to offend 10 smoking 11 seeing 12 to apply 13 paying 14 learning 15 to know 16 cooking 17 to be 18 to fly 19 to see 20 seeing

Exercise 6

1 what other food 2 the other people will 3 correct 4 correct 5 where else would 6 have another cream 7 the other one's 8 correct 9 correct 10 anything else

Exercise 7

1 disappointed 2 interested 3 excited 4 annoying 5 exciting 6 boring 7 annoyed 8 bored 9 relaxing 10 surprised

Exercise 8

1 disappointed 2 boring 3 disappointing 4 interesting 5 bored 6 annoying 7 surprising 8 interested 9 surprised 10 annoyed

Unit 9

Exercise 1

2 Justine's painted the door 3 Andy and Bob have closed the shop
4 We haven't played football today 5 We've organised a party for her
6 Have you watched the film? 7 Has Julie opened the window?
8 Dave hasn't waited for us

Exercise 2

2 Simon's not using the computer 3 Su and Kath are refusing to come
4 Are you looking for the paper? 5 Is Rosemary leaving? 6 Are the
children coming in? 7 Is anyone using this cup? 8 I'm not buying any food
9 Ann's selling her house 10 Is Jenny phoning the office?

Exercise 3

2 fell 3 stole 4 phoned answered 5 called 6 left 7 spoke 8 threw 9 watched
10 went

Exercise 4

2 They didn't help him 3 She opened the window 4 Terry washed the car
5 Did Henry walk to college today? 6 Suzie didn't clean her teeth
7 Did the others arrive late? 8 Did Sandra play the piano?

Exercise 5

1 's fallen 2 went 3 Have you seen 4 have you finished 5 phoned 6 Did you
see 7 've invited 8 's my passport gone 9 have they turned 10 Did you
speak

Exercise 6

2 I had breakfast today 3 Were you late for the meeting? 4 James wasn't
ready 5 They didn't have any money 6 The children were happy 7 Fiona
was in town today 8 My brother didn't have the money

Exercise 7

2 Were you working? 3 We weren't watching the film 4 Dave wasn't
answering his phone today 5 Su was looking after the children 6 Were you
speaking to the teacher? 7 The bus was coming round the corner 8 Were
you listening to your new CD? 9 The kids were playing in the garden
10 Henry wasn't doing his work

Exercise 8

2 was taking landed 3 broke was playing 4 fell was standing 5 saw was queuing 6 was doing dropped 7 cut was cutting 8 was looking saw

Exercise 9

1 a 2 b 3 b 4 b 5 b 6 a

Exercise 10

1 We've just seen 2 I'm still working 3 has never worked 4 homework yet 5 have already passed 6 I still want 7 you ever go 8 you ever been 9 university yet 10 I've already explained

Unit 10

Exercise 1

1 taller 2 more comfortable 3 more valuable 4 heavier 5 faster 6 more interesting 7 bigger 8 more expensive 9 more intelligent 10 sharper

Exercise 2

2 cheaper 3 more difficult *or* harder 4 sweeter 5 more interesting 6 earlier 7 smaller 8 quieter 9 tidier 10 wider

Exercise 3

3 Jack speaks Swedish, and Jill does as well 4 Jack doesn't speak German, but Jill does 5 Jack doesn't speak Arabic, and Jill doesn't either 6 Jack speaks Welsh, and Jill does as well 7 Jack doesn't speak Klingon, and Jill doesn't either 8 Jack speaks French, and Jill does as well 9 Jack doesn't speak Hindi, but Jill does 10 Jack speaks Spanish, but Jill doesn't

Exercise 4

Gorgeous Grind – Bean Bonanza – Cafetière Combo – Froth Fantasy – Coffee Crikey – Steam Surprise – Radical Roast – Percolator II

Exercise 5

2 use the long one 3 The ripe ones 4 The big red one 5 wear the black ones 6 A large one 7 Plastic ones 8 A hot one

Exercise 6

1 one 2 one 3 ones 4 ones 5 one 6 one 7 one 8 one

Exercise 7

2 She'd be better off coming tomorrow 3 She'd be better off doing it with Suzie 4 They'd be better off drinking mineral water 5 We'd be better off writing them a letter 6 She'd be better off sitting next to Gerry 7 She'd be better off eating out 8 We'd be better off watching TV 9 You'd be better off shutting the window 10 We'd be better off visiting them tomorrow

Exercise 8

2 Do you feel like seeing a film in town tonight? 3 Do you feel like flying to the South of France for the weekend? 4 Do you feel like inviting some friends round? 5 Do you feel like running the London Marathon this year? 6 Do you feel like lending me ten pounds? 7 Do you feel like ordering us a pizza? 8 Do you feel like hiring a rowing boat for the afternoon?

Unit 11

Exercise 1

2 It's just coming up to a quarter to four 3 It's twenty to ten 4 It's just coming up to midnight 5 It's ten past seven 6 It's just coming up to five to six 7 It's just gone four o'clock 8 It's twenty-five to three 9 It's just gone twenty-five past ten 10 It's half past three

Exercise 2

1 It's a quarter to nine 2 It's five o'clock 3 It's five past nine 4 It's a quarter past one 5 It's twenty past five 6 It's twenty-five to eleven

Exercise 3

2 Who are you writing to? 3 What is it looking at? 4 What is she worried about? 5 Who are you going with? 6 Who does he play for? 7 Who does she work for? 8 Where does he come from? 9 Who do they live next door to? 10 When have you got to be home by?

Exercise 4

1 since 2 for 3 for 4 for 5 since 6 since 7 since 8 for 9 since 10 for

Exercise 5

2 lived 3 's been learning 4 have you been working 5 haven't seen 6 Have you been 7 've been learning 8 have been

Exercise 6

1 last 2 on 3 at 4 of 5 at 6 at 7 an 8 in 9 out 10 in 11 in 12 to 13 in 14 in 15 of 16 nearly 17 to 18 in 19 for 20 at

Exercise 7

1 asleep 2 afraid 3 alive 4 alone 5 aware 6 awake 7 alike 8 ashamed

Exercise 8

1 when 2 when 3 before 4 when 5 before 6 when 7 when 8 before

Exercise 9

Samantha: 6.45 cinema; Su and Shamira: 7.00 vegan restaurant; Stuart: 7.15 Indian restaurant; Helen: 7.45 theatre; Gerry: 6.30 football match

Unit 12

Exercise 1

2 f 3 b 4 h 5 g 6 a 7 e 8 d

Exercise 2

2 Did we have to show our passports? 3 Have I got to sign the form? 4 The children have to pay 5 They had to pay by cheque 6 Did Greg have to do the work? 7 Keith and Carl have got to play a song 8 Do I have to have my picture taken? 9 Have we got to leave early? 10 Gerry had to work late

Exercise 3

2 James might be ill 3 You can't be right 4 You must be joking! 5 It might snow tonight 6 They must like Indian food 7 This can't be true 8 Terry might come later 9 The rain might stop soon 10 Pete can't think that

Exercise 4

1 You can't be serious! 2 I might phone Julie after dinner 3 It must be very hot in Australia in the summer 4 We've got to do the shopping 5 Did Adrian get to work late yesterday? 6 Did you have to light the fire yourself? 7 correct 8 I've got to get some money from the bank

Exercise 5

2 must have broken 3 can't have connected 4 can't have rung 5 must have thrown 6 must have told 7 can't have done 8 must have closed 9 must have caught 10 can't have understood

Exercise 6

2 It's nice to eat chocolate 3 Having injections is unpleasant 4 Getting phone bills is annoying 5 It's fun to swim under water 6 Getting birthday presents is nice 7 Speaking colloquial English is easy 8 It's polite to write thank you letters 9 It's relaxing to paint pictures 10 It isn't safe to drink the water here

Exercise 7

2 what 3 what 4 who 5 how 6 where 7 how 8 where 9 who 10 what

Exercise 8

2 how to get 3 how to work 4 where to go 5 how to fill in 6 when to be 7 where to plant 8 where to put

Unit 13

Exercise 1

1 f – I'm looking for a man who can mend cars 2 g – I need a pencil that has a sharp point 3 h – I can see a bridge that crosses the river 4 b – This is the road that leads to the town centre 5 a – This is the door that leads to the garden 6 d – I'm looking for a shop that sells cheap chocolate 7 c – Those are the children who broke the window 8 e – That's the pilot who flew us home

Exercise 2

2 The restaurant that did the best food won a prize 3 The students who are learning Russian are very clever 4 The woman who lost her passport phoned the police 5 The train that was late was very full 6 The newsreader who sneezed on camera lost her job 7 The artist who painted the Queen refused to take any money 8 The tree that fell on our house is big 9 The fish that live in the garden pond are pretty 10 The ship that took us to the Caribbean was enormous

Exercise 3

1 remove 2 remove 3 keep 4 keep 5 remove 6 remove 7 remove 8 remove 9 keep 10 keep

Exercise 4

2 that I saw rather boring 3 who was in hospital got better now 4 that we were listening to very loud 5 that Dave bought too short for him 6 that I was sitting on very uncomfortable 7 that we threw away rather smelly 8 that Henry cooked really delicious

Exercise 5

2 This is the office Justine works in 3 That's the chair I was sitting in 4 This is the music we've been listening to all morning 5 This is the piece of paper I wrote the message on 6 This is the town we lived in for five years 7 This is the town Andy comes from 8 These are the people I told you about 9 This is the shop I got my DVD-player from 10 These are the students I came with

Exercise 6

1 done 2 making 3 do 4 do 5 doing 6 do 7 made 8 do

Exercise 7

1 you done with 2 children made a lot 3 I've done 4 correct 5 to make a mistake 6 did 7 done 8 Let's do the rest

Exercise 8

1 often reads 2 You'll probably 3 correct 4 correct 5 Indian food a lot 6 weather often wet 7 Indian food at all 8 Every Saturday we go *or* football match every Saturday 9 correct 10 correct

Exercise 9

1 Is Henry often in the local library? *or* Is Henry in the local library often? 2 Is James always working in the internet café? 3 Have Tom's brother and his wife often visited France? *or* Have Tom's brother and his wife visited France often? 4 Do you usually go to the restaurant next door? 5 Does he often have to go abroad *or* Does he have to go abroad often? 6 Does George go to the pub every Friday evening?

Unit 14

Exercise 1

2 unreal 3 possible 4 unreal 5 possible 6 unreal 7 possible 8 unreal

Exercise 2

2 f 3 a 4 c 5 d 6 b

Exercise 3

2 is 'll leave 3 stand 'll get 4 breaks down 'll repair 5 don't see 'll phone 6 doesn't hurry 'll miss 7 'll be gets 8 won't work don't plug

Exercise 4

2 h 3 a 4 c 5 g 6 b 7 e 8 d

Exercise 5

1 when 2 when 3 if 4 if 5 if 6 if

Exercise 6

2 don't rewrite 3 What did your sister leave early for? 4 don't rewrite 5 What did the Romans invade Britain for? 6 don't rewrite 7 don't rewrite 8 don't rewrite 9 don't rewrite 10 What are you watching the ice hockey for?

Exercise 7

2 You'd be angry if they came home late 3 If you took more exercise, you'd feel healthier 4 Helen would pay the bill if she had any money 5 I'd phone the police if someone stole my car 6 I'd be surprised if she agreed to do that 7 If we left too late we'd miss the train 8 It'd be too dark if we waited till ten o'clock

Exercise 8

1 if I had enough 2 if we came tomorrow 3 if you explained the problem 4 What would you do 5 if she got the job 6 correct 7 would look better if you painted it 8 guests arrived late

Exercise 9

2 You won't pass your English exam if you don't work hard 3 You can't send an email unless you've got a computer 4 We'll go swimming this afternoon unless it rains 5 Start without me if I don't phone 6 I'm going unless he comes in the next ten minutes 7 You can't come in if you're not a member 8 You can't eat here unless you're wearing a tie

Exercise 10

2 g 3 h 4 a 5 b 6 d 7 f 8 c

Unit 15

Exercise 1

2 Fiona had done the shopping 3 James had written six letters 4 Simon had mended the video 5 Liz had paid all the bills 6 Justine had finished her book 7 Adam had done his homework 8 Liam had made some rolls 9 Ann had cleaned four cars 10 Brenda had ordered the pizzas

Exercise 2

2 James had gone out 3 They'd watched the film 4 He'd fed the cat 5 Had Su bought the food? 6 I'd written the letter 7 The bus had left early 8 I hadn't worked in the office 9 Had Henry seen the doctor? 10 Had you phoned them?

Exercise 3

2 she was twenty-four years old 3 she lived in Brighton 4 she'd got two sisters 5 she'd be coming to the party 6 she'd written a poem 7 she'd just joined a yoga class 8 her favourite food was curry 9 she hoped to see me at the party later 10 she'd take a taxi home

Exercise 4

2 it was 3 he wouldn't 4 we could 5 they were 6 she did 7 you had 8 it wouldn't 9 we couldn't 10 he wasn't

Exercise 5

2 'It's too late' 3 It'll rain later' 4 'You can come along' 5 'I've broken my arm' 6 'The box is too heavy for me to lift' 7 'I won't help you' 8 'I can understand why you're angry' 9 'I can't help you' 10 'My computer's broken down'

Exercise 6

1 that's who 2 that's where 3 that's when 4 that's what 5 that's how 6 that's how many 7 that's why 8 hat's where

Exercise 7

1 needn't have 2 may have 3 needn't have 4 can't have 5 may have 6 may have 7 can't have 8 can't have

Exercise 8

1 wonder 2 wondering 3 suppose 4 wonder 5 suppose 6 wondering 7 wonder 8 suppose

Exercise 9

2 The workers are paid by the employers 3 Are the chickens fed by Sarah? 4 Were the letters delivered by the postman? 5 This chair has been broken by James 6 The concert will be cancelled by the organisers 7 The tea was made by Su 8 Big cars are driven by rich people 9 The gardening would be done by Henry 10 Books are written by authors

Exercise 10

2 It was paid 3 It was booked 4 It'll be done 5 It was taken out 6 They were thrown out 7 They were recycled 8 It'll be bought 9 It'll be filled up 10 It was eaten

Reference grammar

Spelling rules

1. drop silent **-e** whe you add the endings **-ed**, **-ing**, **-er**, **-est**
2. after a short stressed single vowel, double **b g m n p r t** when you add the endings **-ed**, **-ing**, **-er**, **-est**
3. change **-y** to **-i** when you add **-ed**, **-es**, **-er**, **-est**, **-ly** *if the letter before the **y** is a consonant*
4. add **-e-** to words ending in **-s**, **-sh**, **-ch**, **-x**, **-z** before you add **-s**

NOUNS are COUNTABLE or UNCOUNTABLE; some uncountable nouns can have a secondary countable meaning.

Countable nouns can be singular or plural – they form their plural by adding **-s** or **-es** (spelling rule 4 above applies). A few nouns have irregular plurals, for example, **man/men**, **woman/women**, **child/children**, **foot/feet**, **tooth/teeth**, **goose/geese**, **sheep/sheep**, **aircraft/aircraft**.

The DEFINITE ARTICLE **the** can be used with both countable and uncountable nouns – it denotes a noun that is already known or has already been referred to.

The INDEFINITE ARTICLE **a** (**an** before vowel sounds) can only be used before singular countable nouns.

PERSONAL PRONOUNS (apart from **you**) have subject and object forms (nouns don't):

SUBJECT	**I**	**you**	**he**	**she**	**we**	**they**
OBJECT	**me**	**you**	**him**	**her**	**us**	**them**

ADJECTIVES come before the noun, or after the verb **be**, and do not change for singular/plural:

the red bus   **the red buses**
this bus is red   **these buses are red**

Adjectives *do* change to show degree:

this bus is bigger   **that bus is the biggest**

Spelling rules 1, 2 and 3 apply to the **-er** and **-est** endings.

Longer adjectives *don't* use the endings, and have **more** and **most** in front of them instead:

this coat is more expensive   **that coat is the most expensive**

A few adjectives have irregular degrees:

good	**better**	**best**
bad	**worse**	**worst**
far	**further**	**furthest**

VERBS – there are REGULAR VERBS and IRREGULAR VERBS. Regular verbs have a past simple *and* a past participle in **-ed**, irregular verbs have an unpredictable past simple, and sometimes a different past participle, also unpredictable. Regular verbs therefore have five forms, while irregular verbs may have five or six. The verb **be** has nine:

base-form	**ask**	**fight**	**speak**	**be**
to-form	**to ask**	**to fight**	**to speak**	**to be**
ing-form	**asking**	**fighting**	**speaking**	**being**
s-form	**asks**	**fights**	**speaks**	**am/is/are**
ed-form				
(PAST SIMPLE)	**asked**	**fought**	**spoke**	**was/were**
PAST PARTICIPLE	**asked**	**fought**	**spoken**	**been**

These spelling rules apply:

ing-form:	1 and 2
s-form:	4
ed-form:	1, 2 and 3

These are the TENSES of the verb covered in this book, illustrated with **I**:

PRESENT SIMPLE	**I ask**	**I speak**
PRESENT CONTINUOUS	**I'm asking**	**I'm speaking**
PAST SIMPLE	**I asked**	**I spoke**
PAST CONTINUOUS	**I was asking**	**I was speaking**
PRESENT PERFECT	**I've asked**	**I've spoken**
PRESENT PERFECT CONTINUOUS	**I've been asking**	**I've been speaking**
PAST PERFECT	**I'd asked**	**I'd spoken**
FUTURE	**I'll ask**	**I'll speak**
CONDITIONAL	**I'd ask**	**I'd speak**

[The present simple uses the s-form for the present simple **he/she/it** – the verbs **be** and **have** have irregular s-forms.

The future can also be expressed in English by the present continuous, the present simple and **going to** – these are *not* interchangeable and are associated with different meanings of the future.]

As well as the STATEMENT forms above, all verbs have QUESTION and NEGATIVE forms:

	Question	*Negative*
PRESENT SIMPLE	**do I ask?**	**I don't ask**
PRESENT CONTINUOUS	**am I asking?**	**I'm not asking**
PAST SIMPLE	**did I ask?**	**I didn't ask**
PAST CONTINUOUS	**was I asking?**	**I wasn't asking**
PRESENT PERFECT	**have I asked?**	**I haven't asked**
PRESENT PERFECT CONTINUOUS	**have I been asking?**	**I haven't been asking**
PAST PERFECT	**had I asked?**	**I hadn't asked**
FUTURE	**will I ask?**	**I won't ask**
CONDITIONAL	**would I ask**	**I wouldn't ask**

Verbs are either ACTION or STATE – action verbs can form all tenses, but state verbs *don't* usually form the continuous tenses.

Even in colloquial English, verbs normally need to have a subject expressed.

ADVERBS describe the manner (how), the time (when) or the place (where) an action or event happens. Manner adverbs are normally formed from adjectives by adding **-ly** (spelling rule 3 applies); time and place adverbs have to be learnt.

The most common PREPOSITIONS are: **about, across, after, against, at, before, behind, below, between, by, during, for, from, in, into, of, on, over, than, through, till, to, under, until, with, without**. When used with PRONOUNS they are followed by the OBJECT form: **with him** not 'with he'.

The normal *order of elements* in a basic statement or negative sentence in English is:

1	2	3	4	5
subject	*(aux)*	*(neg)*	*verb*	*rest of sentence*
Gerry	**'s**		**going**	**to London tomorrow**
She			**reads**	**the paper every day**
We	**'re**	**not**	**catching**	**the bus after all**
The students	**do**	**n't**	**understand**	**the lesson very well**

For a question sentence:

1	2	3	4	5
(wh-word)	*aux*	*subject*	*verb*	*rest of sentence*
	Did	**you**	**see**	**the film?**
	Could	**you**	**help**	**me with these bags?**
What	**are**	**we**	**going**	**to do with it?**
Why	**has**	**Justine**	**bought**	**a clockwork parrot?**

Irregular verbs – alphabetical list

Base-form	Past simple	Past participle
arise	arose	arisen
be	was/were	been
beat	beat	beaten
become	became	become
begin	began	begun
bend	bent	bent
bind	bound	bound
blow	blew	blown
break	broke	broken
bring	brought /brɔːt/	brought
build /bɪld/	built	built
burn	burnt	burnt
buy	bought /bɔːt/	bought
cast	cast	cast
catch	caught /kɔːt/	caught
choose	chose	chosen
come	came	come
cost	cost	cost
cut /kʌt/	cut	cut
deal /diːl/	dealt /dɛlt/	dealt /dɛlt/
do	did	done /dʌn/
draw	drew	drawn
drink	drank	drunk
drive	drove	driven
eat	ate /ɛt/ (*or* /ɛit/)	eaten
fall	fell	fallen
feed	fed	fed
feel	felt	felt
fight	fought /fɔːt/	fought
find	found	found
fit	fit	fit

Base-form	Past simple	Past participle
fly	flew	flown
forget	forgot	forgotten
get	got	got
give	gave	given
go	went	gone /gɔn/
grow	grew	grown
hang	hung	hung
have	had	had
hear	heard	heard
hide	hid	hidden
hit	hit	hit
hold	held	held
hurt	hurt	hurt
keep	kept	kept
know	knew /njuː/	known
lay	laid	laid
lead	led	led
learn	learnt	learnt
leave	left	left
let	let	let
lie	lay	lain
light	lit	lit
lose /luːz/	lost	lost
make	made	made
mean /miːn/	meant /mɛnt/	meant /mɛnt/
meet	met	met
pay	paid	paid
put /pʊt/	put	put
read /riːd/	read /rɛd/	read /rɛd/
ride	rode	ridden
ring	rang	rung
rise	rose	risen
run	ran	run
say /sɛi/	said /sɛd/	said /sɛd/
see	saw /sɔː/	seen
seek	sought /sɔːt/	sought
sell	sold	sold
send	sent	sent
set	set	set
shake	shook	shaken
shoot	shot	shot

Base-form	Past simple	Past participle
show	showed	shown
shut /ʃʌt/	shut	shut
sing	sang	sung
sink	sank	sunk
sit	sat	sat
sleep	slept	slept
speak	spoke	spoken
spend	spent	spent
spread /sprɛd/	spread /sprɛd/	spread /sprɛd/
stand	stood	stood
steal	stole	stolen
stick	stuck	stuck
strike	struck	struck
swing	swung	swung
take	took	taken
teach	taught /tɔːt/	taught
tell	told	told
think	thought /θɔːt/	thought
understand	understood	understood
throw	threw	thrown
wake	woke	woken
wear	wore	worn
win	won /wʌn/	won /wʌn/
write	wrote	written

Irregular verbs by type

Base-form *Past simple* *Past participle*

1 No change in form

cast	cast	cast
cost	cost	cost
cut /kʌt/	cut	cut
fit	fit	fit
hit	hit	hit
hurt	hurt	hurt
let	let	let
put /pʊt/	put	put
read /riːd/	read /rɛd/	read /rɛd/
set	set	set
shut /ʃʌt/	shut	shut
spread /sprɛd/	spread /sprɛd/	spread /sprɛd/

2 Vowel change in past simple

bind	bound	bound
feed	fed	fed
find	found	found
get	got	got
hear	heard	heard
hold	held	held
lay	laid	laid
lead	led	led
light	lit	lit
meet	met	met
sell	sold	sold
shoot	shot	shot
sit	sat	sat
stand	stood	stood
tell	told	told

Base-form	Past simple	Past participle
understand	understood	understood
win	won /wʌn/	won /wʌn/

3 Past tense in -t

bend	bent	bent
build /bɪld/	built	built
burn	burnt	burnt
deal /diːl/	dealt /dɛlt/	dealt /dɛlt/
feel	felt	felt
keep	kept	kept
learn	learnt	learnt
leave	left	left
lose /luːz/	lost	lost
mean /miːn/	meant /mɛnt/	meant /mɛnt/
send	sent	sent
sleep	slept	slept
spend	spent	spent

4 Past simple in -ght

bring	brought /brɔːt/	brought
buy	bought /bɔːt/	bought
catch	caught /kɔːt/	caught
fight	fought /fɔːt/	fought
seek	sought /sɔːt/	sought
teach	taught /tɔːt/	taught
think	thought /θɔːt/	thought

5 Vowel u in past simple

hang	hung	hung
stick	stuck	stuck
strike	struck	struck
swing	swung	swung

6 Vowel a in past simple, vowel u in past participle

begin	began	begun
drink	drank	drunk
ring	rang	rung
run	ran	run
sing	sang	sung
sink	sank	sunk

Base-form	Past simple	Past participle

7 – Past participle ends in -n

arise	arose	arisen
be	was/were	been
beat	beat	beaten
blow	blew	blown
break	broke	broken
choose	chose	chosen
draw	drew	drawn
drive	drove	driven
eat	ate /ɛt/ (or /ɛit/)	eaten
fall	fell	fallen
fly	flew	flown
forget	forgot	forgotten
give	gave	given
grow	grew	grown
hide	hid	hidden
know	knew /njuː/	known
lie	lay	lain
ride	rode	ridden
rise	rose	risen
see	saw /sɔː/	seen
shake	shook	shaken
show	showed	shown
speak	spoke	spoken
steal	stole	stolen
take	took	taken
throw	threw	thrown
wake	woke	woken
wear	wore	worn
write	wrote	written

8 Miscellaneous

become	became	become
come	came	come
do	did	done /dʌn/
go	went	gone /gɔn/
have	had	had
make	made	made
lay	laid	laid
pay	paid	paid
say /sɛi/	said /sɛd/	said /sɛd/

Grammar index

The first number gives the unit, the second number gives the Language point: e.g. 3.21 means Unit 3, Language point 21.

a/an 1.9
a-adjectives 11.69
active versus passive 15.90
adjectives, comparative 10.59
adjectives, superlative 10.59
adjectives in **-ed** 8.52
adjectives in **-ing** 8.52
adjectives with prepositions 6.40
adverb position 13.78
after 11.70
another 4.28
article, indefinite 1.9
as soon as 6.37
auxiliary **did** 4.24

base-form 2.14, 3.18, 6.38
before 11.70
bet 14.83
better off ... -ing 10.64
bring 7.46

C1 conditional 14.79
C2 conditional 14.82
can 8.47
can't 8.47, 12.72
can't have 12.73, 15.88
certainty 12.72
choosing 5.34

commands 3.17
comparative 10.59
conditionals 14.79, 14.82
could 8.47
Could you ...? 3.18
countable nouns 4.23

degree words 10.62
did auxiliary 4.24
direct object pronouns 6.36
do, versus **make** 13.77
Don't ... 3.17
don't think 4.27

-ed adjectives 8.52
ed-form 9.54
either 10.61
else 8.51
empty **it** 7.42

for (time) 11.67
forms of the verb 2.14
future 7.41, 7.43, 11.70

genitive 3.19
get 3.22
going to 7.41
goodbye 1.10

had 9.56
have 4.25
have to 12.71

if 8.48, 14.80, 14.83
if only 14.83
in case 14.84
indefinite article 1.9
indirect object pronouns 6.36
indirect speech 15.86
-ing 3.21, 8.50, 10.64
-ing adjectives 8.52
ing-form after verbs 8.50
introducing people 1.3
it, empty 7.42

Let's . . . 1.8, 5.29
likes and dislikes 5.32
liking doing things 5.33
liking things 5.30

make, versus **do** 13.77
may 12.72
may have 15.88
May I . . . ? (formal) 6.38
might 12.72
mine, **yours**, etc. 2.16
money see Unit 4, Life and living
must 12.71
must have 12.73
my, **your**, etc. 1.6

needn't have 15.88
negative short forms 2.11
nouns, countable 4.23
nouns uncountable 4.23, 4.26
n't 2.11
numbers see Unit 4, Life and living

object pronouns 6.36
obligation 12.71
of genitive 3.19

offering 5.30, 5.31
one 4.28, 10.63
other 4.28

passive 15.90
past continuous 9.57
past perfect 15.85
past simple 4.24, 9.54, 9.55, 9.56
personal pronouns 1.5
phone language 6.35
phrasal verbs 3.20, 7.44
pointing out 1.7, 5.34
position of adverbs 13.78
possessive adjectives 1.6
possessive pronouns 2.16
possibility 12.72
prepositions after adjectives 6.40
prepositions at the end with
   wh-words 11.66
prepositions in relative clauses
   13.76
present continuous 3.21
present perfect 9.53, 9.55
present simple 2.12, 6.37, 8.48,
   11.70, 14.79
pronouns, object 6.36
pronouns, personal 1.5
pronouns, possessive 2.16

quantity 4.23
questions with **be** 1.4
quite 10.62

relative clauses 13.75
relative clauses with prepositions
   13.76
reported speech 15.86

saying goodbye 1.10
's genitive 3.19
Shall I . . . ? 3.18
short forms 1.1

short forms, negative 2.11
should 8.47
since 11.67
some 10.63
state verbs 7.45, 8.49
suggestions 5.29
superlative 10.59
suppose 15.89

tags, questions 1.2
tag responses 1.2
take 7.46
telling the time 11.65
that relative 13.75
that's with wh-words 15.87
this, **that**, **these**, **those** 1.7
time 11.65
time expressions 6.39, 9.58, 11.68
to-form 2.14, 8.50, 12.74
to-form after verbs 8.50, 12.74
too 10.62

uncountable nouns 4.23, 4.26
unless 14.84

verb, forms 2.14
verbs, state 7.45, 8.49
very 10.62

was 9.56
weak forms 2.13
were 9.56
What . . . for? 14.81
What if . . .? 8.48
when 11.70, 14.80
which 10.60
who relative 13.75
wh-questions 2.15, 11.66
wh-words 2.15, 11.66 12.74
Why don't you . . .? 6.38
will-future 7.43
wish 14.83
wonder 15.89
would 14.82